EMOTIONAL
RULERSHIP

EMOTIONAL RULERSHIP

HOW EMOTIONS, PRINCIPLES, LAWS, AND EMOTIONAL INTELLIGENCE AFFECT YOU AS A LEADER

DR EMMANUEL ENI AMADI

Copyright © 2022 Dr Emmanuel Eni Amadi.

Unless otherwise indicated, Scripture quotations in this book are from the Holy Bible, New International Version (NIV, Anglicised edition) Copyright ©1979, 1984, 2011 by Biblica (formerly International Bible Society). Used by permission of Hodder & Stoughton Publishers, a Hachette UK Company. All rights reserved. Scripture quotations taken from The Message (MSG) Bible. Copyright © 1993, 1994, 1995, 1996, 2000, 2001, 2002. Used by permission of NavPress Publishing Group.

EMOTIONAL RULERSHIP: How Emotions, Principles, Laws, and Emotional Intelligence Affect You as a LEADER.

First published in the United Kingdom © 2022 by
Amadi Global Publishing (AGP), an imprint of:
AMADI GLOBAL LTD, United Kingdom.
Global Centre, United Kingdom.
www.amadiglobal.com
Email: info@amadiglobal.com

Paperback ISBN: 978-1-7398778-0-4
Dust Jacket Hardcover: ISBN: 978-1-7398778-1-1

The moral right of the author, **Dr Emmanuel Eni Amadi**, has been asserted. This book is protected by the copyright laws of the United Kingdom of Great Britain. This book may not be copied or reprinted for commercial gain or profit. The use of short quotations or occasional page copying for personal, or group use is permitted and encouraged. Permission would be granted upon request.
All enquiries to: info@amadiglobal.com

British Library Cataloguing in Publication Data.
A catalogue record for this book is available from the British Library.

About Amadi Global Publishing (AGP)
AGP is an imprint of **Amadi Global Ltd**, a UK Company Registered in England & Wale. The ultimate design, book contents, editorial precision, and views expressed or implied in this work are those of the author.

Cover design & formatting: Dr E. E. Amadi

Contents

Dedication	VII
Preface	IX
Introduction	1
SECTION 1: THE POWER & INFLUENCE OF HUMAN EMOTIONS	11
1. Emotions Matter	13
2. Emotions at the Heart of Leadership	27
SECTION 2: THE FOUNDATION OF EFFECTIVE LEADERSHIP	39
3. Emotional Intelligence	41
4. Models of Emotional Intelligence	57
5. The Benefits of Emotional Intelligence	65
SECTION 3: DOMINION RULERSHIP	77
6. The Concept of Emotional Rulership	79
7. Emotional Rulership: The Divine Form of Leadership	111
8. The Benefits of Emotional Rulership	117
9. Five Laws of Emotional Intelligence	127
10. Interplay of Laws, Religion & Politics in Our	159

Society

SECTION 4: SCIENTIFIC EXPLANATION OF HUMAN EMOTIONS	167
11. The Brain Science of Human Emotions	169
12. Two Kinds of Human Brain	183
13. Domains of Success Competences	197
14. ANGER: The Perfect Gift from the Manufacturer	205
15. The Benefits of Anger in Leadership	233
SECTION 5: CHANGE MANAGEMENT	249
16. Introduction to Change Management	251
17. S.O.W.S. Strategies for Managing Change	257
18. Five Principles of Emotional Intelligence	265
19. Emotional Hacking	273
Conclusion	281
Reference	285
About the Author	291
Books Published By the Author	295
How to Contact us	297

Dedication

THIS BOOK is dedicated to God Almighty for the special gift of articulating my mind, my emotions, and my will into writing this book.

To my beloved wife, Mrs Ewa Amadi (Nee Klosowska), who had been the source of my encouragement and inspiration to follow my passion for business, entrepreneurship, and leadership.

To our two sons, Michael Chidozie Amadi (Dodo) and Anthony Chibuike Amadi (Chibyke), for their tolerance, and maturity during the many years of my travel to various cities in the UK for work, and overseas away from home to deliver my vision, helping others discover their purpose in life following my mission, which is: *"To transform the Mindset of Today's Managers into tomorrow's Leadership vessels through the instrument of leadership"* – the reason I discovered I was born to accomplish.

To my late leadership mentor, Dr. Myles Munroe, whose teachings and leadership philosophies had inspired me to become the leader I was born to be in my area of gifting.

To the millions of people all over the world, teenagers, and undergraduates whose potentials are awaiting to manifest.

To graduates, employees, and potential entrepreneurs who are too afraid to think and believe that they are born leaders.

Your inability to control CHANGE or Life circumstances within your environment is what makes you live a life of mediocrity. You were not born to live an ordinary life.

Therefore, I urge you to engineer your Emotions and your Thinking to sync as a single entity and use them as catalysts for CHANGE.

In the words of King Solomon, "For as a man thinketh in his heart, so he is" (Proverbs 23:7 (KJV)).

Preface

THE MOST powerful forces in the world for effective leadership or for the sustainability of leadership and organizational growth in challenging times are not found in the leaders' visions, planning, nor in the Office they occupy. They are neither found in the leaders' influence, political rhetoric and in their charisma.

Possessing over-confidence, humility, or political manipulative skills have constantly failed to qualify some past Kings, Prime Ministers, Presidents, or CEOs as effective leaders.

The most powerful forces on the planet earth are not the fundamental forces of nature, such as the electromagnetics, weak nuclear forces, or the force of gravity – even though the Earth's gravitational force alone is capable of pulling down the heaviest rocket from the surface of the Earth's orbit down to the ground.

The Saturn V Rocket, built as part of the NASA's Apollo programmes, is considered by the Guinness World Records, as the biggest rocket ever built by space engineers, standing at more than 100 metres tall (363 ft.), and weighing approx. 3,000 tonnes when fully fuelled and ready to launch (Guinness World Records 2021).

Despite its enormous weight, this rocket is too light to defy the Earth's law of gravity. This gravitational force can pull this gigantic rocket down in a matter of minutes. And yet, the force of gravity is not the most powerful force on the Earth. Therefore, the most powerful forces in the World are: **HUMAN EMOTIONS.**

Human Emotions are the only gifts on the planet Earth that the Creator of the universe cannot take away from humanity. When the Creator created human beings from the dust of the grounds, made of earthly raw materials, He implanted His own Spirit unto our dead body, and it became a living Soul in a bodysuit. The last thing He did was to infuse His Seal of authority and ownership on the Soul of everyone with His **IMAGE** - His likeness or character – and Emotions were part of that image. Emotions make up the trinity of the human Soul – the Mind, the Will, and Emotions.

The Creator could not erase these powerful forces called emotions from humans, even though humanity has continuously used their gift of emotions such as anger, frustration, and jealousy as weapons to harm others when they fail to accomplish their ambitions and selfish desires.

How do domestic violence, divorce, and murder first start? How do wars and crimes against humanity first start? Are uncontrolled emotions not the reason why strong nations wage wars against weak nations? Why do people impose their belief systems, religion, culture, and democracy on other nations, and rob the indigenous people off their natural resources with impunity? Wherever jealousy and selfish ambitions cross paths, there you'll find emotional distress appearing in the form of discord, tension, bitterness, disagreement, or conflicts - and evil of all sorts begin to take shape and manifest themselves.

Were these events not due to the emotions of individuals who want to lord it upon others, or the people we call leaders, who want to impose their desires on other nations just to feel superior in their minds? They have ambitions they cannot satisfy, and the only option left for them is not dialogue, but war and might against their brothers just to get their way by force.

Why are our young, British Black teenagers disproportionately the victims of a knife crime in the streets of

London, Manchester, and Liverpool? Is this not due to the "unguarded" and "unguided" emotions of these young brains – who, we thought, were once innocent schoolchildren? But it turned out that some of these teenagers were responding to the impacts of some "alien, powerful forces" they could not control. And those powerful forces are "superimposed-emotions" as substitutes to their original sources due to societal deprivation and the absence of fathers in broken homes.

Therefore, broken homes in British families had led to not only bitter divorce rates, but also gave birth to increased rates of atrocities in the streets near you. Unless the foundation of crime is dealt with from the root causes, and unless the foundation of our homes is fortified with emotional concretes and metal structures, our teenagers would continue to mismanage or misuse their private emotions.

Although human emotions are being deployed to kill and destroy properties around the world, yet the Creator of the universe could not remove these important forces from our Souls. Why? Because, hidden inside human emotions, are the keys to life – the secrets for survival. The Creator uses the same emotions, just like humans, when He wants to cause changes in His Earthly territory. Emotions are not primarily designed as tools to cause mayhem, but as secrets to influence positive changes in our environment here on Earth.

The keys to turning every adversity into a business opportunity are found in **Emotional Rulership**. In times of adversity, when the fire alarm in your business goes off, it becomes natural for human beings to lose their power of effective thinking and imagination. Therefore, we need Emotional Rulership as the solution to keep us on track and thrive in difficult times.

Many CEOs of today believe that Boardroom-Thinking alone, or sitting around a table, isolating themselves from the junior staff, discussing serious issues affecting their organizations can save their companies from financial crises. Long hours of executive meetings, rational or deliberate thinking, and decision-making processes may not even protect your leadership from ruin, when you violate your leadership mandate. Why? Because when leaders are submerged in a crisis, rational thinking becomes irrational and useless.

I offer this book as a resource to help you develop, not just as a leader, but an **Effective Leader** when facing your storms of life. A leader deficient in **Emotional Rulership** is a weakling in the face of adversity. Human *Emotions* are the ONLY KEYS to save us from decay when our leadership styles and ability become questionable.

Dr Emmanuel E. Amadi, January 2022

Introduction

The Missing Ingredient In LEADERSHIP

"The difference between the bad Leader and an Effective Leader is in the contents of their emotions."

– Dr Emmanuel E. Amadi

WE HAVE heard about exceptional business leaders, and how impactful they are at inspiring those under their charge to achieve targets for their departments, organizations, or their countries.

In 2018, the UK's gross domestic product (GDP) stood at 2.86 trillion U.S. dollars. The GDP is the total value of all goods and services produced in the country within a specified time, usually one year. In other words, it's simply the "SCALE" or the "barometer" to measure the blood pressure of the country's economy. It answers the question of "how fatty, meaty, bulkier, or leaner" the economy is in terms of value.

In the pre-pandemic months of 2019, the figure in the previous paragraph had shrunk to 2.833 trillion U.S. dollars. In

2020 during the full-blown Covid-19 pandemic, the economy further nosedived to 2.7 trillion dollars (O'Neill 2021). However, when the lockdown restriction was lifted in 2021, the UK economy had shown a great sign of recovery, with the GDP anticipated to grow by 9% up to 3.124 trillion dollars by the end of 2021.

While some jobs had evaporated into thin air, and gone with their companies going burst, others had survived the financial storms caused by the COVID-19 pandemic. Many businesses were swept off their feet by waves of bankruptcy and redundancy. Others took the furlough scheme, but couldn't make it to 2021. Surprisingly, thousands of new job opportunities were created as a result of the crisis.

Despite the challenging times, through thick and thin, the year 2021 had proved to the world that a crisis doesn't come to destroy you. Rather, a crisis comes to shape you and your economy. Between January and March 2021, and April to June 2021, there was a record-high net flow of 299,000 individuals who migrated from the city of "Unemployment" as "Jobseekers" to the city of "Employment" as "employees" (Office for National Statistics 2021). This change in people's life circumstances had injected fresh red blood cells into the British economy, contributing to over 2.308 trillion dollars in GDP per Capita anticipated by the end of 2021.

When we asked our leaders – our Prime Minister, Boris Johnson, the CEOs of businesses, Entrepreneurs, and Investors - how they fixed the British Economy and restored people's trust and hope in the Service sector, Production, and Construction sectors, the traditional answers were always predictable:

- Good vision.
- Good planning, and
- Good financial management.

When we asked them how they became so effective as political and business leaders when other economies in Europe were in tatters, and most African nations in dire need of blood for economic survival while paying foreign debts, such as loan repayments from China, we were often told it was due to:

- 🌀 Budgeting.
- 🌀 Sound strategies, and
- 🌀 Hard work.

But you cannot achieve anything without people – the employees - who had worked so hard to engage with customers, increase sales and deliver profitability on the shop floor for the shareholders and CEOs living big on the top floor! These talented employees might have been motivated and inspired to commit to your vision – which is the companies' vision.

Because every person has emotions and our body is a mobile emotional chemical reactor, your staff couldn't have improved the company's overall performance without first working on their emotions. The secrets for thriving in life – whether in our relationships, business, achieving goals, and managing people are found in this book:

Emotional Rulership.

First 100-Days of the Adrenalin Rush

Let's talk about politics and the first-100 days of the "adrenalin rush" to fulfil the political party manifesto, and see how human emotions had been used to influence policies and political outcomes. My observations for the past forty years, about people seeking political power, is this: They "rush in" to power with emotional energy and rhetoric, but fail to sustain the steam, or adrenalin required to maintain efficient, and effective leadership, when the pressures of office demands start to take their tolls.

Before I commenced writing this manuscript, I had studied the emotions and mindsets of some of the world's great leaders, politicians, the craziest dictators, and warlords from Africa to

England, including King George III; the Americas, including George W. Bush, Barack Obama, and Donald J. Trump; and from Asia to Europe, one thing that stood common among these leaders was their performance in the first-100 days in office.

In the political arena, we are familiar with the "first 100 days" in office as coined by the 32nd President of the U.S. - Franklin D. Roosevelt (1882-1945) (Walsh 2009). This simple model evaluates the effectiveness of potential leaders. This period is classified as the most important or the leading term in office. This period is the most challenging time for leaders to be "seen" by the citizens as effective leaders. They also feed the appetite of the crazy camera crew, news media, and journalists as the leaders tackle the needs of their citizens by converting their political manifesto into legislation through the power of their emotional experiences.

Most of the greatest achievements in the first term of a leading president are almost achieved with the speed of light, within the first-100 Days. President Roosevelt was noted to have passed 76 laws during his first-100 days to revive the economy of the US (Walsh 2009).

In 2019, the UK Prime Minister, Boris Johnson set out his plan to take the UK out of the European Union (EU) and promised to pass the best post-Brexit budget within 100 days of taking office if he wins the General Election. His popular slogan - Get Brexit Done - warmed the hearts of the people, and helped him win the December 2020 General election. The UK officially left the EU on 31 January 2020 at 23:00 GMT after many years of wasted debate by politicians, whose business interests in the EU were under threat by Brexit.

Whatever political debate that was dissected and hammered out in the House of Commons by Members of Parliament (MPs), they did not do so by the power of their THINKING alone. They debated so ferociously as a result of their emotions and their feelings. Although they were influenced by their thinking and spoke through the vibrations of their lips, they were greatly empowered and energized by the contents of their emotions.

The popular votes that decided the outcome of the UK Brexit (52% vs. 48%) weren't by accident (The Electoral Commission 2021). They came from the power of human emotions. Thus, on the polling day, the British people carried their emotions with them, not in their heads this time, but in their hands. Some even had their emotions hidden and sealed in envelopes, in the form of ballot papers, and finally dropped into the polling box – like the postman.

Brexit, therefore, was the result of both thoughts and emotional feelings through the ballot box. Below are some of the driving forces – the areas of emotional interest closer to the heart of the British people - which compelled 48% of the population (the Remainers) to submit and vacate their mandate in favour of the emotional forces of the 52 % of the population who voted to leave (the Brexiteers).

❶ **The UK Sovereignty** as an independent nation governed by its parliamentary constitution.

❷ **The Economy:** The EU States depended hugely on funding from the top-four nations, Germany, France, Italy, and Britain. According to the UK House of Commons Library, it was estimated that in 2019 alone, the UK net public sector contribution to the EU budget stood approx. at £9.4 billion (House of Commons 2021).

❸ **Political Decisions** for the UK by the UK: Decisions concerning the UK were made in Brussels, not in England.

❹ **Immigration Policies**: To regain control over immigration and its borders.

❺ **EU Bureaucracy:** It was difficult for the UK to deport foreign criminals under the EU Human Rights Laws.

⑤ Social Security and Benefits: The Social Security and Benefits, such as Tax Credits, Free NHS (Health care service), and social care meant for the UK citizens are claimed by other EU members. When they arrived freely in the UK, they immediately have access to some of these services, while the British citizens living in other EU nations don't have immediate access to the same volume of benefits, including free cash when they migrate to other EU states.

These points listed above, among others, were the key driving emotional forces that moved the mountain from its foundation without shaking the mountain top.

Everyone is a Good Leader in Good times

In good times, everything seems to work as planned. In good times, anyone could be a good leader. The ability to lead people in good times remains unquestionable only for a few months or years. Leadership abilities grew exponentially for only a limited time. After this limited expiry date, the leadership ability plateaus or levels up, mostly by the end of the 1-2 years. But the ability to sustain performance at this level becomes critical as we get past the second year in office as a leader.

The intensity of energy and focus, fall below standards, and leadership capability becomes questionable. Suddenly, when the wind of a crisis blows across the nation - from the North to the South, or from the East to the West, they lose it completely. Governance becomes tough, and the reality of leadership turns into a dreamland. Old traditions, such as academic qualifications, skills, expertise, or experiences begin to erode and cancel out.

Although, our leaders may appear capable and fit on the outside, but are empty from the inside, and lack the real ingredient of Leadership under pressure. When this happens, they go back to their old skills and past experiences hoping to find new solutions. But the results remain the same.

New problems require innovative thinking or new ways of solving problems. The best explanation for the lack of sustainable leadership in difficult times is that they are either deficient or poor in some of the Hidden ingredients of Leadership found in Emotional Rulership including knowledge of the Principles and Laws of Emotional Intelligence which are essential for thriving during leadership crises.

Unanswered Leadership Questions

When I completed my Strategic Leadership Professional Development Programmes in September 2019 at Harvard University, Extension School, Harvard Division of Continuing Education, Cambridge, USA, and returned to my hometown in Manchester, England, UK, I had more burden in my heart than I had before leaving for the U.S.

On the last day of the leadership training held at 51 Brattle Street Cambridge, MA, I left the training room at 18:00 hours asking myself hundreds of rhetorical questions. As I left the Boston Airport the next day and flew to Texas, my heart was full of questions I couldn't find answers to while at Harvard. Flying long haul back to Manchester UK, from Dallas Love Field en route to Philadelphia Int'l Airport, I became a victim of my emotional circumstances.

Every part of my emotion was fighting for self-recognition and significance in my heart, as I craved for more answers to some of the leading questions that had bothered me for the past twenty-one years or so. The more I tried to provide the answers, the more the questions kept throwing themselves out on my face like the Euro Million Lottery Balls! Below are some of the thousand questions that haunted me for more than 21 years, but kept me fixated throughout my long-haul flight back to the UK:

❶ Why do some leaders become successful while others stay dormant as failures?

❷ How do leaders feel when governance is at stake?

❸ Is there any MISSING INGREDIENT between bad leaders and exceptionally great leaders? If yes, what is that missing link that converts cowards into Leaders par excellent?

❹ Why do leaders of nations wage war against other nations, with innocent civilians killed, and properties destroyed? What goes on in their minds and their thinking?

❺ Can emotions, conceived privately at home, in the comfort of our bedrooms have an impact on our public functions and performance? Why are crimes on the increase: murder, homicide, rape, child abuse or abduction, street demonstrations, terrorism in the name of religion, anarchy and rebellion - to name but a few?

❻ Can humans leverage EMOTIONS and THINKING in their daily decision-making processes?

❼ Can we integrate EMOTIONS and THINKING like Symphony Harmonica as ONE Package, so that people of any race, religion, or culture can ALWAYS apply this package simultaneously in their daily lives, utterances, actions, or inactions?

❽ Is it possible to understand other people's emotions without personally being judgmental?

❾ Why are some people poor, and a minority Rich and Wealthy?

❿ Why have many marriages broken down, and divorce rates becoming more relevant?

❶ Despite the increases in innovative technology, medicine, surgery, and pharmaceuticals, why are diseases such as cancer or Covid-19 still have control over humans, and crimes such as murder and rape still on the rise? Why?

Asking myself these ELEVEN questions and searching for answers had led to the publication of this book: **Emotional Rulership.**

This book will help you to:
❶ Understand emotion as a powerful tool for effective leadership in hard times.

❷ Understand emotions, feelings, and moods.

❸ Understand the Concept of Emotional Rulership, and how the mastery of human emotions leads to an emotionally intelligent leader.

❹ Apply the Principles and LAWS of Emotional Intelligence with other tools to help you in times of Change. Principles and Laws are vital in sustaining effective leadership in your daily activities and allow you to remain atop your game.

❺ Understand Anger as the ultimate catalyst for Change. The inability to regulate CHANGE in your life circumstances leads to stagnation and failure.

SECTION 1

THE POWER
&
INFLUENCE
of
HUMAN EMOTIONS

"How you deal with the situations at hand determines how you'll succeed in life."

- Dr Emmanuel E. Amadi

Chapter One

Emotions Matter

"A man without no feelings is a heartless man who never understands anyone."

~Aaditya

EMOTIONS MATTER more in the World System than **THINKING**, and here is why. About 6,000 years ago, the modern man – Homo Sapiens - relied extensively on one part of the brain - the prefrontal lobe (i.e., the Neocortex) - for making business decisions. Do you know what? It worked! Hidden deep, just a few steps above the ear zone is a small portion of the brain known as the limbic system. This limbic system houses an almond-shaped object known as the Amygdala, which in turn is responsible for human emotions and the regulation of stress hormones. Despite its vital role in the circuitry of emotions, it's always relegated to the background. Poor thing!

Emotions from the amygdala were considered "personal" or "private," yet, it is the heart and soul of humanity in terms of regulating human emotions and how we respond to stressful events. The amygdala is regarded as "second-class" or "primitive," just like what it is in wild animals in the jungle. That means, our government – the politicians, the economists, religious leaders, and the CEOs of businesses – had led the people from the forehead, rather than from the heart – the soul, comprising the Mind, the Will, and Emotions.

HOW DO YOU FEEL when people in Leadership positions had lost ideas on how to lead the people under their charge and save the world? The Year 2020 is a year that would remain indelible in the sand of history for many generations to come. It was a year littered with one crisis upon crisis. COVID-19 pandemic which started as a small, tiny virus crisis in Wuhan China in early March 2020, started as a local crisis but moved on quickly to a national crisis, and from a national crisis to a global crisis. According to an unpublished Chinese Government data, the Guardian Newspaper of March 13, 2020, reported that the first case of COVID-19 outbreak was actually recorded in China on November 17, 2019, but was not disclosed to the public. By 11th March, it became a global crisis with Italy, Iran, South Korea, and Japan recording the highest number of cases within a matter of months, compared to all cases inside China.

Even those in Wall Street could not see the economic crisis coming through the pandemic. According to the Press Release by the World Bank in Washington on June 8, 2020, termed "Global Economic Prospects" it was predicted that by the end of 2020, "the global economy [caused by the COVID1-9 pandemic] will shrink by 5.2%, which represents the deepest recession since the Second World War, with the largest fraction of economies experiencing declines in per capita output since 1870" (Davidson 2020).

Four months later, the same alarm bell continued to chime in the ears of the economies of the world. By October 2020, the World Bank Chief Economist, Carmen Reinhart, was quoted in an interview granted to Bloomberg Television that "the Coronavirus pandemic is turning into a major economic crisis", and that "this did not start as a financial crisis but it is morphing into a major economic crisis, with very serious financial consequences" (Heath and Hays 2020). What Carmen did not realize was that the virus had already caused global economic devastations, with thousands of deaths, business closures, redundancies, and abject poverty to millions of people around the world.

HOW DO YOU FEEL when the World's Leaders – the Prime Ministers, Presidents, Kings and Queens, and CEOs and top Business Executives around the globe, had failed to communicate effectively in times of crisis - leading to loss of trust and vote of no confidence by the citizens? Businesses no longer trust the Government, and many businesses going burst with redundancies and bankruptcy proceedings.

HOW DO YOU FEEL when Scientists - immunologists and Virologists - from some of the world's best virology and immunology research Universities including Harvard, Stanford, and Cambridge, Oxford, MIT, and Imperial, Yale, Munich (Germany) and so on – could not find a new answer, a new vaccine for a new disease?

According to the data from the WHO (World Health Organization) COVID-19 which I watched live on the WHO Dashboard on 18th October 2020 in my study room in Manchester, England at 10:38 am CEST (Central European Summer Time), equivalent to our 9:38 am British Summer Time (BST), globally, there were 39,442,444 confirmed cases of COVID-19, including 1,106,181 deaths, reported to WHO.

HOW DO YOU FEEL when the lives of your family members were taken away in a flash with no fault of theirs - your wife, husband, your mum, and dad, or even your young ones and children? How do you feel, when you wake up the next morning, and everyone is gone?

How do you feel and react when things you had worked for all your life were destroyed by a disaster in a split of a second? How do you feel, when many businesses are shut down, and thousands of people lose their jobs with no alternative sources of income for the entire family?

In your job as the Manager or CEO of the AZ company, do you understand how your customers, your employees, and the stakeholders feel emotionally about the company's brand, products, and organizational culture?

HOW DO YOU FEEL when redundancies and furloughs loom, and the company you had worked for, for more than 3 decades couldn't know how to get rid of you, and suddenly crisis came, it was an opportunity to lay you off? How do you feel when the government, which had promised to protect you throughout your life had taken away your pensions with nothing to show for your hard work when you're retired?

How do you "**feel and respond**," when many marriages and relationships of 2 years, 10 years, or even 30 years are crumbling due to money worries, caused by the emotional crisis that could have been managed, but allowed to rave havoc in your family? How do you feel when you can't afford the mortgage repayments, with interest rates going up, and your house repossessed by the bank due to a job crisis which was never your fault?

HOW DO YOU FEEL when the Police Force, which is meant to preserve and protect the life of their Citizens, turn their back against the ordinary people, killing and sucking life away from innocent civilians trying to survive and make a living from nothing? No one is safe. From the Black Lives Matter Movement (BLM) from the US to the **#EndSARs** public demonstrations across Nigeria (Lagos, Abuja, Enugu, Port Harcourt, etc.) against Police brutality of her Citizens; and to the anti-monarchy demonstrations in Spain (2014), in Bangkok, Thailand (October 2020), and Hong Kong antigovernmental protests, and so on.

For the last time, let me ask you once more: **HOW DO YOU FEEL** when friends and family members had rejected you, simply because of money, and they have brushed you to the backside?

These are real-life emotional crises that had happened across the world in the past 18 years since September 2002, and most recently between 2019 and December 2020. Some of them were personal, and the most were global. These crises had come to impact the emotions of humanity. But how you deal with the situations at hand will determine how you'll succeed in life. By embracing the fact that the only constant thing that never stops changing is CHANGE. But Change will always happen. Emotions do really matter.

Emotions vs. Feelings & Mood

Emotions, Feelings, and Moods are not the same. Frequently, we have misused these words interchangeably. I was once a victim of the same misuse of these three words until I took time to study them carefully. While one serves the **internal** aspect of our body, the other serves the **external** environment of the same body.

EMOTIONS

Emotional experiences are the "SUBCONSCIOUS", "natural", and "neurological reactions" to an **external stimulus**, constructed with "biochemical" and "electrical reactions" triggered by "neuro-transmitters" and "hormones" released in the brain and our body forming a "feedback-loop system". In other words, Emotions are unconscious processes and don't require conscious arousal to react to defensive mode against harmful events. Emotions are aroused first before feelings, and their presence is manifested through our physical reactions.

When we encounter emotional triggers, it takes the brain (i.e., the amygdala) about ¼ second to detect the source and characterize those emotions, and another ¼ second to induce chemicals to enable us to give them names (Miller 2015). A good example is when you are terrified by a stray dog running towards you along the street. Your emotions will manifest as both "conscious" and "subconscious."

FEELINGS

Feelings are the CONSCIOUS, cognitive-emotional experiences (i.e., intellectual, thoughts, thinking, rational, or perception) and the physical sensations we have encountered and give them names based on our present and past experiences, memories, our thoughts, belief systems, and cultural influences. Feelings are hidden and more durable than emotions which are always visible to a certain degree.

MOODS

Moods are the collection or precipitation of human responses and feedbacks of events - past, present or future expectations. They are influenced by our emotions and feelings. In other words, Moods are the sum of our emotions and feelings, i.e., **Moods** = Emotions + Feelings.

Moods = Emotions + Feelings are shaped by various factors, such as:

1. **Physiological Activities**: Our appetite, health status, and exercise play crucial roles in how our body responds to emotions.

2. **Mental Status**: Our thinking influences our emotions, and our emotions give birth to our attitudes, and attitudes give birth to our lifestyle.

3. **Environmental Factors**: The People we interact with – at home with our children, the team at the workplace and the friends we keep in our social circle - could sometimes get on our nerves and influence our mood on daily basis.

While feelings last longer than emotions, moods could last for minutes, hours, or days depending on the intensity of the feeling at the time. Understanding emotions, feelings, and moods will help you integrate these vital components as the centrepiece of your leadership.

Bridging The Gap Between Thinking and Emotions

As I have watched the entire world dive into one crisis upon crisis, and yet nothing seems to work anymore, it is now pertinent that in times of adversity, the World Leaders - in corporate organizations and those running the affairs of our government need to find another way of thinking; another way of strategizing, or another way of planning to resolve our lingering global problems.

Right from the creation of mankind on the planet earth, people in leadership positions had relied enormously on one part of the brain, The Thinking Brain or Neocortex (the frontal lobe), to make rational decisions. It may be in the way we relate with members of our families at home or the way we relate with members of staff in your organization to achieve your vision and mission.

In good times, we think normal and rational. Anyone can be an effective leader in good times. But under immense pressure, our emotions rule over our thinking ability, and our performance begins to disintegrate from within. Therefore, the key to surviving under pressure is simply by connecting our thoughts with our emotions.

Thinking Without Feelings

Throughout our life, the neocortex (the frontal lobe in the forehead) had been trained to think in one direction without emotions interfering with logical thoughts. Our attitude (behaviours or actions) had been "conditioned" by our environments, such as corporate culture, nurtured by our educational system, enslaved mentally and spiritually by our religious or non-religious teachings, coated by our belief system like cake-toppings, and made manifest in our lifestyles.

So, for over 6,000 years, the human race had constantly trained their brain to think, reason, and respond to the world CRISES in a certain, predictable pattern, and get the same, predictable old results. We have equally trained our brain (the Neocortex) to function at its best in complex decision-making processes when everything is going on well – from algebra to calculus, and from biology to chemistry, we had mastered the equations in colleges or universities, and followed the same formula to get the same results anywhere in the world.

From Africa to China to the USA, and back to England, the same equation works everywhere. From management to leadership, executives had been "programmed" inside the boardroom to think strategically without involving our emotions. Our Institutions of Higher Learning require leaders with practical political experience to formulate creative ideas through THINKING to solve intractable industry problems and end global conflicts. Yet, nobody talks about synching thoughts with emotions or mixing our minds with our thinking to bring out the best in us.

I call the Neocortex, the Executive Business Centre. Thus, we have developed this Executive Business Centre so well that we placed 100% of our trust in this department. It handles 100% of our business responses and statistics and uses old financial data to make informed or uninformed revenue predictions. When we face challenges in our personal life or revenue begins to slump in our businesses, we rush to the same old Executive Business Centre for assistance. Why? Because that's the only place we know that works.

Humans are like children, who, for the first time, run to their parents for help after ingesting a harmless seed from juicy apple fruit! We ignore the Amygdala or the Feeling Centre – even though we had felt these strong emotions just a few seconds ago. We cry for help from other people when we're angry, disappointed, or challenged in life. We hug our children as a sign of love and care for them when they're in their tiny, difficult moments. Everyone needs hugs to feel good when under stress.

The bad news is that the Neocortex isn't the right place to seek refuge and hugs. It's not a BIG warehouse, and it doesn't know how to deal with human stressful conditions either. Practically, the neocortex can handle approx. 80-90 % of the job of the entire brain - the Cerebral Cortex or "Cerebral Mantle." Because we had trained our body to respond ONLY to the neocortex, automatically we reject the Limbic System, the *Amygdala,* the small fraction of our brain (the 10-20%) hidden in a bunker, just a few steps above the ears.

But, when we encounter serious problems in our businesses or relationships, the stress level begins to enslave our thinking. We, therefore, need a solution from the bottom of the brain to restore our sanity.

Let's make it clear that the limbic system is the first station to receive emotionally stressful signals from inside and within our external environment, and relay them to our body as feelings. Although the Amygdala might seem too small in size (10-20%) to make an impact, compared to the big size of the cerebral mantle (80-90%), it is more powerful than the frontal lobe in dealing with difficult conversations.

Never underestimate the size of the amygdala relative to the neocortex. In the words of Dalai Lama XIV,

> *"If you think you are too small to make a difference, try sleeping with a mosquito."*

No matter how tiny in size the amygdala is, this centre of human emotions is the primary solution for human survival. When we feel stressed, the Amygdala is released immediately to protect us from harm. It shuts the door BOOM! in the face of the perceived stress. The Thinking Brain is jobless when CHANGE arrives at your front door. Therefore, the first place to rush for safety is not in your head. The best place to seek refuge in difficult times is the limbic system: the human underground bunker.

On Wednesday, 6 January 2021, here in the UK, I watched live on YouTube the invasion of the U.S. Capitol by the pro-Donald Trump supporters. Fear gripped me when I saw a group of the mob manoeuvre their way to the atrium of the Senate Rotunda, carrying the flag of "another nation" with them. Instead of the American Flag, they consciously chose to carry the Confederate flag with them into the American seat of power. What a shame! It was utter chaos, confusion, and a breach of U.S. democracy.

The first thing that came to mind was their emotional states at the time. I saw emotions being transformed into instruments of destruction: anger and rage-filled atmosphere. As I watched the Capitol police been outnumbered, some were killed, while journalists covering the scene were attacked, what was going on in my head was one thing: Safety.

How safe were the American government leaders – the Senators, the members of Congress, and employees who were holed up inside the Capitol? What were the mental states of the rioters? Which emotional state was President Donald Trump when he encouraged them to move on through his tweeter handle? What about the emotional state of Joe Biden – who was taking over the presidency? What about the Senators?

The security breach of the American seat of government shows that, historically, no matter how powerful militarily a nation might be, people's emotions will always triumph over the muzzle of a gun. From the state of apprehension to the state of calm – was the feeling right inside me when I saw the Senators being ushered into a safety vault – away from the centre of the crisis. That was a display of Emotional Rulership.

Predictably, Leaders without Emotional Rulership do the opposite. They don't run to the bunker for safety when the enemy throws stones at them on the blindside. When they begin to suffer a leadership crisis, the first thing they do is rush to their thinking brain. They'll become philosophical and speak logic and grammar ad infinitum.

Like the dying fish, they quickly use up their 80-90% for thoughts and dump the small portion of the brain (10-20%) where oxygen = life is locked up. The same goes for the personal choices we make in life, and the strategic business decisions we make on daily basis as the CEOs, Company Directors, or Entrepreneurs.

Over Expectation Breeds Mental Exploitation

Too many unrealistic expectations lead to too much curiosity and invasion of other people's private lives. Curiosity, they say, kills the cat. When you set business targets for your employees, you expect them to accomplish them on time, and within the expected company deadline. Sometimes, the procedures for completing these projects are provided by the employer, and the strategies may form part of the company's business plan for that specific target.

They might have seen the end from the beginning, through projections and statistics. What they see is the revenue – how much income the target will generate in their millions for the season. But there's a problem here. The CEOs or Directors of Strategies had forgotten that there are people on the shop floor whose *abilities* to get the job done are powered by passion and the state of their heart – their mind and their emotions.

What the CEOs had forgotten is that they can't force people to get the job done, if they can't inspire trust and loyalty in their employees. What your boss [the employer] had forgotten, too, is that you [the employees] see the business targets through different eyesight. The employees have to first, like the CEO, or manager through the eyes of "confidence", how "passionate" their "vision" is, and how that vision aligns with the corporate vision of the organization.

Managers and CEOs consistently make the following mistakes:

#1: They instruct their junior staff to commit 100% of their brain – their thinking, their time (including over-time) and their attention into the organization's business, even though the employees cannot naturally afford to do so. When stress is built into the target, the results are increased absence, increased sick leave, and delayed completion.

#2: Your boss may fail to establish an emotional connection with the employees. Emotional connections, such as empathy, or good listener, but less talk, could help reduce the perceived threats seen through the tasks.

The truth of the matter is that managers, and business leaders – the CEOs, and Entrepreneurs - commit 80-90% of their think tank to their businesses, their jobs, or their careers. Everyone is born to give 80-90%, nothing more. But your Boss expects 100% commitment from those under their charge. What hypocrisy!

When a business fails to deliver on annual targets, that's a crisis for the manager. It's an indicator that CHANGE has arrived. Your job, which you thought was permanent, may soon begin to acquire an expiry date. Feelings of underperformance, if not controlled, can impact your teams. When a crisis of life hits us from the blind side, and we fail in our duties to deliver good governance to the people, rather than stepping aside from the public domain, to reflect and think privately about how to use our strengths to improve our weaknesses or convert the perceived threats into real opportunities for innovative ideas, we always find someone to blame. We blame others – not ourselves nor in our thinking.

The solution to derailing business revenue and profitability doesn't lie in the company's marketing strategies. It doesn't depend on buy 1-get-1 FREE promotional offers. Rather, it depends on how you "manage" your team's emotions, and inspire them to achieve beyond sales targets.

In the area of politics, this scenario I'd just painted above is very common among African leaders: Presidents, Governors, and heads of Governments and Institutions. If you are a leader or a politician, this question is for you. Have you ever seen or heard of a politician from African nations – South Africa, Kenya, Nigeria, South Sudan, among others - to have ever resigned from office due to their leadership failures? The answer is Nope! Their emotions influence their thinking.

There is an urgent call to change this self-gratifying paradigm of political thinking into emotional thinking. Even those we call our leaders had been charged with corruption charges, money laundering, and human trafficking. They are still walking freely, parading themselves as leaders who are deficient in Emotional Rulership in Leadership.

To achieve greater than the average, and live above ordinary life, making impactful decisions in your business helping others to achieve success, or becoming influential - both in private and in public life – the answer lies in your ability to merge the Thinking Brain with the Emotional Brain in a kind of relationship akin to marriage. Two becoming one.

Once your thoughts and emotions sync as a single, powerful corporate entity, whatever you desire out of a task will surely come to pass. Great leaders are not known for the upheavals they'd suffered, they are known for the emotional crises they've survived.

To solve our economic problems, improve the GDP and our healthcare sector (The NHS), the Government, through the people we've voted into power, should provide the enabling environments for businesses to thrive through innovative thinking in tandem with Emotional Rulership. Therefore, in difficult times, the destination for your survival is not in your thinking, but in your EMOTIONS. Emotions set the path, humans walk the walk.

Chapter Two

Emotions at the Heart of Leadership

"What lies behind us and what lies ahead of us are tiny matters compared to what lives within us."
~Henry David Thoreau

EVERY HUMAN ENDEAVOUR is driven and powered to a certain degree by the contents, shapes, and size of our emotions. While leaders make decisions through their thinking brain to shape the direction, success, and safety of their businesses, organizations, and countries, or parents as leaders guiding their children to grow into adults, we cannot achieve all these without the help of emotions which are the key drivers of success or failure as a leader. We need Emotional Rulership to remain on top of our role in difficult times.

The results of my research activities on Emotions and their impacts on leadership were astonishing and insightful, and reveal the central role of emotions in human pursuits. I have personally applied my concept of Emotional Rulership at the workplace as I worked with a team of over 100 employees in the past two years. My wife and I equally deploy this concept at home as we engage in family discussions. I have also personally applied it when resolving issues between our two children and their behaviours, especially when their emotions began to nosedive and malfunction into gigantic monsters!

The Benefits of Emotions For Effective Leadership

Emotions have unique characters, which can only be observed by people gifted in this department. Below are my FOURTEEN research findings on this forgotten, crucial element that makes people appear smart, and leaders outstanding compared to those who lack it, or are deficient in Emotional Rulership.

#1: Emotions Protect Your Sanity

The opposite of sanity is insanity. Emotions are there for your survival. Imagine in your business, you keep applying the same ineffective business strategies repeatedly and getting the same old results repeatedly while anticipating better results than the status quo. Albert Einstein calls it "insanity." Madness! But when emotions step into the scene, they change your mind and restore your sanity to its original setting.

#2: Emotions Protect Your Thinking

In difficult times, when crises begin to manifest in your leadership, it means your old thinking habit is no longer sustainable or capable of getting results. When emotions step in, they stop the brain from thinking itself to death. We are as safe as we think.

#3: Emotions are the Progenitor of Habit Formation Known as "Chunking"

Some Neuroscientists - Nuné Martiros, Alexandra Burgess, and Professor Ann Graybiel - at the Massachusetts Institute of Technology (MIT) have discovered that certain neurons in our brain are accountable for the assemblage of our behaviours into a single, habitual, and automatic routine known as "chunking"(Trafton 2018).

Every routine habit is made up of various minor activities. For instance, applying your favourite moisturizer in the morning involves several sequences, such as picking up your moisturizer, taking a portion of the cream smoothly with your forefinger in a fluid-flowing motion, rubbing it between your palms, and finally unto your face (up and down) and neck (upward stroke to defy gravity). This habit of routinely applying your moisturizer, initiated by your emotions, causes your neurons to fire at the beginning, when you first pick up the moisturizer and then fires and the end of that routine, bracketing each step as "chunks", and forming units that constitute a single behaviour. Once these habitual patterns of behaviour are formed, breaking such habits will be as difficult as trying to extract water from hard rock.

#4: Emotions Are the True Rulers of The World

People don't lead others through their powerful oratory and charisma that pull the crowd together. People are simply led by the emotions of their leaders. The decisions we take on a daily basis regarding our circumstances and the actions we take resolving life situations are literally fuelled by the contents of our emotions. For instance, the hiring of a new member of staff, or the firing of the "tired" employees. This action is influenced by the personal and private emotions we have held briefly or stationed in our minds for a very long time. Even in our private lives at home as parents, or on the outside as business executives, we are the results of our emotions.

#5: Emotional Intelligence Precedes Emotional Rulership

No leader, irrespective of their title or office, can truly regulate their emotions and feelings without adopting some of the elements of emotional intelligence. Understanding the roles of emotions in humanity is the foundation to success in times of adversity. No business will ever thrive without the CEOs understanding the mood of the customers (demand and supply). The mood of the customer is measured by their shopping habits, which gives you an insight into their loyalty to the company.

If you're a politician, you may never survive the next general election if you don't carry in your heart, the emotions, and feelings of the local people who voted you in during the last election. If you're a religious leader or a cleric, if you don't study the emotions of your members, gain insight into their emotional and spiritual wellbeing, and seek understanding of what makes them attracted to your teaching programmes, you might lose them when you need them most, especially during the next fundraising projects.

If your business or charity is not generating the right amount of revenue or tithe required to run the affairs of your organization, here are some rich emotional questions you could ask yourself:

1. Why is my organization attracting poor people against the wealthy?

2. Why are my teachings or services attractive to the elderly, but not the younger generation who spend their weekends at the pubs?

3. Why do parents with children attend my services, but the singletons, are absent?

4. Why is it that the organization is overfilled to its capacity with people of all sorts during particular events such as weddings, burials, baptism, or Holy Communion - only for the

premises to dry up with empty seats during other normal activities?

Emotional Rulership is the starting point to finding solutions to your business problems.

#6: Life void of Emotional Intelligence Leads to Self-Destruction

You get a mortgage for a big house you never lived in. You get married to your lovely wife or husband and have children, but you never really had time for them. Even the partner you were in a haste to get married to, when parties are over, you leave that partner at home in your empty house. You buy a big TV screen to keep him/her busy, and a new mobile handset to browse the internet. But you never had time to enjoy the union. Why? Because you're too busy working three jobs to pay off the mortgage or maintain the loans on luxury cars you only drive twice a month on Sundays.

The above illustrations are personal experiences – and we call them life! What do we gain from all these labours every day? One day, these jobs will kill you, and when this happens, you pass on your debts to your children as an inheritance. Others leave landed properties and assets to their children and great-grandchildren, but you work hard for others (banks, mortgage companies, credit cards, utility bills, and so forth) just to maintain a lifestyle. You'll leave a broken home and accrue unpaid loans to your family if you ignore to acknowledge your emotions and emotions of others, manage, and regulate them effectively for the benefit of the entire family. Emotional Rulership is the key to helping you thrive in life circumstances.

#7: Emotional Rulership in Leadership Leads to High Team Productivity

When the people you lead in your organization always feel good to work on their jobs, they are more likely to be productive with 100% commitment to the business. On the other hand, when the team perceive emotional conflicts, deceit, manipulation, or they "feel" that their views are less important than others, it is likely to cause cracks in the emotional wellbeing of the group.

Here is an example of one of the incidences I encountered when I consulted at a third party's organization here in England, UK. I had witnessed an employee of an XYZ company in the Northwest of England, UK, who was under pressure to complete a mentally demanding task for eight hours (9:00 am - 5:00 pm). While the store manager had assisted other members of staff to complete their assigned roles, the manager could not assist this particular employee. Why? Because the manager had thought the junior staff was just "doing fine." This was a wrong perception. This employee was not the type of employee who liked to complain about their jobs and carried on with the task at hand.

The problem is that nobody ever spotted the contents of his mind - his emotions, and his feelings. This employee 'felt' undervalued inside, but couldn't voice his opinion. When the manager had gone home for the day, this employee was filled with anger and frustration. Rhetorically, this staff asked questions repeatedly; "Why couldn't the manager help me when my colleagues received some form of assistance?"

By the end of the business day, this fellow was fed up and threatened resignation the next day. However, I decided to step into his emotional fragments and link them up with his thoughts. I managed to calm him down and allowed him to view this scenario from another perspective. By the following day, he was happy to return to work and save his job. This was the power of guided emotions at work.

#8: Absence of Human Emotions is the Absence of Innovative Thinking

King Solomon, the formerly wealthy and wise King of the United Kingdom of Israel is famous for his quote, "there is nothing new under the sun" (Eccl 1:9). In other words, innovations are not really new per se as they were already in existence in the mind of the Creator. Humans are as creative as the heights of their emotions. Innovative thinking is simply a different way of thinking deeply about solving emerging problems. It involves the integration of old ideas with old products - combining them efficiently to develop new concepts. For instance, this generation is gradually moving from driving cars to automation ("self-driving cars, robots), landlines to mobile phones, letters to emails and text messages. All these innovations are the results of human emotions in action.

#9: No Emotions, No Business Growth

Without emotions, it is impossible to experience growth in any sphere of life. No growth means no progress. Stagnation in the business revenue stream, year-on-year is a sign of no progress. When leaders begin to connect their emotions with their thinking and begin to feel the impact of poor revenue structure, the idea of growth or expansion – either organically or by acquisition - will begin to arise.

#10: Uncontrolled Emotions are as Dangerous as Weapons

Unguided emotions can render the most powerful Kings and great leaders into useless nonentities. Despite their wealth, power, and authority, some of the world's Heads of Government, Kings and presidents had gone down in history as deluded in times of challenging times. Some had attempted suicide as a means of escaping from the pains of adversity, while others were described as having mental health disorders such as panic disorders, social anxiety, and bipolar to psychopaths. Why? Because unguided emotions are as dangerous as military warfare. Uncontrolled emotional stress at home, workplace/business, political environment (political anxiety disorder), finances, and relationships can spiral into depressive mental states. In some cases, no medical help could cure these emotional states.

#11 Emotions Birthed the USA

The United States of America is the product of the emotional state of one man. It was not the invention of the Italian explorer Christopher Columbus - the first man in records to set his foot in the US on October 12, 1492 – even though the geographical location of the United States had been there where God left it. The birth of the US was not from the sixty delegates elected from the thirteen United Colonies that made up the Second Continental Congress. Even the formal change of name from "United Colonies" to the "United States of America" on 9th September 1776, was not the genesis of the USA we know today. The Sovereignty of the states of the USA did not emerge from the declaration of independence by Thomas Jefferson and the Committee of Five. The real birth of the USA was the result of the emotions of one man, a British King: King George III.

#12 Nothing Changes in Your Lifetime Until Your Emotions Change

Emotions can sway the minds from right to left, and left to right in a repeated fashion akin to a pendulum. Let us back-track to the emotions and the mindset of this 16th century King George III of England, his Kingdom, and his thirteen American colonial territories which make up the present-day USA: Connecticut, Delaware, Georgia, Maryland, Massachusetts, New Hampshire, New Jersey, New York, North Carolina, South Carolina, Pennsylvania, Rhode Island, and Virginia.

A Kingdom operates by Laws, and not by emotions: In an Empire or a Kingdom Government (not in a democracy) such as the former British Empire (the United Kingdom of Great Britain), the nation is ruled by a King or a Queen (the Monarchy).

To become relevant and powerful, a Kingdom Government (the colonizer) must have dominions: colonies, protectorates, provinces, mandates, and other territories. The colonizer is supposed to provide basic needs and protect the colonized territories. Through the process of colonization, these dominions are governed, ruled, or administered by Governors and Councils (Councillors) appointed only by the Kingdom Government (not voted by the people).

In a democracy, these Kingdom representatives (Governors and Councillors) are called Ambassadors. They exercise power and control over the territories on behalf of the King. They don't represent the interest of the people, but the interest of the King. They simply implement the King's mind! Whatever the King says or promises in the public domain becomes law and is transcribed as such. Those promises or utterances in the laws must be "executed to the fullest" to the satisfaction of one person: The King or Queen.

In a Kingdom rulership, here are some of the rules: The King is not opposed both in private and in public. The King is the Lord of the land, and whoever occupies the land owned by the King automatically becomes the property of the King. His views and utterances remain supreme.

When King George of England "imposed" many stringent policies on the British American colonies without their consent and representation in the British Parliament - such as:

1. The Stamp Act of 1765 for taxation.

2. The Townshend Revenue Acts in 1767.

3. The Tea Act in 1773 (the Tea Party started in Boston).

He expected them to be executed to their fullest - and for his satisfaction. Surprisingly for the King, his policies were utterly opposed by the colonies - a "rebellion of the highest order" ever experienced by the King and a blow to his authority and influence. In other words, the King was a ghost sitting on His throne! The King went into a state of "amygdala hijack" and disbelief that his "colonial subjects" could oppose the laws of a King – which they shouldn't. Why? Because whatever the King says becomes laws.

#13: Emotions are the Incubator of our Actions

Let's continue with the story of King George who was pregnant with his unborn child called the USA. His personal belief was that any opposition to the King or Queen is an act of 'rebellion." This mindset kept the King locked down with an emotional state of extreme anxiety. And of course, King George, without joining his thinking with his emotions, labelled the opposition as a " 'traitorous action' against himself and Great Britain" (History.com Editors 2009).

In a father-and-son relationship that hit the rocks, the only option left for the father would've been to call for dialogue or slap his son on the wrist, rather than waging a war. For disloyalty to him only, the King, with the approval of the British Parliament descended on his colonies. He deployed the British Army against his own people in a Revolutionary War that lasted for eight years, hoping the outcome could bring increased "Royalty and Loyalty" to the British Crown. He even considered abdication at one point as a means to save his shame. But he was wrong. Our emotions are the incubator of our actions. It was King George's emotions that birthed the USA we know today.

The Whigs in the Parliament once called The British King "an autocrat" while Thomas Jefferson – a delegate of the Second Continental Congress who later became the 3rd US President - once described King George as a "blundering tyrant" (Adams and Adams 1996-2021).

#14: Nothing Succeeds in Life Without Emotions

When Britain took the war to the back gardens of the British American colonies, George Washington (the American Supreme Military Commander) had a different mindset. In his vision, he saw the war coming but remained resolute and unshakable. He saw the war crisis as an "opportunity" (not a threat) to carve a new, strong nation. Therefore, the success of the Revolutionary War was the result of the emotional state of one man: George Washington.

When the British army invaded its colonial American subjects in the Summer of 1776, Washington had only one option in his mind as he led his team against the British invaders (Sheerin 2019). That option was clear: DEATH! He never considered Life as an option. Rather, he saw death, not as "the end of Life," but as the means to the "beginning" of a New life for the colonies. He saw a vision no one else ever saw. He was never distracted from his dreams and vision by circumstances of "nearly" losing the war to the British Army. That vision was the birth of a new World Superpower: The USA.

It was his emotions that led to his conviction, in his mind, that he would rather be dead than alive and see his people – the American colonies - remain under the British colonial occupation and subjugation. As the outcome was so grave for the Americans, Washington couldn't handle his emotions anymore. It's on record that George Washington theoretically tried to commit "suicide by redcoat" (Sheerin 2019). In the words of Nathanael Greene, one of Washington's Generals, he once described Washington as a man who "sought death rather than life" in the face of crisis. That's great leadership.

In the words of the greatest leader and teacher ever recorded in the history of mankind, He was quoted as saying, "Very truly I tell you, unless a grain of wheat falls to the ground and dies, it remains only a single seed. But if it dies, it produces many seeds." He further stated that: "anyone who loves their life will lose it, while anyone who hates their life in this world will keep it for eternal life" (John 12: 24-25). In other words, Washington had found a vision he was willing to die for, and a vision he would declare, "It is finished."

SECTION 2

THE FOUNDATION
of
EFFECTIVE
LEADERSHIP

"Everybody has access to the Conscious Mind, but not everybody can control what goes on in their Subconscious Mind."

- Dr Emmanuel E. Amadi

Chapter Three

Emotional Intelligence

"It is very important to understand that Emotional Intelligence, is not the opposite of Intelligence, it is not the triumph of heart over head. It is the unique intersection of both."
~David Caruso

WHETHER YOU ARE military personnel, Navy Seal, Olympic athletes, Boxers, or Medical personnel (doctors, nurses, pharmacists, or Physiotherapists), you need Emotional Intelligence to survive in your area of life. Whether you're the CEO, President, or Prime Minister; Cleaners, babysitters, mechanics, or parents with young children – Emotional Intelligence is the foundation for effective leadership.

Right now, the world is still wrestling with Covid-19, and the current global solutions aren't working. Our leaders are struggling to keep their promises and manifestos. On 7th September 2021, the British Prime Minister failed to keep to this party's manifesto by announcing the opposite – that from April

2022, all UK pensioners must receive economic punishment for their hard labour. That punishment is that all the 1.5 million UK pensioners from the age of 65 - who are still in good health but wish to help the UK economy grow through work must be penalized for the first time. But how will his government carry out this task - you might ask? By hiking the National insurance contributions by 1.25% – in what he termed Health and Social Care Tax (BBC News 2021).

Our religious ministers are grappling with their image - their character - and what they stand for. Parents are struggling to keep their children safe from the insanity and depression induced by our constant exposure to the internet – searching for answers to their life problems.

The masses are searching for people with extraordinary powers, leaders with inbuilt artificial intelligence above other humans to solve our internal, economic crises. Our emotions and emotional intelligence seem to be the gateways to running for safety.

There is More to Emotional Intelligence than Meets the Eyes

The original idea for this manuscript was to conduct simple research on human Emotions and Emotional Intelligence. The aim was to find out how human emotions influence the mind and the thoughts of world leaders.

As I surrounded myself with Daniel Goleman's books on Emotional Intelligence, such as "Emotional Intelligence: Why It Can Matter More Than IQ," "Working with Emotional Intelligence," and "Primal Leadership" – as well as other books written by established authors in the field of Emotional Intelligence, including the "Emotional Brain" by Joseph Ledoux. I didn't look at emotions with the same "eyeballs" of a psychologist. Rather, I looked at emotions differently - at an angle of 45 degrees - using the microscopic lenses of a Philosopher, Entrepreneur of multiple businesses, and a Leadership Consultant.

I have, therefore, concluded that Emotional Intelligence is the foundation of Emotional Rulership, taking its base from the last letter "R" = RULER or "Regulation"– which forms part of the definition of Emotional Intelligence as we'd see shortly in this book.

Emotional Rulership is, therefore, the continuation of where Emotional Intelligence stops, expanding the Gospel of the huge amount of power, energy, information, and leadership influence one could gain and tap into when you study this unique, secret package, called Emotions.

The emotional experiences gained studying and dissecting emotions in the contexts of "leadership" and "paradigm shift" have enormous impact on the way we think and reason. It is more powerful than just studying emotions on the periphery for the sake of becoming emotionally intelligent.

During the two year study of human emotions in leadership, I saw emotions simply as the keys or catalysts for CHANGE. Approaching emotions this way, had equipped me with the grace to change any circumstances I find myself in. It allows you to see the future from the beginning and provides the path towards leading a life of which you had dreamt of as a young toddler.

By understanding your **Conscious** and **Subconscious** minds, you can turn your life around = CHANGE. That means, CHANGING from a life of mental poverty, moral deficiency, a life of ordinary, uncreatively or boredom, stagnation or poor growth, to the next higher level of fulfilment – living a life of productivity, influence and growth – wealth and riches.

I do believe that everybody is emotionally intelligent! Yes, I mean everyone. But the question is this: How often do we apply this emotional intelligence concept in our everyday life?

Think of how you treat your children at home when they are naughty – shouting or screaming at them, ditching out instructions to them to tidy up their bedrooms?

What about your manager and workplace pressure? How often do we deploy the emotional brain, just like we deploy our thinking brain for making daily decisions at work?

What do you do, with the intelligence, information, or knowledge you've just acquired after completing your education – college or university? Becoming emotionally intelligent is not quite easy. It might take several steps and training to decongest our old mindset, keeping watch over the subconscious mind and regulating how our conscious mind controls, imposes or dumps every garbage into the subconscious mind.

The conscious mind is bombarded with all sorts of information from the outside environment on daily basis - from the news media (TVs, Newspapers, or videos), Society, Educational System, Religion, and Culture. Everybody has access to the conscious mind, but not everybody can control what goes on in their subconscious mind.

Whatever information you allow to leak, or drop into the subconscious mind, will always, and predictably act on your body to produce RESULTS. But that result cannot manifest without you activating it - by taking action and working on it.

If you believe that starting a business from scratch is hard, but getting a job as an employee with minimum wage is easy, and you internalize this belief into your subconscious mind, your subconscious mind will guide your body towards the easy option. But the easy option is the final bus stop for the 95% of the population - living a life of ordinary. This is where Emotional Rulership comes in – to help you move closer to the 5% of the population - where wealth dwells.

It was my two-year spiritual journey, researching, and searching for answers to control my circumstances that eventually led to coining this Emotional Rulership concept.

What you do with your God-given INTELLIGENCE is what this book is trying to address. Nothing more! Nothing less!!

Unlike Emotional Intelligence which can be learnt or thought in the classroom, you don't have to attend a seminar to learn Emotional Rulership. It was naturally endowed on everybody on Earth. We were born with the God-given mandate to "rule over" bad circumstances around us – from poverty to a life of abundance and opulence. You just have to ACTIVATE your dominion mandate and "rule over" life events in your domain.

No matter how smart you're, or how intelligent you might be, what you do with your life circumstances is where the tyre meets the road. Millions of people around the world are too afraid to follow their minds and their dreams. Why? Because it is difficult to follow the "unseen" visions – the virtual sight you cannot see objectively with your physical senses. Rather, people, follow their heads – because it is easy to see the head wallowing in the pit of dirt and uncertainty.

As an employee in that organization, you're sure of your salary hitting your bank account at the end of the week or month. But as an entrepreneur who had just started a new business venture from scratch, the chances of drawing an income from that new business, in the first month, 6th month or even after the 12 month is very low.

As long as the earth rotates around the Sun, and there're days and nights, and there are seasons all year round - Spring, Summer, Autumn, and Winter - humans will never escape from the emotional CHANGES in life.

- Sickness will come: - How do you restore yourself to good health? You go to the hospital to be fixed.

- If you're single and want to be in a relationship: What do you do differently to attract, and meet the right person – not the wrong person - whom you had dreamt of? You dress up and hit the town!

- If you're broke and don't have money to pay your rent or mortgage: - What do you do to save yourself from financial disgrace? You look for a job – ready-made waiting for you.

- You have a PhD and a Business degree, yet can't find a job like me? What do you do to transform your situation into a life of glory? Rather than folding your hands and waiting for years for job vacancies to become available, you follow my footstep as an entrepreneur, create businesses, and become an employer of people. I couldn't find a job, so I registered a company. I couldn't get a job as a lecturer, so I registered a Leadership Academy ‖ Executive Education from scratch and employed PhD and MBA holders to teach in the programme. You're who you think you are!

My question to you is this: How do you change this paradigm of living a life of mediocrity into a life of abundance? The answer lies in your emotions. By leveraging the power of your emotions with your thoughts, you can use them to influence positive changes in your life circumstances through planning and design.

Since the last 200,000 years when the modern man evolved up to this day in 2021 writing up this manuscript, humans had continuously relied heavily on one part of the brain – the Neocortex or frontal cortex - for decision-making processes, while our emotions, from a different planet in the brain (the limbic system), which provide us with crucial information to help us make those wise decisions are relegated and neglected. Now is the time to bring your emotions to the boardroom to influence change and let your thinking rest for a little while.

Definition of Emotional Intelligence

The internet is riddled with different definitions of Emotional Intelligence (EI). Since 1999 when Professor Daniel Goleman made EI a global success, thousands upon thousands of books had been written on the topic relating to leadership, businesses, parents, and relationships. This goes on to show the importance of EI, and how impactful it is to the global community.

But how do we define this important concept, known as Emotional Intelligence, since everyone has EI, and defines it in his or her terms? In defining EI, one should be careful to avoid losing the crucial meaning, and how it practically relates to business activities and relationships with people around us.

On a Saturday morning, being 31 July 2021, while writing this book chapter, my younger son, Anthony Chibuike Amadi, a 10-year old boy in Year 5, but will be in year 6 by September 2021 at the St. John Bosco R.C. Primary School, Blackley, North Manchester, entered our bedroom, followed by his older brother, Michael Amadi, who's in Yr. 7, at the Co-Operative Academy, Blackley, North Manchester. My wife, and the mother of our children, was busy browsing the internet with her mobile phone at the far end of the bed, while I was busy working on this manuscript chapter on my desk towards the other end of the bed.

Anthony came forward and asked me, "Dad. What are you writing?" Anthony is fond of asking me intellectually engaging questions. In my mind, I said to myself, "this boy has started again with his troubles." I composed myself and replied: "I'm still working on this 'Emotional Rulership manuscript.' It doesn't seem to end."

He was quiet. I decided to break the silence and test his intelligence. I asked him this question which I thought would be difficult, and surprising. It went like this:

> "Son, what is the difference between Emotional Intelligence and Emotional Rulership?"

It didn't take him time to respond. I was excited at his response, and I have reproduced his statement here with his permission. His answer was:

> "Emotional Intelligence is about how SMART you're in your head, or your thoughts."
> - Anthony Chibuike Amadi

"What about Emotional Rulership? What do you have to say about it?" I asked further. He replied without hesitation, saying: 'Dad, I think that:

> "Emotional Rulership is about how SMART you're in regulating your emotions and joining your THINKING with your FEELINGS."
> - Anthony Chibuike Amadi

This guy is SMART. I was shocked that children as young as 10 knew much better than the adults. As a star, he was able to answer this question, boldly and confidently. This is the computer age. Our children are now too smart than their parents!

Okay! Let's jump to the mind of Professor Daniel Goleman to see what he has to say about emotional intelligence.

DANIEL GOLEMAN'S DEFINITION

Daniel Goleman defined Emotional Intelligence as ...

"the capacity for recognizing our feelings and those of others, for motivating ourselves, and for managing emotions well in ourselves and our relationships." (Goleman 1999).

Emotional Intelligence in Leadership Development

Emotional Intelligence (EI) has a huge role to play in leadership development. Understanding its true impacts can help shape the mindset of anyone aspiring to great leadership that exceeds human expectations. In their book entitled, Primal Leadership: Unleashing the Power of Emotional Intelligence, Goleman, et al. portray EI as the number one trait any leader should possess to become exceptional both in good times and bad times (Goleman et al. 2013: pp. 253-256).

The EI is an active ingredient, akin to the productive force hidden within the individual workforce, the leaders, and the organizations. It is responsible for driving outstanding performance, and thus, this hidden talent must be 'reactivated' through personal training to develop the emotional brain to align itself in resonance with the frequencies of their thinking brain.

What do I mean by being 'reactivated'? It is like the Human **Leadership Spirit**, which is suppressed by 99 per cent of the population who become followers based on long-term 'conditioning' of their minds and beliefs that leadership is reserved for others. They don't grasp the idea that every human being is born to be a leader too.

It is a common knowledge that humans don't use 100% of their brain for thinking and decision-making on daily basis. We use only ≈80% of our brain, the size of the Neocortex, for thinking and decision-making processes. Everyone has a level of intelligence quotient (IQ) with which they were born. The level of this IQ determines the level of your cognitive abilities such as memory, thinking, and reasoning.

The average IQ score is 100, but those with a score of more than 140 (e.g., doctors, pharmacists, lawyers, etc.) are deemed genius or nearly genius. While it was previously thought that our IQ from birth remains the same throughout life, what I found during my research was quite amazing.

In 2018 two psychologists from the University of Edinburgh, UK, and the University of Texan at Austin, USA, had disproved this long-held belief that our IQ is constant from conception to the grave. In their research entitled, "How Much does education Improve Intelligence? A Meta-Analysis", and using six hundred thousand participants, the authors found that for being in School or education for just one year, our IQ is bumped up, from 1 to 5 points (Ritchie and Tucker-Drob 2018). In other words, people who had spent up to 11 years in academic studies - academic environments, and stretching their intellect through organized thoughts, including undergraduate, postgraduate masters, and up to a doctorate - are more likely to possess IQs greater than 140 akin to 'super genius' in their areas of expertise. This is amazing, isn't it?

Apart from IQ, Emotional Quotient (EQ) is the higher level of intelligence which is critical for exceptional leadership and personal development. Therefore, great leaders strive to possess high levels of IQ and EQ combined.

While we spend our entire life learning new skills and training our frontal lobe (neocortex/the thinking brain) to think and reason in tandem with our skills, less time and effort are spent developing our limbic system – the amygdala - the emotional brain.

The amygdala, vis-à-vis the limbic system (LS), is the domicile of our EQ - located just a few inches away from both sides of the ears. Although everyone was born with the EQ, not everyone can access this region. The reason is that the Creator hid the amygdala from our sight; locked up inside a gated vault of the LS – the residence of emotional intelligence.

Emotions are the Superheroes

For the past 3 decades or so, Scientists have been searching for **Superheroes** from another planet – with ideas on how our government leaders can lead the economy effectively in difficult times. The good news is that we don't have to look outwards in space to find the answers for our poor team performance. The answer was never in other planets – Mercury, Venus, Mars, Jupiter, Saturn, or the Moon. The answer is hidden within us - in your emotional brain.

That human planet is the limbic system. Effective leadership communication, successful business strategies, inspiration and team motivation, and relationship with others are controlled, not by thinking, but by our emotions which conjure thoughts in our minds.

The Psychologists found that the answer to extreme performance under pressure was in the planetary human body, hidden a few steps down from the front of the human brain (Neo-cortex) to the ground floor of our brain, in a warehouse where all emotions are stored under lock and key.

Emotional Warehouse

The Emotional Warehouse is the Emotional Brain or the Limbic System which houses an "almond-shaped" biological Security Alert System, known as the Amygdala. Just as business leaders rely on their people – the employees – to deliver results or sales, the amygdala shares an *emotional neighbourhood* with other parts of the brain such as the THH - *Thalamus, Hypothalamus,* and *Hippocampus*. They work in a coordinated fashion to "protect" humans from emotional stress and fragility.

The Limbic System is a primitive, uncivilized, and uneducated part of the brain. Even if you take humans without the frontal lobe, but massively loaded with the limbic system, to Harvard or Cambridge University, they will never learn how to think like normal human beings. Although the limbic system is part of the brain, it has no "rational brain" of its own. Ordinarily, we could say that it is brainless in this department.

What do I mean that the Emotional Brain is brainless? This is because it only has one duty in his job description: **Protection**. In the most difficult situations or crises such as anxiety, anger, and frustrations, the emotional brain becomes the leader of the entire human body, just like the CEO looks after the business of the organization and the team. It controls us and holds the thinking Brain (Neocortex) hostage. It holds the thinking brain to ransom. Under pressure, the Amygdala shuts down our Thinking Brain. How can the CEO shut down his company when in difficult times? To preserve you and keep you safe.

In difficult times, the emotional brain floods our body with the stress hormone – cortisol. It sends signals in the form of feelings. We perceive them differently depending on our moods at the time. We respond by 'reacting without thinking.'

The first signal goes straight to the buccal, or oral cavity (i.e. the mouth). We respond with loud shouts, swearing, stamping our feet in anger, or banging the desk like my first son does when he couldn't figure out how to fix his Lego pieces or Spiderman.

When we face difficult challenges, we scream with anger in such a tone that the other person next to us could virtually see the word ~~I HATE YOU~~ written boldly across our face. We complain without minding whose ox is gored, instead of taking steps to consciously RULE our emotions and take up the good mantle of leadership which we are born to be.

Types of Emotions

In 2017, two Scientists - Alan S. Cowen and Dacher Keltner (PhD) from the University of California, Berkeley, USA - published 27 distinct types of emotions in the Proceedings of the National Academy of Sciences (PNAS) journal. This journal was edited by Joseph LeDoux of New York University – who is also the author of Emotional Brain (Cowen and Keltner 2017). The 27 emotions they identified are Admiration, Adoration, Aesthetic Appreciation, Amusement, Anxiety, Awe, Awkwardness, Boredom, Calmness, Confusion, Craving, Disgust, Empathetic Pain, Entrancement, Envy, Excitement, Fear, Horror, Interest, Joy, Nostalgia, Romance, Sadness, Satisfaction, Sexual desire, Sympathy, and Triumph.

As we can see from the list above, the three emotions - *anger, happiness,* and *surprise* - which we regard as part of "the six basic emotions" were not even listed!

We express over 2,500 emotional responses a day. This translates to a minimum of 104 emotions per hour or 2 emotions per minute - this is just a rough estimate. Emotions are, in fact, due to the type of chemicals we generate from our brain to our body in response to our perception of events: how we feel at the time, and how we want to regard, name, tag or call that eventful experience.

The Emotional Brain is the Manager of Human Behaviour

Our Emotional Brain is responsible for managing the psychological responses (emotional, mental, spiritual) to the stimuli our brain creates for us, and we interpret the stimuli as "crises." The Amygdala is the Governor of our emotions. Therefore, the emotional brain or the Amygdala is the ruler of our mind, our emotions, and thus influence the actions we take every single minute of our lives.

To be one step ahead of your colleagues in the same environment, classroom, culture, office, or the Boardroom as the CEO, Business Leader or Coffee Shop Owners and to perform exceptionally well above the ordinary, we must hack into another territory or hierarchy of intelligence above the average to harness that exceptional knowledge and wisdom to succeed where others had tried and failed.

That territory is not outside the Earth or another planet. It is not even in your chest or in your thinking brain. Rather, the key to exceptional leadership lies inside the Limbic System – the Amygdala. In the words of Dr. Myles Munroe:

> "Your future is not ahead of you; it is trapped within you."

Furthermore, Emotional Intelligence is about having a relationship with people in your charge. It's about showing them empathy and sympathy in their emotional crisis. It's also about not being the first to make judgements, as well as not imposing your perceptions or beliefs on others.

Finally, Emotional Intelligence is about establishing *Emotional Intimacy* - wearing other people's shoes, tying the laces tight, and walking around with the same shoes so we could "feel" their pains without being judgmental.

Chapter Four

Models of Emotional Intelligence

"As more and more artificial intelligence is entering into the world, more and more emotional intelligence must enter into leadership."
~Amit Ray

THERE ARE various models which explicitly simplify Emotional Intelligence in Leadership, making it easier for everyone to understand this uniquely high level of intelligence. In this chapter, I'll focus my interest on the two "fundamental" Leadership models which I think make common sense, and stand out uniquely to simplify my understanding of Emotional Intelligence.

The two models are:

1. The ICEBERG Model.
2. The RULER Model.

#1: The Iceberg Model for Leadership Development

An iceberg is simply a huge, freely-floating solid chunk of freshwater ice which fragmented from a glacier or an ice shelf. It is like a military submarine with two components: The "small visible tip" on the surface and the large "unseen component" buried inside the body of the ocean.

The "Tip" of the Iceberg: The Visibility of the Human Action

The small "visible tip" of the iceberg is the only tip people around you can see, observe, or feel. It's the fraction of whom you are. It is only visible "only" to the outsiders – the intruders, the enemies who want to pull you down – who are not members of your leadership team or the inner caucus of your political party. Although some of them might be members of your parliament, this group on the surface are not members of your cabinet or committee – the selected few Ministers and Secretaries - to whom the secrets of the Government and governance are revealed.

In other words, the "tip of the iceberg" is for those who only see the "mango fruit," or your "success," but forget there is a mango *seed* buried inside the fruit. This seed is filled with hard work, dedication, failures, heartbreak, etc. you had encountered in life before manifesting your success superficially.

This tiny tip influences the perceptions, opinions, views, judgements, feelings, or insights other people have about you. This tiny, "visible component", make up 10-20% of our skill set: educational qualifications, IQ, professional skills, work experience, and expertise.

Beneath The Iceberg: The Invincibility of the Human Action

Submerged below the surface of the iceberg is the bulky, hidden component beneath the water which is much greater than what is visible above the water - the Hidden Potential. It is submerged under the ice like a powerful nuclear submarine loaded with nuclear warheads unseen by the enemy - which represents a much more lethal and dangerous threat above the surface.

Beneath the iceberg is the most vital component of your life to which only you have access. It represents some of your worst moments - tidal waves of life, failures, breakdowns, deceptions, values, beliefs, morals, ethics, helplessness in the face of adversity, crises, and ideas conceived that are yet to be released to the world.

This hidden component makes up the 80-90% of your EQ - which you and members of your Cabinet or Ministers have access to. In other words, the rest of your intelligence – the 80-90% EQ – and your "natural talents" are buried beneath the heart of your mind. You can control these talents in your terms and conditions wherever you're domiciled around the world – anytime – anywhere. Political geography or your country's economy cannot control what the Creator has hidden on the inside of your iceberg.

The Government of the day owes you nothing, and cannot control this warehouse, except the provision of the right enabling environments for you to manifest this hidden gift, so you can prosper in any area of life - business, management, or leadership. Yet, you owe the world your hidden gifts – because the world needs them.

I believe that everyone is like an iceberg described in this passage. Deep-rooted inside each person, are a great attitude, aptitude, beliefs, and life philosophies that make us who we are, and what we are meant to be in this world. The taste of a piece of cake is dependent on the contents of its ingredients.

The "Ideal" Situations

When I finished my PhD in 2019, all I wanted at the time was to find work as a postdoc, researcher, or lecturer in the UK or US universities so I can help impart knowledge to others during the course of my work.

Some of the feedback I received after each interview (some never offered feedback) was: "You don't have the relevant teaching experience", "We have selected another applicant whose "experiences" fit the role."

One professor from a UK university School of Pharmacy asked me during the interview: "Why are you applying for the job at this age?" I was 48! This can be described legally as institutional discrimination. That's when I knew I wasn't meant to be there!

When I phoned a friend in the US who is in academia to discuss the concerns I have in the UK, he couldn't believe that I wasn't absorbed by some of the universities from where I had obtained my degrees. This is what he told me over the phone: "Dr Amadi, when companies need you, they will hire you to work for them 'if they "like" you." He went further to state that: "if you possess the relevant educational qualification without the relevant work experience, they can still go-ahead to hire you – but "only if" they "need" you".

In other words, in an ideal situation, any company that hires you will train you as their assets so you can perform well on the job. They know that your future potential doesn't lie in your old CV, but is hidden as an "untapped" talent within you.

These statements above were just enough to convince me that I wasn't meant to be an employee – rather, I was born to be an "employer of people" and an entrepreneur – leading to the birth of my business: AMADI GLOBAL LEADERSHIP ACADEMY ‖ Executive Education - on 1st November 2019.

The illustration above is in ideal situations. But the mistake thousands of recruiters - employers and leaders - make in life leading to management's bad performance is one factor: Over EXPECTATION from new employees with previous work experiences with little or no concern regarding the "Hidden Component" of the Iceberg. Companies will always expect a higher performance by up to x10 from employees without first giving x 10 equivalent amounts in professional training to the employees.

In computer science, we are all familiar with the computer language – GIGO: Garbage In, Garbage Out. If you input the wrong data to the system, it throws the wrong results back to your face. However, because we don't dwell in ideal situations, during job recruitment drives, recruitment executives place more emphasis on the visible components of the iceberg required to get the job done such as academic intelligence, technical skills, and work experience. However, they overlook what is hidden inside your iceberg - which is your true potential.

From high school to college or university, we are challenged to be the best and get good grades to make progress in the educational system. Hence, our parents, teachers, and even our potential employers are delighted in our academic performance than in our hidden potentials.

Nobody thinks of you as the next entrepreneurs. No employer thinks of employees as potential business owners or the future presidents of global corporations. They are only interested on what you can bring to them in terms of value and revenue in the next 10 years, with attractive offers such as pension, holiday allowance, professional feed paid, etc.

Allow your emotions and your thinking into your boardroom - and let them work in sync before accepting or rejecting an offer. Why? Because what is hidden inside you is richer, and more powerful than what is seen and exposed externally on the outside. But remember that employment was never designed to make you rich or wealthier, but just enough wage to cover your basic needs!

Iceberg Model:

The Concept of "Rarity" in Leadership

What lies beneath the surface of the Earth (the iceberg) is more valuable than what lies above the ground. Apart from precious metals (silver and gold), and petrochemicals (petrol, diesel, petroleum, etc.) hidden under the soil, inside the rocks, and beneath the oceans and seas, the Creator of the universe hid more than 300 precious stones or gemstones underground according to the findings from the International Gem Society (IGS). They include actinolite, adamite, agate, Alexandrite, Amazonite, Amber, Amblygonite, Anglesite, Anhydrite, Apatite, Sapphire, Zircon, and so forth (IGS 2021). Yet thousands of them are not discovered by the human race. Our geologists, geophysicists, and engineers are sleepless exploring our mineral sites - rocks, oceans, and rivers - in search of hidden minerals.

Their secret locations make them very difficult for the ordinary man or woman from the street of London or New York to dig them up and harvest them. They are so rare and hidden from the sights of the poor. It takes certain grades of people with financial muscles to search for precious metals and find them.

The Creator of the universe was the one who hid them under the ground - like the bottom of the iceberg. It takes the brave to find them.

As of 19th December 2021, the price of diesel in the UK was 149.7p per Litre. In the bullion global market, the UK bid prices per gram for Gold, Palladium, Platinum and Silver were £43.5814, £42.7536, £22.6719, 22.6719, and £0.5410, respectively [1] compared to a 500-ml bottle of Still Spring Water from Aldi Supermarket that costs 0.9p per 100ml.

The only reason why prices of all products processed from underground are so high lies in the concept of "RARITY." The rarer they are, the higher their value in monetary terms - and so are your hidden talents in your iceberg. They are so valuable that their prices are higher than the prices of our basic needs: water, air, and food.

Likewise in our lives. While our academic studies and hard work at school are good for us to get the grades required to get into college or university or gain our first management-level jobs, the fact is that they remain the tips of the iceberg!

Therefore, what lies below the iceberg is what makes us "Super Intelligent" especially when we reach the climax in our careers. What keeps you climbing to the top of your career, and makes you more impactful than other people in your group, your classmates or colleagues is "rare," - the concept of rarity - and thus hidden inside you – away from the public view.

#2: The "RULER" Model

The Yale Centre for Emotional Intelligence defined Emotional Intelligence (YCEI) using the "RULER" acronym derived from the FIVE Emotional Intelligence competencies contained in Daniel Goleman's definition of EI- recognize, understand, label, express and regulate emotions - needed by anyone who leads a team.

A leader must, therefore, possess these five keys to achieve success under pressure where other people deficient in this department had failed woefully. While studying Emotional Intelligence, I have concluded that the foundation of **Emotional Rulership** is, in fact, Emotional Intelligence.

When you become emotionally intelligent on any life events, occurrences or circumstances which cause changes in the status quo, and make you think differently, the next step in handling those events is to dominate the Change through the concept of "rulership" -which is what this book is all about. You simply turn your life circumstances around into what you'd desired previously.

Therefore, emotional intelligence is: "the ability to recognize your own emotions, and the emotions of others, Understand your emotions and other people's emotion; Label emotions as accurately as possible; Express them effectively, and Regulate all emotions" (YCEI?).

---

1. Source: https://www.ukbullion.com/live-chart/gold/gbp/.

Chapter Five

The Benefits of Emotional Intelligence

"You can conquer almost any fear if you will only make up your mind to do so. For remember, fear doesn't exist anywhere except in the mind."

~ Dale Carnegie

WHEN IT comes to the overall company bottom line, there are SIX key questions business leaders must ask themselves.

1. Have you ever considered the impacts of emotions on your employee-workplace experiences, and how their personal emotions affect their job performance – their ability to reach company goals?

2. Have you ever considered the impacts of emotions on the organization as a whole? What about workplace tension? Have you ever considered how a lack of empathy (emotional connection and emotional management) between senior managers and junior employees could

impact the company's business - its name, image, brand, its values, vision, and mission?

3. What about organizational culture? Have you thought about the impacts of emotions on the organizational culture and the way the organization does its business with the public?

4. Have you considered that the emotions of your staff on the front-line customer service or telephone etiquette could impact the overall customer experience? And how do you measure customer experience - their wants, and their needs?

5. Have you ever considered the impact of emotions on the senior leadership of the organization – from the CEO down to the line managers, and how their private lives and emotional states conceived in the privacy of their own homes could impact them publicly and venomously affect the performance of the Boss the next day?

6. Finally, have you also ever asked yourself, "why should customers visit my business, my website, or buy my products or services, instead of visiting my competitors' next door? What values of unique significance have you created to attract high-value customers through your door?

You don't have to answer these SIX questions right now, but these questions are here to help you understand the importance of Emotional Intelligence training for the benefit of your organization. Below are TWELVE research activities on EI, and their effects on financial performance.

1: Achievement in College Or Job

Increased levels of EI can help you circumnavigate the social difficulties and pressure each student encounters throughout their academic years. Preparing and sitting for examinations could be mentally tough for everyone. Even in the workplace, employees are constantly going through various forms of training or learning. Being "tested" doesn't seem to end any time soon!

Understanding the Principles and Laws of Emotional Intelligence in Leadership, will help you to lead, and inspire your team to outshine in their profession. While measuring key job applicants, many organizations now rank EI as high as technical skills and apply EQ testing before an appointment.

2: Your Mental Health in the State of Crisis

When your emotions and stress levels are unregulated over time, they can affect your mental wellbeing. From being vulnerable to suffering from anxiety and panic attacks, one's mental health could nosedive to deep depression due to chemicals generated in our brain. It can have an impact on your relationship with your wife or husband or even on your children and your social circle. When you find yourself trapped in a chain of events that compel you to the state of 'feeling' lonely and 'isolated,' it can further induce depression and escalate any hidden mental health problems.

3: Your Health Might Be at Risk

If it is practically impossible to manage your own private and personal emotions at home or collegiately while working in a group, you might find it hard to manage and deal with stress effectively. Emotional stress is a silent activator of cortisol stress hormones.

Your inability to handle stressful events or experiences exposes the fragility of the human body to a host of healthcare problems, ranging from high blood pressure to kidney failure, diabetes, and suppressed immune system; infertility, strokes, and congestive heart failure (CHF), as well as amplified speedy ageing processes. You become mentally geriatric (old) but physically adolescent. The best way to improve your overall stress management is to destress and manage your emotions effectively.

4: Your Relationship Might Suffer from Haemorrhage

Understanding the source of haemorrhage in your relationship is one step away from finding the solution. Learning to manage your own emotions first, means you can manage and understand other people's emotions thereafter, and manage them for the benefit of your relationship. Since you are the only one that can understand your "inner feelings," and "changes" happening in your organization, you will be in a better position as the CEO, Manager, or Entrepreneur to know how best to communicate your feelings, ideas, or innovative solutions to others. You'll be able to know when to press the brake pedal without having a car crash in your life and build a good, sustainable relationship both at work and in your private life.

5: Employees' Job Performance

Your employees' ability to work well and meet the company's targets is one of the keys to success in your organization. How do you feel when all your employees give you 30, 40 or 50% of their talents (abilities) and their time, leading to so many projects being half-completed or missing deadlines? More than anyone else, the only one person in your organization who is responsible for creating the "conditions" - the climate - which directly or indirectly determine people's ability to work well is the boss: the CEO, the Senior Manager or the Line Manager.

I believe that Emotions are contagious. The low emotions of employees at the forefront of customer service could impact negatively on company revenue, repeat purchase, and recommendations. For instance, when a member of your staff who had fallen out with a Senior Manager carries their emotions in their hearts while serving customers, the chances are that their personal emotions may directly or indirectly affect customer service and impacts the customer's excitement and emotional wellbeing for increased linked sales.

The lack of emotional connection and attitude of the business leaders and senior managers towards employees in the workplace are some of the keys to poor financial performance in the organization. But in organizations with a positive culture and employee engagement, evidence shows that employees' performance increases by 10 to 30% above those with poor workplace engagement.

6: Business Performance

As a business leader in your organization, have you ever considered the business case of emotional intelligence training, and how this would benefit your team, your organization, and the shareholders? What does success mean to you, in your organization? How do you know when performance is high? How do you define success? Because what you classify as success may, in fact, not be a success after all for your employees. How do you measure success in your organization and what are the key performance indicators (KPI)?

Businesses that are dedicated to emotional intelligence outperform the competition. They continuously increase their performance and deliver exceptional customer experience. They reach this feat by providing enabling environments by allocating resources – finances, people, and materials – for leadership training, performance management, and emotional intelligence.

7: Organizational Climate

Organizational climate can be defined as the common perceptions, views, experiences, opinions, culture, or way of life or norms which exist in an organization and the way an organization carries out its businesses with members of the public. Research shows that about 53-72% of organizational climate as "perceived" by employees is traceable to the responses, actions, or inactions of only one person: The Leader (Kelner et al. 1996).

Poor organizational culture is a major contributory factor on why employees resign from their jobs. People leave managers, not companies. Research shows that more than fifty per cent of Americans have left a job just to "get away from their managers at some point in their career" (Gallup 2015).

8: Customer Experience

Have you ever considered what your customers have to do to enjoy a high customer experience in your organization? This is because good customer service could be the single reason why your customers keep shopping on your premises, while poor customer service could be the wall standing between your business and the wallet of your potential customers. Poor customer experience, vis-à-vis the poor emotional management of your team, could affect customer service either directly or indirectly.

Because our emotions are contagious, when your employees are happy and well-engaged by the senior management, they automatically transfer the same energy, the same emotions, and the same attitude to serve the customer - on the counter, on the shop floor, or over the phone.

9: Poor Workplace Tension

The prolonged period of poor workplace tension is the common cause of the company's poor financial performance leading to:

- Increased staff absence.
- Increased staff resignation.
- Increased de-motivated employees.
- Decreased output/productivity, and
- A fall in financial performance.

From the guru himself, DANIEL GOLEMAN, in his 'Working with Emotional Intelligence' book, his research activities across various organizations showed that

> *"for leadership positions, Emotional Intelligence competencies account for up to 85% of what sets outstanding managers apart from the average."*

10: Impacts on Leadership

It is no longer a secret that EI is the key to high performance under pressure. The CEOs, Business leaders, Entrepreneurs, Presidents of Governments, School Headteachers, Vice-Chancellors, and so forth - are all expected to be "superheroes," but not the supervillains to remain in control or achieve results when other leaders had failed in similar circumstances.

Great leaders achieve extraordinary results not by magic or juju or manipulation, but by deploying the mysterious combination of psychological proficiencies available to the human race, but to those who seek knowledge in this department. The high level of intelligence is Emotional Intelligence.

Whether we approve of it or not, our great leaders and entrepreneurs have to manage tough business climates and decision-making processes through this blend of proficiencies. Some of these skills are natural or inborn, and can never be learnt or taught in the classroom. Others could be acquired through life experiences, age, exposure, etc. while a small fraction can be gained through outdated leadership training.

I believe that with my experience managing people and multi-million-pound pharmacy businesses, and being an entrepreneur and employer of people in the UK, I would say that I have gotten pretty much better, with on-hand-experience reading other people's emotions on daily basis. We can improve our emotional intelligence through observation of body language, reading books, and listening to vocal variations and tones as people interact with one another.

As I stated earlier in this book, I would like to emphasize that human emotions are contagious. Like viruses, emotions can spiral from the top to the bottom. Thus emotions can be transmitted from the top management to the junior managers, from managers to frontline employees, and finally to the customers on the counter or the phone.

Research by Randall Beck and Jim Harter (April 2015) shows that leaders and their leadership styles are accountable for up to 70% of changes in Employee Engagement in workplace environments. Poor emotional leadership is attributable to the deficiency of emotional intelligence among senior managers who influence the employees.

In another research conducted by the same authors in 2012, their findings showed that about 13% of the Global workforce were engaged by their managers. What do these statistics tell us? The big question that I'm asking business managers is this: What happened to the 87% of the workforce who were not engaged?

In practical terms, this old data means that the vast majority of employees worldwide were failed by their managers who did not care to develop their staff effectively to contribute maximally at work. All managers, irrespective of their location or type of industry, are responsible for the training and development of their junior employees.

Therefore, managers should be held responsible for employees' inefficiency to carry out daily work routines. Why? Because these groups of the workforce should have been "trained" properly, or "prepared in advance" to work efficiently anyway. The eighty-seven per cent of the workforce who were underdeveloped could be one of the contributory factors for organizational and leadership failures around the world.

Finally, if applied with knowledge, understanding, and wisdom, Emotional Intelligence can serve as a stimulant for leaders, their people, and their organization to achieve outstanding business performance. However, if applied unwisely, it can weaken the leaders' integrity, character, and trustworthiness.

11: Value Creation

There is nothing new in this world, no matter how innovative the inventions are. There is no need of thinking out new ideas which have never existed in the world. Why? Because the Creator of the university had already put the solutions to the world's problems in the minds of the human race. "Let them have dominion" - He says!

As of 28 December 2021, the World population stood at 7.9 Billion people. If each person has one unique solution for one unique problem, this translates to 7.9 Billion problems waiting for the 7.9 billion people to solve 7.9 Billion crises.

NEW Problems - New Solutions - New Businesses

This is how to solve new problems: we borrow one or two old ideas which had been tested and proved to be effective in solving problems elsewhere. Then, we mix them differently with new stuff (such as adjuvant) to yield a unique blend resulting in astonishing results. This is how vaccines are developed using an old base - with adjuvants added! To us, the result of the mixture becomes the new solution to the current problems.

Once a new solution emerges, a new business with a new value proposition has arrived and resources management creeps in. Just as bees are attracted to the flower nectar, so will people be attracted to your new business solution. They will travel miles away to test if your new concept or mixture can wipe off their earthly problems.

Therefore, to create value in your business or organization, the leadership must adapt and manage available resources effectively. Such resources include humans or people management; financial budgeting, cash flow; technology, and other environmental factors to create something - a product or service - of significant value which the customer wants or needs in exchange for revenue.

Your value, which comprises your image, character, name, product quality, culture, uniqueness, customer relations and so forth, are some of the value-created assets - both tangible and intangible - which attract your customers to your organizations.

Those who desire your services will have the will and power to pay you heavily in return for your efforts. Value creation is one of the key reasons many emerging entrepreneurs start new businesses from scratch. The aim of starting new businesses is not necessarily to make profits, but to make a difference in the world and contribute to the national economy.

12: Increases in Revenue

We will not complete this chapter without mentioning the bottom line. Emotional Intelligence is responsible for improved revenue generation if the organizational culture is good. Research shows that:

> *"for every 1% improvement in the service climate, there is a 2% increase in revenue."*
> (Spencer 2001; Gallup 2015).

That service climate is not just the embodiment of your customers, stakeholders, shareholders, members of the public, and your competitors, but more especially the emotions of your employees.

SECTION 3

DOMINION RULERSHIP

"Millions have nurtured great innovative ideas, dreams, or ambitions, but not many have the mental toughness or agility to pursue those dreams above the norm."

- Dr Emmanuel E. Amadi

Chapter Six

The Concept of Emotional Rulership

> "A Leader Without Emotional Control is like a Navy Seal who lost his shotguns on the battlefield. The enemy snuffs him out like a coward."
>
> ~Dr Emmanuel E. Amadi

THE MOST ELUSIVE form of Leadership or Governance is "Rulership." Leadership in the public domain has been "*misunderstood*" or "*misconceived*" in the mental womb of our political leaders. The quest for Power, Sovereignty, Dominion, or Rulership "over people" is the most dangerous form of leadership or governance which has been *misunderstood* and *misinterpreted* in the history of mankind.

It is this *"misunderstanding"* or "*misconception*" of what Rulership concept is, and what it isn't, that makes Rulership appear dangerous on the surface, but magnificent inside.

When I use the term, RULERSHIP, I'm not referring to the despotic, repressive, and dictatorial domination of the people under your charge. Rather, I'm referring to your ability to influence or change your environments and life circumstances through the Power of Emotions and the instrument of Leadership.

I am not referring to the political monarchy existing in various forms and nomenclature - Emperors, Pharaohs, Chiefs, tsars, khans, Sultans, Sheikhs, Kings or the Queen of the United Kingdom sitting on her throne in Buckingham Palace, London - neither am I referring to certain ever-powerful "deities" or "mini-gods", who control their "subjects" or "proletariat" rather than "serving" their "Citizens."

I am referring to your own personal "kingship experience" – which is your ability to control or dominate the Earth's resources in your environment, culture, job or profession. I'm referring to your capacity to influence the world or the Cosmos. And that Cosmos is the System of control, power, or influence which controls everyone that lives on the surface of this very planet Earth in any area of life, whether in business (Commerce or eCommerce), economics, politics, or government, Law / Legislature, Healthcare - Medicine & pharmaceuticals.

The guys in healthcare are like demigods. That's what I mean by taking control of your fields in life. They can revive your sick body into a healthy one when you visit them in their place of practice (they are still practising), or they can end your life at − 10 to -150 degrees Celsius while experimenting on your body. They call it "medical negligence" instead of "murder" or "manslaughter."

They will do these things without anyone questioning them. Very powerful mini-gods – they think they are! Yes, the brain surgeons can rip off your brain, feed it with cholate and hamburger, or stamp it with their logo or name without anyone questioning their authority. That's how influential some of the World Systems are, especially in the World of Healthcare.

By Rulership, I am also referring to your personal influence in your domain such as the worlds of Arts; Entertainment industry (such as music); the World of Sports; the World of Civic –

which creates value for the benefit of its citizens; the World of Society or Social life - which controls people's lifestyle, as well as the "Religious World" – which influences our faith, righteousness, and dictates how we worship our God.

Millions have nurtured great innovative ideas, dreams, or ambitions, but not many have the mental toughness or agility to pursue those dreams above the norm. Some people are confused in life that they don't seem to grasp what they want out of life. Most are not living a purposeful life. Many know what they were born to fulfil on Earth, but don't have the courage to take risks in business and innovation.

The world is full of past leaders in the corridors of Power and Authority who had fallen as victims of their personal emotions conceived privately in the comfort of their homes resulting in the public display of dysfunctional leadership. I am convinced that some of the reasons for failure in life are either **deficiency, insufficiency** or the **total loss of effectiveness** in Emotional Rulership in Leadership.

Although this concept of controlling life circumstances evolves naturally and gradually over time, Emotional Rulership can be "activated" or "accelerated" through the instrument of personal leadership and training.

The loss of effective leadership in governance is a global pandemic with increasing prevalence among low-income earning employees that has long-term consequences for societal development. Unless our leaders recognize this deficiency or lack of effective leadership in areas of concern and commit to global incorporation of leadership in our academic curriculum, and address it as a priority, many will retire without fulfilling their purpose on Earth.

Thousands of books will be buried in the cemetery this year without hitting the shelves. And many talents that were never served to the world may soon turn into ashes in our crematorium.

Emotional Rulership also refers to organizational wide-approach and culture of promoting mentorship programmes.

This involves transforming employees as future leaders of their time to preserve their inherent leadership and its effectiveness in our society.

Life is like the Rat-Race we all seem to run at different lanes of life:
Go to high school, college or university.
Get a Job and a Big House + the mortgage you can't afford.
Get a wife or a husband you can afford to drive nuts.
Or a partner you don't have time
to spend quality time with.
Why? Because you love your job. You work hard to pay off the mortgage.
From 9 am to 5 pm on a Minimum Wage,
You will retire at 60, 67, 68, or 70.
To help you get alone,
The government pays you £200 a week as a pension.

I believe that these illustrations are not the kind of life we had dreamt to live. For me, billions of employees don't seem to know their purpose in life – the reason they were born to accomplish in this world, or the problems they were assigned to solve in their local communities.

Many ideas have been trapped in the World System known as *Employment* and many had died in their jobs without finding what problems they were born to solve. I also believe that you can change lives, create jobs, build schools, donate to charity, and control your life circumstances.

For those of you, who are managers, leaders, or CEOs in your organizations, you cannot achieve success, without first controlling your private emotions and feelings. Your private feelings, if not "ruled" by you, can 'spill-over' into the public domain as venoms that could harm the mental health of your employees. The future consequences may be damning as well and diminish the ***trust*** you had worked hard to achieve in life.

Here are the five statements that define a "trusted" leader:

Your Emotions give birth to Your Character.
Your Character gives birth to Your Personality.
Your Personality gives birth to your Integrity.
Your Integrity gives birth to TRUST.
And TRUST carves you as the Trusted LEADER.

These four qualities – character, personality, integrity, and trust - are the building blocks that define you from within. Whether you like it or not, your private, secret life might overflow its boundaries if not well controlled. Your secret lifestyle may one day, become public and influence people around you.

Living a Life of Success

Living life fully and successfully doesn't happen by default. Success stories of Self-made Millionaires don't happen by chance either. Rather, they happen by DESIGN or PLANNING. When you live your life by default, you drift on the tidal wave of shallow waters of life, without any specific dreams or vision, and without purpose or destination.

Living a Life of Mediocrity

This is how people live a life by default. They have no dreams. When they have dreams, it's just like other night dreams or daydreams, but no plans. Although some may have dreams + Plans, they lack the "willpower" to act on them. They're too tired, or too afraid of uncertainties to take risks starting new businesses, becoming entrepreneurs, going into real estate, or educating themselves.

Some might have Dreams + Plans + Actions, but lack Consistency of purpose. Why? Because they're distracted by too many visions from the enemy, that flashes luxury life – expensive cars, houses, and fashion - across their sight. Their real vision is blurred to occlude their real destination. This sort of life is a life of mediocrity, boredom, and crumbling into the abysmal valley of poverty.

But when you live your life by DESIGN, you know who you're, your purpose in life, where you're from, and where you want to be in real-time. A Life by DESIGN is a life with:

1. PLANNING.

2. ACTION (active and proactive, not reactive by default).

3. CONSISTENCY of Purpose – in the pursuit of a SINGLE Vision.

It is our failure or inability to control our daily personal circumstances, conditions, and event that compels us into feelings of vulnerability and hopelessness in the face of difficulties, and we live as remnants of life casualties.

For some of us seeking to survive the issues of life and live a decent lifestyle, we work on two low-paid jobs just to pay the bills, credit cards, and big mortgage repayments for a house we don't live in. Life has become a daily struggle as we attempt to remain buoyant in the waves of doubts and stressful conditions of all kinds.

Concurrently, we grapple with the feelings of servitude, bondage, and subjugation in our jobs as we find ourselves mentally chained to the jobs we hate, but financially hooked like "drugs" or "cocaine" to the establishments in our communities which had tied us down in a relationship next to economic slavery.

What is Emotional Rulership?

How do you define this important concept, which had been forgotten in the fabric of leadership for more than 2,000 years? Since Emotional Rulership is the practical application of Emotional Intelligence (EI), it is imperative to define and distinguish Emotional Rulership without juxtaposing its meaning on EI.

Therefore, I define Emotional RULERSHIP as this:

> "Emotional Rulership is the ability to control or influence CHANGE in your environment, circumstances, or destiny with your EMOTIONS and THOUGHTS through the instrument of LEADERSHIP."

Below is the body of 10 points that summarize the definition of Emotional Rulership. They're details of what Emotional Rulership is all about. They'll help you improve your leadership in your family, relationships, and organizations so that you can live your life to the fullest by DESIGN, not by Default.

1. Emotional Rulership is "the ability to control or influence CHANGE in your environment, circumstances, or destiny with your EMOTIONS and THOUGHTS through the instrument of LEADER-SHIP." Where there is Leadership, automatically, there is a Followership. In-between a Leader and a Follower is INFLUENCE built-in. Therefore, the only difference between a Leader and a Follower is their mindset, known as Influence. The question you might begin to ask yourself is this: "How can I convince people to follow my vision for a minute? How can I influence them,

or shift their mindset - to abandon their visions and to willingly follow my passion without imposing my doctrine or belief on them? How can I cause a positive CHANGE in my community, society, the culture of the people, their CHOICES, or their PREFERENCES without manipulating their minds: their will-power, and their emotions?

2. Rulership is the capacity to become a person of value in your area of gifting. Your job in life is to find that area in your work, job, or profession – so you can add value to it, refine it, redefine it, dominate it, and serve it to the world.

3. Emotional Rulership is the ability to INFLUENCE "the world" around you, make it better, and maximize resources for the benefit of the people under your service.

4. Rulership = Leadership of the people in the areas of life that matter most to the people in your local community, city, or country, such as the economy, GDP, employment, labour market, infrastructure, education, religion, and culture.

5. Emotional Rulership in Leadership is the capacity to exercise the kingdom of heaven experience in ONE AREA of Life, better than you were in the previous years. You don't have to master and dominate all industries, but you MUST focus on one industry, solve one problem in that industry, and finally dominate it. Here is the Number ONE Life Secret to adopt to become successful. When you follow this simple trick, your life will be CHANGED forever: One Dream, One Vision, One Mission, and One industry. The next step is to take Dominion = Rulership over a domain of life. You'll rule your world – just like Elon Musk, Jeff Bezos, and Richard Branson are ruling their own "World" of Space Tourism.

6. Rulership is not about INTIMIDATION, but INSPIRATION. You cannot bully work colleagues into

obeying your terms and condition, rather they have to be "inspired" to work on your Ts & Cs.

7. Emotional Rulership is not IMPOSITION, but IMPARTATION. How do you embrace the culture of other people, the minority ethnic groups, the people of colour, people of different religions or faiths or languages? How do you lead people of diverse backgrounds in your organization without being judgemental? How do you accept the notion that "it is good to be different" without imposing your belief systems on them?

8. "Emotional Rulership in Leadership" is about seeking the right or "uncorrupted" information from the right source, and communicating the same in the right LANGUAGE to the right people, in the right PLACE, and at the right TIME that builds cohesion and unity. By Right language, I mean the common language of a certain group of people (nations, culture, business, profession, etc.) that they understand. Just as every culture, society, or country has its language or terminologies, so does every profession or career. You can see that I have used the word "right" very frequently. Make no mistakes about this. There's a difference between "doing good" and "doing right."

KNOWLEDGE OF THE LANGUAGE OF YOUR DISCIPLINE

Let us dive a little into this idea called Language. Everything in life has its own language for communication. The cells in your body have their own language. Birds and other beasts of the jungle have their own language. Law as a profession has its language - the Legalese - very confusing and not ordinary language. Medicine, pharmacy, and dentistry - all have their confusing languages and terminologies borrowed from the ideas of old dead men - Aristotle and Plato of the ancient Greeks. For instance, when your doctor, nurse or pharmacist prescribes your medicine to be taken One "in the morning", it will be written thus: "i mane." Instead of advising you to take your medicines twice a day, they will write "BD." If you don't understand the language and culture of this profession, you have a 100% chance of killing your patients under your care.

9. Rulership in Political Leadership is not about making political statements to the sweet romance and darling of political party members, rather it's about creating fertile business opportunities to encourage existing or potential entrepreneurs to start or expand their businesses, decrease the unemployment rate, and reduce crime or divorce due to lack of earned incomes.

10. Finally, Rulership in Government is about providing a healthy economy for businesses to flourish and survive in turbulent times. It's also about improving profitability in the manufacturing sector, the service industry, and international trade relationships, such as the exportation of locally made goods to other nations that balance our importation of foreign products in a bilateral relationship akin to marriage.

Characters of Rulership

Rulership has two inherent characters or characteristics – AUTHORITY and POWER. These two characteristics – authority and power – are different, and they too had been *misconceived* and *abused* by humans in their quest for true Leadership. If we don't understand these two words from their roots or foundation, it would be impossible for us to truly understand Emotional RULERSHIP as an effective means of LEADERSHIP.

AUTHORITY is about responsibility, orderliness, accountability, domain, territory, legitimacy, influence, right, i.e., righteousness, or "official permission", while POWER is the ability or capacity to do something. While AUTHORITY is about the empowerment of the people in your charge, POWER is the instrument for enforcing that authority.

POWER is hidden inside AUTHORITY. Therefore, when you see a man with Authority in the physical realm, such as Her Majesty the Queen, Elizabeth, or the President of the USA, and so forth, they carry their Governments or Authority along with them. Their power is hidden inside them. The amount of power or influence they exhibit is proportional to the POWER of that nation they are coming from or representing.

Here is another example of how authority works. When I travel to the US as a British Citizen with my British passport (please note that the British passport is the property of the Crown – Her Majesty), although I'm travelling as an individual, I'm carrying an authority – a nation – along with me. I'm carrying an entire Sovereign Nation in my hand in the form of a booklet from the original source: The United Kingdom. If my life is threatened or I need some help while in the US, I have the legal right = authority = to demand consulate and diplomatic assistance from the UK Government, through the British Embassy in the US or anywhere in the world, just like any other British Citizen in a foreign country.

When I open my British Passport, the first thing I see written inside the left page of the hardcover is this statement:

> "Her Britannic Majesty's Secretary of State requests and requires in the name of Her Majesty all those whom it may concern to allow the bearer to pass freely without let or hindrance, and to afford the bearer such assistance and protection as may be necessary."

However, if you're a dual citizen and something wrong happens to you - whether legally or illegally - in your other country of nationality, the Government Authority you possessed a few minutes earlier is now under threat. Here is what the British Crown says (see Notes on page 4 of the New British Passport, section 3: Consular Assistance Abroad):

> "Consular assistance is NOT routinely provided to dual nationals in their other country of nationality."
> It went further to state thus: "A person who has dual nationality may be subject to the LAWS of the other county. It is your RESPONSIBILITY to determine what responsibilities you may have with that other Country."

In other words, the Government of the country you're in, and possess their nationality can activate her POWER through its Legal Authority over the Power and Authority of the British Crown. Therefore, authority lends power to the legality to function. In other words, power is powerless in the absence of authority.

Let me explain this difference further, on how Authority and Power share the same corridors in government, governance, or leadership. For instance, the UK Prime Minister, Boris Johnson, has the legitimate right = authority - to function as the Prime Minister of the United Kingdom.

Secondly, behind every authority, is a hidden power. The Prime Minister, once confirmed by the Queen automatically has POWER by the virtue of his Office - "The Office of the Prime Minister" - to change the laws of the land through legislation, or parliament. Such powers in a democracy are not obtained by inheritance, nobility, or birth. Rather, the authority is "given" to "whom" "thou has voted in" through the ballot box. But in an undemocratic government, power can be "taken" by usurpation through "military force," also known as "Stratocracy." In Stratocracy, the citizens are not "ruled" or "governed" by the army, rather 'dictated' by "dictators" in comparison to a democratically elected government.

The Beginning of Modern Rulership

Our UK imperial history is shrouded with the colonial past of the early empires: colonial masters, dynasties, emperors, Kings and Queens. It is filled with sordid tales of how Kingdoms later dissolved into obscurity and turned themselves into history lessons for our young children. From Alexander the Great (Greek Empire) to Julius Ceaser and Augustus Caesar (Octavian) of the ancient Roman Empire - their successes in military power for over 5,000 years could not save both empires from ruin or self-decay.

Wars after wars – the Roman Empire was doomed economically due to many reasons, including costly colonial expansion strategies, while their rulers, empires and Kingdoms gradually declined in moral values. Their leaders and former military commanders decayed from the inside through their loins. They died from immorality and failed to provide the best Rulership or governance for their people. Rome was not defeated by any known army; it was defeated internally from the contents of their emotions: their bedrooms.

The Greeks invented the old leadership philosophy which has continued to rule the world till this day. The Greeks, such as Aristotle, Plato, or Socrates (the **APS** as I call them) were the best thinkers of their times. Even though they are dead, their ideas and philosophies from the graveyard had continued to control humanity. Our government, industries, science and technology; engineering, medicines, and pharmaceuticals as well as leadership ideas have continued to influence the world of today.

These founders of modern thinking - **APS**– 'believed' and 'acted' upon their belief system, that leadership is "the result of natural endowment or birth traits: a person of charismatic (god-given) personality and possess forceful personalities. They also believed that leaders are extroverts, have specialist training and are demi-gods (providence) shaped by divine power over other humans graded as sub-humans.

By providence, they theorized that leaders are chosen by certain deities, or gods, which are wiser, most powerful, benevolent, and divine than humans. In other words, if you're short, naturally the Greeks will not pick you as a leader. If you don't possess compelling "attractiveness" in terms of beauty, high-pitched voice, masculinity, or if you're not from a particular "race, certain skin" colour: whites versus blacks; blue eyes versus brown eyes; extroverts versus introverts; pointed nose versus flat nose; long hairs versus short hairs; Europeans versus Africans, and so forth, you have been automatically cancelled to be a leader. If you can't inspire "devotion", "reverence" or "worship" from the people in any form or shape, the Greeks believed that you're not born a leader, but born "naturally" to be led as "followers."

In his Theory of Evolution and natural selection, entitled "On the Origin of Species by Means of Natural Selection Or The Preservation of Favoured Races in the Struggle for Life," Charles Darwin in 1859, hyped or popularized the above stated Greek philosophies of leadership and brought them to life in our corridors of Governments.

Darwin showcased this idea using the "survival of the fittest" model, where strong animals in the jungle thrive over the weak ones. When applied to humans, this statement means that only the "elected," or "selected" class of people, such as the 'wealthy aristocrats,' political class, the clergy, businesspeople, etc., are suitable for survival. He infused blood to the idea that some races are more equal than others.

With his theory of Evolution, vis-à-vis natural selection, social Darwinism supported "Scientific Racism" to the core in the 21st century of corporate Britain. In the words of Lindsay

Pressman of the Trinity College, Hartford, Connecticut, USA, she made the following statement regarding Darwinism:

> "When applied to imperialist societies, this concept asserts that groups who are more economically, technologically, or politically advanced than neighbouring groups will naturally dominate and conquer" (Pressman [2011-Present (2017)]).

The social Darwinism theory of *racial dominance* and *subjugation* of other people only acted as a booster to "the belief that a group or species' position in society is fixed, or has minimal capacity for improvement," as stated by Pressman in the Trinity Papers of 2011.

Back to the Greek philosophers, they not only invented leadership ideas, but also invented *Demokratia* (Greek: dēmokratía) in what we call *democracy*, and *Politiká* or *Politeia*, derived from the word *polis* (which means affairs of the city-states) – in what we call "politics."

The Greek was very strong intellectually, transforming ideas into beliefs, and beliefs into life philosophies. They were not only strong in their heads (thinking) but also in their hands militarily - as demonstrated by the military tactics of Alexander the Great. His tactics were phenomenal that he conquered the world by the age of 20!

For years, the Romans watched these Great Thinkers with great passion, and carefully studied their weaknesses without undermining their strengths. Aware of their targets, Augustus Caesar of Rome invaded Greece (first converting Macedonia – the Northern territory into a Roman "province" or "colony") with advanced military tactics stolen from Alexander the Great plus other superior tactics unknown to the Greek military might. Rome seized the treasured gift of the Greeks back to the

Roman Emperor. That treasured gift was not their armoury - the warehouse of their weapons - but rather their LIBRARY.

What the Romans did to the Greeks is similar to what the virus does to the human body when it enters the victim's body to colonize it. It takes control of the victim's nucleus and uses the victim's DNA or genome to colonize and control the entire body. Once inside, the virus multiplies itself into various armies or soldiers. It uses your DNA as its own, and sends coded instructions to your body to shut it down. At this stage, the virus rules your body into submission through domination. That's exactly what the Romans did to the Greeks.

Thus, Rome invaded Greece and took all Greek's ideas to Caesar. The library contained recorded life philosophies – leadership ideas, governance, Ecclesia, or Senate in what we call in English "Church," and thousands of innovative ideas, complex equations, algebra, calculus, and formulas (formulae) that had never been touched, and which had continued to influence our industries today. Rome controlled the world for 2,000 years.

The word "Ecclesia" or "Church," as used by the Greeks, is a political term. It was never intended to be used as a religious word. The Greeks used "Ecclesia" or "church" to refer to the Roman Government's Cabinet or the Senate – the seat of power. "Ecclesia" or "Church" also means the "the selected few", "the chosen", "the appointed", or "picked out" of others. It is the same meaning that Jesus "intended" in his mind when he said to Peter:

> "And I tell you that you are Peter[1] and on this rock, I will build my church [*ecclesia*][2], and the gates of Hades[3] will not overcome it."
> (Mathew 16:18, NIV; *emphasis italicized*).

Our religious leaders have misunderstood the word "Ecclesia" or "Church" thinking that Jesus had meant "religion" - even though his primary assignment on Earth was to restore the kingdom of God's Government on Earth. About 700 years before the birth of Jesus, one certain Hebrew prophet known as Isaiah, correctly predicted the birth of Jesus Christ in the year of King Uzziah's death - the former King of the United Kingdom of Israel - when he said:

> "For to us a child is born, to us, a son is given, and the government will be on his shoulders." He continued, "Of the greatness of his government and peace there will be no end. He will reign on David's throne and over his kingdom, establishing and upholding it with justice and righteousness from that time on and forever." (Isaiah 9:6-7).

The Greeks used the word, "Senate" to refer to the body of Administrators of God's government, leadership, rulership, or authority on the Earth. Members of the Senate were appointed, not voted. Because an Emperor was regarded as a demi-god, representing God's authority on Earth, Cabinet Ministers were to serve as God's "Ambassador" or "diplomatic force" to pursue God's agenda on Earth through Caesar.

The Greeks were not taken to Rome as conquered slaves or war prisoners, rather they were allowed to remain in their cities in Greece as a "Roman Colony." To control the Greeks in their own lands, Caesar, therefore, adopted the same Greeks leadership philosophies, Government, Senate, etc.

Therefore, the Roman Empire was the first empire to establish the SENATE or Member of the Governing Council. They implemented these borrowed ideas in Rome for the first time. No other empire had ever done so previously. Members of the

Senate were not voted in by the people, rather they were selected by Caesar to work with him in the same caucus, inner circle, or cabinet. Remember that "Caesar" was not a name, but an official title given to a ruler at the time. In our modern democracy, that title akin to "The President" or "Office of the President."

The Greeks and the Romans believed that Caesar was the "King of the World" who ruled the whole world. They also believed that Caesar was a "demi-god" - who was superior to ordinary humans. Whatsoever Caesar said publicly, members of his cabinets took notes and converted Cesar's words into written laws. Therefore, the Roman Empire, I would say, was an "imitation" of the Kingdom of God on Earth. Whatever the king says becomes a law.

The Disintegration of the Roman Empire

The European countries we have today, such as the United Kingdom of Great Britain (Anglo-Britain), Belgium, and the Kingdoms of Denmark, Netherlands, Norway, and Sweden were once the conquered colonies of the former Roman Empire. When Julius Caesar of Rome conquered the Celtic region, the country we know today as France, Rome was originally called it *Gaul*.

The geographical size of Gaul was a huge landmass, spanning from France to Belgium, Luxembourg, and some areas of the Netherlands, Switzerland, and Germany. *Hispania*, the landmass of the Iberian Peninsula, presently occupied by Spain and Portugal - was once a Roman colony.

But when Rome imploded, the once big-time empire disintegrated into several pieces, leading to these former colonies forming smaller Kingdoms of their own, collectively known as *Europa*, or Europe. As the smaller kingdoms developed over time, they carried with them the same old leadership philosophies of their former Colonial Masters (Rome).

To remain relevant and influential, Kingdoms must have territories or colonies, just like God created the Earth as his personal territory, but to be ruled by humans. When the new seven "European Kingdom" Powers - Britain, Belgium, France, Germany, Italy, Spain, and Portugal - decided to expand their territories, they invaded smaller nations, including Canada, the USA, and the continent of Africa through the same concept of "colonization" just as Rome did to them and the Greeks.

Now, the new rulers of Europe deployed the same Roman "ideas" and "philosophies," adopted the same Roman "colonization blueprint", and became Colonial Slave Masters themselves only in African nations. They deployed the same ancient Roman ideology of "divide-and-rule" to invade and control their colonies in the name of bringing "Western culture" and "Civilization," trade, Christianity, and democracy, "rational thinking" and "capitalism" as well as "modern weapons" of war, photography, and processed food.

They did so at the expense of these smaller nations. They looted Africa's natural resources and those of the US back to their Kingdoms – including Great Britain, such as minerals, gold (from South Africa), diamond, ivory, Benin Bronzes and artifacts from Nigeria, oil and gas, bauxite (the chief source of gallium and aluminium) and timber.

In Africa, we had the following "divide-and-rule" strategies that made it easier for the Colonial Masters to enslave African nations with brutal control. Thus, Britain divided the continent of African nations they held hostage into three and lorded it over the indigenous people.

1. British West Africa: Nigeria, Southern Cameroon, Ghana, Gambia, and Sierra Leone.

2. British East Africa: Kenya, Uganda, Tanganyika and Zanzibar (Both Tanganyika and Zanzibar merged in 1964

and rebranded themselves as the Republic of Tanzania with the hope of getting rid of their colonial past); and

3. South Africa: Botswana, Lesotho, Swaziland, Southern Africa (now South Africa), Southern Rhodesia (now Zimbabwe), Northern Rhodesia (now Zambia), and Nyasaland (now Malawi).

Independence Without Freedom

The same Kingdoms that claimed to save Africa, took from Africans but never taught African leaders the principles of leadership and character, and resources management, thereby opening another dimension of slavery known as economic slavery. Hence, The Scramble For Africa.

Although they gave Africa **INDEPENDENCE** but forgot to give Africa **FREEDOM**. One shouldn't be confused about the difference between the two words. On one hand, INDEPENDENCE is about Sovereignty, dominion, **self-government or self-governance**, or "self-determination."

By independence, you as a person, group, or nation becomes "free" from external influence, control, or governance. You have control of your own internal and external affairs: Security, immigration/Border Control, Military, currency, and enact your own Constitution and Rule of Law. In independence, you may be a people of the same culture, the same language, and the same religion. It also means that you can do what you decide to do on your own Will, Mind, and Soul without "depending" on the approval or rejection from others.

FREEDOM, on the other hand, can mean different things to different people. For me, freedom is the ability to take risks where others had tried and failed. Freedom also means the ability to free yourself from the shackles of poverty and "the prison of employment" which has kept millions of people poorer throughout their working life.

Finally, for me, freedom means having the time to do what pleases my emotions such as writing my books, teaching other people how to start a new business from scratch, and inspiring young ones to re-discover their purpose in life.

EU Laws versus Domestic Laws

As I sat down in my study room here in Manchester, UK writing this section of my book on 31st December 2021, the European Union (EU) - made up of the former colonies of the Roman Empire - appears as a sinking ship in the eyes of the outside world following the UK Brexit.

Originally conceived by its founding fathers as an instrument to bolster trades across Europe and the rest of the world, that instrument of unity is now "metamorphosing" itself into a "gigantic elephant" attempting to tramp upon the "mud baths" outside its constitutional boundaries.

The EU, under the influence of France and Germany, is now wagging its finger of "legal supremacy" in the faces of smaller Sovereign states like Poland, Romania, and Hungary. Its dream is to trap and enslave the smaller nations within its borders with the EU Law through the shackles of the European Court of Justice (ECJ) in a process akin to "Modern Colonization" - as they did in Africa.

Subjugating fully-fledged Sovereign nations into accepting the primacy of a third-party, ECJ judiciary system over domestic legitimate, legal systems is inappropriate and uncalled for. This attempt should be resisted and remedied pronto. It is like telling Poland, Romania, and Hungary that, "although I have given you INDEPENDENCE, you're NOT really FREE per se!"

With the departure of Angela Merkel, the former Chancellor of Germany, coupled with the economic difficulties ravaging the German economy after Brexit, plus the clutches of the Covid-19 pandemic, the EU Commission in Brussels is in dire need of a supreme leader.

Under the influence of the French President, Mr Emmanuel Macron, who thinks he can take over the EU leadership and as a substitute for Mrs Merkel and the driving force in EU, is simply breeding a collection of 21st Century "Colonial Masters" dressed in "Santa Claus costumes" as political leaders. They are simply "re-enacting," "re-activating" or "glorifying" the same leadership ideology of the ancient Roman Empire as previously discussed from where all EU kingdom Governments were first conceived and delivered as progenies or descendants of the old block.

By withholding blood supply to the heart of a Christmas chicken to wrestle life out of its existence, the EU has deliberately withheld its recovery fund payment of 36 Billion Euros (£30.2 Billion) to Poland and 7.2 Billion Euros (£6.05 Billion) requested as grants by Hungary[4] in an attempt to "autocratically" subdue them into "modern slavery" and ridicule their countries' Rule of Law and Constitution.

I would leave this international political topic for now with one eye closed, as the world watches the EU political dramas unfold in 2022. But, I will keep the second eye open, without ignoring the ongoing fear of intimidation and military might that one day, the Russian forces under Putin, might invade Ukraine by early 2022.

Imitations of Kingdom Government

From Kings of Kingdoms to Governors of territories, and from politicians to the electorates, all have *misinterpreted* this fundamental concept of Rulership, leading to other "imitations"

of Governance and Political systems such as feudalism, dictatorship, communism, socialism, monarchy, and democracy.

Now, let's dive into each of these copies of Government, and see how they compare with each other.

1. **Feudalism:** An exploitative system of government through the power of land ownership and nobility. During the Middle Ages, societal power, or influence was likened to agriculture. Whoever owns the land, controls the people. Therefore, the noble or wealthy individuals in the society took land ownership from the monarchy in exchange for military service. They were called land-lords or feudal lords, as they became rulers of the society. They rented out their lands to their occupants or tenants in exchange for their loyalty, devotion, allegiance, or services culminating in the concept of "real estate."

2. **Dictatorship:** A form of government where a single leader, a **dictator**, or a small group of tyrants have absolute powers without regard to others or constitutional limitations. The word, **dictator**, was originally used by the Roman Republic as a **Title** for a ***Judge*** or ***Justice Minister*** appointed by the Legislature, who declares Emergency Rule and *dictated* governance for the Roman Republic in times of crisis. This political leadership style has proved to be an unpopular form of leadership and has been abused by despots for personal wealth and oppression of the opposition.

3. **Communism:** This is the marital union between Feudalism and Dictatorship, i.e., Communism = Feudalism + Dictatorship. When both systems of government failed, it became paramount that mankind needed another form of government to salvage itself. Some of the great thinkers at the time, such as Karl Marx and Friedrich Engels, seemed to have found the alternative form of governance - leading to the theory of Communism - where the government owns most landed properties and controls the people and

economic resources. In communism, the political parties in power are the **Feudal Lords** in principle, but **dictatorship** in their mindset.

Between 1945 (after WW II) and 1980, Poland as a nation had communist rule imposed on it against the wishes of the people. In communist states currently experienced in China, Cuba, Laos, and Vietnam, ownership of land and properties is greatly restricted to the most influential = the feudal. In other words, no individuals own landed properties as the government can demand them if they wish to do so.

In communism, the citizens work hard in government-owned enterprises and industries and get paid for their abilities and time. In return, the government provides them with "subsidized" basic needs, such as water, food, healthcare, and education. That means if electricity supply is not considered a basic need, the entire nation will remain in darkness for life. What a tragedy!

4. **Socialism:** Man's attempt to bring governance closer to the people. It's a cover-up of communism. Here, the government controls almost all the society's functions as a commonwealth. The economic resources of the state, i.e., the means of production, such as factories, farms, raw materials, and tools, are owned by the state. Work is conducted as a "Cooperative entity." Here, goods and services are produced solely for consumption by its citizens, unlike in Capitalist economies (UK and USA) where production of goods and services are in private hands and generate profits and wealth for the owners.

This brings us to the last two forms of governments which are still practised by some of the former Roman colonies which later became Kingdoms and are ruled by the Monarchy on one side, and democracy on another.

5. **Monarchy:** A system of government where utmost authority is entrusted in the hands of one person, the Monarch – the King or the Queen – who rules over a kingdom or empire. A Kingdom government is the only "imitation of Government" on Earth that closely resembles the government of the Kingdom of Heaven. In a Kingdom government, first established by God, the King is the LORD, and everybody is his citizen (Eph. 2:19; Colossians 1:13). The King owns everything in his domain, while the citizens own nothing. However, the wealth of the citizens, i.e., the commonwealth, is in the Kingdom. Hence, we have the Commonwealth of Nations.

The King provides resources and protection to his citizens. Thus, every citizen in a Kingdom has access to that commonwealth. But in a kingdom ruled by humans - mere mortals - this form of government will not survive fatalities forever because of its limitations. Our history is littered with various Kingdoms rooted in human slavery, racism, and colonial mindset. Only a Kingdom ruled and initiated by the Creator of the world – whose leaders are "appointed by Him as Senates and Ambassadors of Heaven", and who receive instructions directly from the King Himself - is bound to survive forever.

6. **Democracy:** Democracy was conceived as a child of necessity. It is defined as the "government of the people, for the people, and by the people." It sounds good, right? I regard democracy as a "child of necessity" because democracy evolved in man's attempt to wrestle power from the hands of one powerful individual, in the likes of the Feudal Lords, Dictators, Communists, Socialists, and Kingdom Rulership of the Monarchy to "the Power of the people."

Democracy was introduced closer to the people to enable them "partake" in making distant-political decisions away from the corridors of government, and from their communities on who should take up the leadership of the people through the instrument of the ballot system. Democracy encourages people to voice their minds by casting their votes from the comfort of their communities, while leaving the most difficult areas of governance to the politicians whose jobs are to manage government affairs according to their abilities, but at the expense of the taxpayers.

However, the problem with this system of government is that it has its inherent limitations. For instance, your power to elect or to be elected into office is only limited to some years, let's say 4 years. Secondly, governance in the hands of humans has always failed compared to the divine rulership of the Creator. Last but not least, electoral results can be manipulated to favour a particular party.

Democracy only emerged because people "rebelled" against their King and his Kingdom. For instance, the birth of the US is one of them as previously discussed in this book. The USA was the direct result of Americans' "rebellion" against their King and his Kingdom: King George III of England - who toyed with the emotions of the American colonies.

Wilson Church, who led Britain successfully during the Second World War, strongly supported the argument that democracy isn't the best form of governance after he was angrily voted out of power as the British Prime Minister a few months after taking Britain out of the war. That's the paradox of leadership in the hands of mortal men!

In his honest cynicism about democracy, he said that:

> *"Many forms of Government have been tried and will be tried in this world of sin and woe.*
> *- Winston S Churchill, 11 November 1947*

He went further to criticize democratic government with this statement:

"No one pretends that democracy is perfect or all-wise",

and that:

"democracy is the worst form of Government except for all those other forms that have been tried from time to time"

While democracy might not be the best form of governance by itself, yet, it is the preferred form of leadership by the people for the people compared to other forms of government where people's opinions are suppressed through dictatorship, tyranny, communism or socialism.

One Power, two Government Systems: How the Constitutional Monarchy and Parliamentary Democracy Function as One System of Government

Our so-called modern democracy is shrouded with its gross limitations, including voting frauds and other manipulations to remain in power. Even Plato knew that the "government of the people, for the people, and by the people" is not immune from human failure.

To avoid internal decay in the kingdoms of Europe just like their Roman colonial rulers, some European countries (UK, Belgium, Denmark, Luxembourg, the Netherlands, Norway, Spain, and Sweden, as well as Australia, Bahrain, Jordan, Kuwait, Liechtenstein, Monaco, and Morocco) conspired among themselves to practice an alternative form of government, in what I have termed *"innovative government"* - a kind of *hybrid* - whereby two forms of "old government systems" are blended in a mortar and pestle of the political system forming one Powerful Government under one Authority.

That alternative form of government was the combination of Constitutional Monarchy (democratic monarchy, or parliamentary monarchy) on one hand with the Parliamentary Democracy on the other hand to tighten their grip on the same old tradition of government practised by their Roman Empire ancestors.

In the UK where I live with my wife and our two children, our Government practises the Constitutional Monarchy in a Parliamentary Democracy. On one hand, the Monarch, our present queen, Queen Elizabeth II, is the Head of State for life with no executive functions. She was never voted into power by members of the public, rather, she was born into Royalty. In other words, Royalty flows in her blood. Her Crown can only be transferred over to another royal - her son, Prince Charles, the next in line to the throne - when she passes on to another glorious life.

On the other hand, we have the Prime Minister (Boris Johnson) as the Head of the UK Government with executive powers. He was voted into power by the people. As a result, his term in office is temporary. He's limited by his ability to shift the mindsets of the UK voters and win their emotions and their will through the ballot box. All voted politicians win through the "majority" votes, even though the majority might have voted wrongly depending on their emotional states the previous night before the voting day.

I believe that the idea of having two kinds of Government structures under one Authority, and under one roof, is peradventure, 'just in case,' if one Government system fails, they have another "tested" government system as a backup. They cling and refine the ideas of their colonial masters – the Roman Empire.

Irrespective of the POWER of these two systems of government under one AUTHORITY, they are guaranteed to fail. Why? Because those in power are still struggling to understand what true rulership is all about. So, they had invented their own systems of government for their personal gains, and then wobble in shame as they play party politics.

All political parties in governments around the world that practise "Absolute Democracy" or "quasi-democracy" are vulnerable to one single leadership disease known as 'elective dictatorship' – a phenomenon in the world of politics whereby a leading political party in government wants to "lord it over" other smaller parties whom they consider as weaker parties. They boldly introduce the same old Greek philosophy that the stronger the trait, the better you're as a leader. They give trash talks during political debates against political opponents and regard them as "sub-humans" who're incapable of leadership.

The British politicians suffer from this disease. The Americans embrace it. And African nations marinate themselves in the pool of shame that democracy brings. Even the People's Republic of China with its one-party state under the leadership of the Chinese Communist Party (CCP), and Russia with its federal, semi-presidential republic, filled with promises for the people, ambitions for good moral, public and fairer society - they are not safe from failure as they are "mere mortals" in the corridors of POWER.

Trust:
The Leadership Lesson from a Wooden Ruler

As a primary school pupil during one of my first lessons in arithmetic (Mathematics), one of the first wooden equipment the teacher used in my classroom was the Wooden "RULER." Forty-two years later, and due to innovation, this piece of equipment now comes in other forms such as metal and plastic rulers.

The wooden ruler was used to draw straight lines, parallel lines, or measure a distance from point A to point B. The unique thing about the ruler was that it gave us accurate dimensions of our measurements. It never lies. The ruler has the Power and Authority to deliver what it's known for - Straight lines.

The manufacturer never made it to draw circles or spheres, but a straight line. We drew straight lines, even with our eyes closed. We trusted this piece of wood. That line was guaranteed to be straight. However, when it comes to Human Rulership, that high level of trust cannot be found in human rulers.

The Human Rulers vs. Kingdom Rulership

When "rulership" is in the hands of humans, it means power, authority, and influence have been transferred to that person. Many nations suffer from one leadership crisis to another as a result of governance being in the wrong hands of the selected few.

When this happens, leading people can turn into aristocracy, tyranny, or oppression of the people they are meant to protect and provide for. A Ruler is anyone who is in a position of power, trust, authority, or influence over a domain or territory. Whether you're the King, Prime Minister, a Governor, Parents, business leaders, entrepreneurs, doctors, nurses, cleaners, kitchen porters, footballers, chefs, and so forth, you're a leader in your field of calling – through your work, which becomes your territory. Territories other than nations may include land, assets, businesses, professional jobs or careers.

Rulers have characteristics similar to kings of Kingdoms or countries. A kingdom is ruled by a monarch – a Royal family of King or Queen, which controls a domain (a country or territory) and influences his or her territory with power and influence. It has decrees, statutes or constitutions to guarantee orderliness. In a kingdom government, not a democracy, the people are the King's subjects, and the King or the Queen owns the land - and everything standing – below and above the ground.

Rulership cannot exist in the absence of the subjects, i.e., the businesses, the fields, or disciplines - that the ruler controls. When you become the ruler, the King, the expert, or consultant in your profession, that profession automatically becomes your "subject" under your control - to the Glory of our Creator.

Because you've dominated your field as a physician, business or leadership consultant, you fix your consulting fee in thousands of British pounds, and the people pay to experience your services. Therefore, "Emotional Rulership" is not autocracy, tyranny, or dictatorship. Emotional Rulership is about ownership, responsibility, and accountability in the areas of your natural gifting.

Leadership Begins at Home

To become an exceptional leader, we must first rule ourselves from within - which is self-governance. We have to become the RULER of our minds and our emotions. It's only after we have mastered and understood our own emotions that we can control them and help others overcome their adversities. For instance, you cannot really become a marriage counsellor while your marriage is in shambles.

Furthermore, we can use our leadership abilities to manage and control the Change, and the emotions of other people for the benefit of all – the family, friendship, the organization, or the nation as a whole. To do this, we must first take control of our minds, manage our emotions, before connecting with other people's emotions.

In the next chapter, I would re-introduce the concept of Emotional Rulership as a divine form of leadership where everyone is expected to lead effectively from within and control life circumstances.

---

1. The Greek word for Peter means rock
2. The Greek word for "Church" means "Ecclesia" - which is an assembly of citizens in a city-state, Senate. It can also mean representatives, Ambassadors, Cabinet members of political parties or government.
3. Hades in the ancient Greek's religion or myth refers to god of the dead, the realm of the dead, or the king of the underworld
4. Skolimowski, Piotr (2021) 'Poland, Hungary Likely to Miss EU Recovery Funds in 2021', Bloomberg. Available at: https://www.bloomberg.com/news/articles/2021-12-07/poland-likely-to-miss-out-on-eu-pandemic-aid-payments-this-year (Accessed: 31 December 2021).

Chapter Seven

Emotional Rulership: The Divine Form of Leadership

"Only A Crisis, Actual or Perceived, Produces Real Change."
~Milton Friedman

HERE IN this book, I wish to *"re-introduce"* another paradigm of leadership or government that originates from another planetary body – the human planet - your minds, your thoughts, and your emotions. That system of leadership or governance is what I had termed: **Emotional Rulership.**

You can see from the paragraph above that I'd used the word, *"re-introduce."* By re-introduction, it means re-introducing, re-storing, or re-instating. It also means renewing, returning, re-establishing, or reviving what was originally introduced at some point in the past.

In other words, I'm bringing back the leadership or rulership mandate over the Earth's territory which was lost to the enemy of the Creator during the Fall of Adam. And that Creator's arch-enemy had turned against His creatures on earth.

It was God's System of Government, which He had intended for His children to practice on Earth and "rule-over" our life circumstances or events - businesses, jobs, families, or our relationships. I believe that God's original intention for human success is inherent in this concept termed Emotional Rulership, and His intention for mankind was for us to rule ourselves from the inside through the process of Self-Government or Governance.

My conviction is clear when the Creator spoke through Moses to the people of Israelites that, although "the whole earth is mine, you will be for me a kingdom of priests [leaders] and a holy nation" (Exodus 19:6; See also Isaiah 61:6, Rev 1:6, 1 Peter 2:9; emphasis added).

In other words, God intended to establish a Holy country on Earth where all citizens are collectively kings, queens, leaders or Ministers of the Lord in their own rights, with direct influence of the Kingdom of Heaven on Earth. His idea was for kingdom leadership principles to spread and multiply with the same "ideology" across the rest of the world - just as He had planned it before the beginning of time inside the Garden of Eden (the presence of the Lord).

No sickness. No poverty. No crime. In a nation where everyone lives a quality life, where everything is in absolute order: educational system, road network, infrastructure, healthcare, security, economy, and industries.

That is why the signs, wonders, and miracles recorded to have been performed by some of the prophetic leaders in history - Moses and his stick in his encounter with Pharaoh, Elijah vs. Elisha (his miraculous jar of oil in 2 Kings 4:2), and Jesus Christ vs. His disciples - casting out devils, healing the sick, resurrecting Lazarus, etc., all the miracles did not trigger excitement, or euphoria in the mindset of these leaders, neither were they new in their sights. Why? Because they simply demonstrated the kind of life which already exists on another planet - the Kingdom of Heaven.

The concept of Emotional Rulership has been called various names, including:
- Self-Awareness.
- Self-worth.
- Self-Wealth.
- Self-knowledge.
- Self-Government.

The Creator of the universe never wanted humans to be "ruled" externally from the outside – which is what democracy and other imitations of Government is all about. Democracy was never the invention of God, but leadership and governance. Therefore, the concept of Emotional Rulership originates from the inside – from controlling our minds, our emotions, and our will-power, which ultimately dictates how we function externally in the outside world, helping other people to reach their full potential in life - passionately and effectively.

The concept of Emotional Rulership is not a brand-new idea. In fact, "Dominion-Rulership" is as old as mankind, finding its foundations in the Creation narrative of Heavens and Earth and our ancestors (see Gen. 1 & 2).

The Rulership mandate was the Royal Charter, officially decreed by the King of Heavens and Earth, who granted men and women the perpetual right, power, and authority as individuals, institutions, or corporate organizations to take 'dominion,' 'rulership,' 'leadership,' or 'management' of the Earth's territories and resources – both the seen and the unseen, on the surface of the ground, above the ground, and below the ground.

In the words of King Solomon, he said:

> "What has been will be again, what has been done will be done again." "There is nothing new under the sun." (Ecclesiastes 1:9, NIV).

Humans, with a Spirit living in a dirt body, are the only species on the planet Earth with the legal rights to inhabit it, manage its resources, and make them much better than they met it on Earth on behalf of the Lord (landowner) – the Creator. For that reason, God, with His three business partners – God the Father, God the Son, and God the Holy Spirit - declared to themselves saying:

> "Let us make mankind in our image, in our likeness, so that they may "rule over" the fish in the sea and the birds in the sky, over the livestock and all the wild animals, and over all the creatures that move along the ground" (Gen 1:26).

Thus, we are legally obligated and authorized to "rule over" our professional territories in the areas of our gifting - either in medicine, law, pharmacy, architecture, leadership, entrepreneurship, carpentry, joinery, cleaner, and so forth. (Gen 1: 26 & 28).

But true leadership cannot really start if we can't control and regulate ourselves with discipline and trust. That is why if you re-"discover" yourself and your purpose in life, you're on your way to "becoming" true yourself – the true leader in the area of your natural gifting.

When you find that field in your job where your gift is, train yourself to "become" the best in that job, and become a person of value. As you progress in that job or profession, you may upgrade yourself to the next higher level to "become" a "consultant," "specialist," "adviser," "pundit," "wizard," or "authority" in that profession.

When you've reached the peak of your career or field, the last step is simply to dominate that profession. That is where the idea of DOMINION comes in. You'll rule supreme as an authority, and become an "industry-standard" or "Reference Point" in your field.

When that happens, automatically, you have become a King or Queen in that job. As a consultant in your field, people will seek your valued services. In return, they will pay you a premium on your terms and conditions. You will no longer be paid salaries or wages, rather you'll charge them FEES!

The "dominion mandate" of RULERSHIP, therefore, is about governance, and government. You can observe that I have repeated these two words very often in this book. The reason is to emphasize the importance of this subject of self-governance.

Emotional Rulership is guaranteed to bring peace, productivity, equality versus inequality in your personal life. If we collectively practise Emotional Rulership and indoctrinate it as a lifestyle, we will wipe off all manner of racism from its roots. It will wife off hate crimes and failures in our society. When light appears, darkness has no strength of its own to stand against it, but will soon disappear into oblivion.

Bad times are always parts of life on Earth, but success will emerge thereafter. If we can control and regulate our anger, feelings of hate, and the distrust of others, we will wipe away terrorism, the fear of the unknown, hunger as an instrument of war, child abuse, and sexual predatory behaviours.

Emotional RULERSHIP is neither in dominating other people in your charge nor manipulative attempts to coerce the minds of people to buy into your ideas for your benefit. Emotional RULERSHIP is about Leadership and Management over the Earth's resources.

However, without putting your emotions to work, it is impossible to manage your staff effectively, manage resources, reduce waste, improve customer service and customer retention. Emotional RULERSHIP, therefore, is for others – the emotional management of the employees in our charge, meeting your business targets in the organizations you work for.

In the following chapter (Chapter 8), I will dig deep into human emotions to find out some of the hidden benefits of human emotions, and how Emotional Rulership can positively help us improve as LEADERS.

Chapter Eight

The Benefits of Emotional Rulership

"A Leader is One Who Knows the Way, Goes The Way, and Shows the Way."

- John C. Maxwell

THE BEAUTY of Emotional Rulership is its wide applications and influence across various human endeavours:

- Influence on Business Policies and Procedures.
- Influence in our Families and Relationships.
- Influence in Political Leadership.
- Influence in Educational Institutions; and
- Influence in Religious Organizations.

Let's have a little discussion on how this Concept of Emotional Rulership influences the following SIX areas of life:

1. **Families:** It's so important in families so that parents could be the best in parenting their children, and when our

children need their parents for emotional support.

2. **Relationships:** so that friends could connect, avoid undesirable feelings against each other; and wear each other's shoes, tie the lace, and tighten it hard so we could feel their discomfort and pains where it matters most.

3. **Businesses:** so that business leaders could lead with exceptional precocity to manage the team and operations with poise.

4. **Politics and Politicians:** For political leaders such as Presidents, Prime Ministers, Ministers of Government parastatals, and those in Governance - to lead, communicate, and govern effectively under pressure.

5. **Educational Institutions:** for teachers to impact positive influence on their students; and

6. **Religious Organizations:** For our Religious Leaders to lead with exemplary leadership where others without these skills of EI have failed woefully under pressure.

Leadership is not about yourself – self-esteem or self-centeredness. Leadership is about other people. When the Creator blesses your business, He does so for the benefit of other people - in your city, country, and globally. He had other people in mind and wants them to receive their blessings through you. You become the earthen vessel (2 Cor. 4:7).

In the Creation story, as written by Moses, the Creator of the universe told the first man to "manage" and to "rule" the Earth's resources – land, rivers, rocks, trees, gold, onyx, minerals, animals (wild and domestic). Since then, only humans have had the power of "dominion" over Earthly resources, but not to rule or manage other humans. You cannot manage people, neither can you rule over humans. attempts to control human emotions had always backfired through rebellious actions. It wasn't the primary assignment of God for mankind to rule mankind. Rulership over people, therefore, is tantamount to oppression, subjugation, dehumanization, or in the case of controlling the citizens through financial jobs, employment, or financial slavery.

The application of the emotional brain helps us to regulate the Amygdala Hijack (Limbic System) by controlling our thoughts in difficult times. In other words, Great leaders instruct the human Amygdala to hold the Neocortex to account.

We are all familiar with these three powerful adages below:

"He Who Rules Your Mind - Is The King."

"He Who Rules Your Emotions - Controls Your Life."

"He Who Plays the tunes - dictates the Dance."

The above three statements almost mean the same thing. In a Kingdom Government, the ruler - King or the Queen - makes laws and principles that guarantee success for the citizens. On the other hand, in a democratic Government, the legislators or the members of parliament are responsible for enacting laws and passing them.

Your Mind is Your Boardroom

Your mind is the boardroom where all executive decisions take place. Emotions are the key drivers of change, and that change might be in the form of our behaviour and the daily decisions we make. Our emotions originate from our amygdala – the centre of our emotions. Everybody makes decisions using the frontal facing part of our brain (the frontal lobe). We only arrive at a final decision only after we've deliberately thought about the events, over and over again.

Our decisions are based on our personal feelings at the time. Take, for instance, you've interviewed 20 job applicants yesterday. You took notes, felt the vibes, and then decided whom to select. You took your time out to think it through over and over again. You had "the 'feel-good' moments" or "the 'feel bad' moments" in your mind.

Finally, you feel emotionally connected with one particular applicant, who "you think" (using the Thinking Brain) that met the "criteria" set by your organization. The mindset of the organization, and not the untapped potential of the candidate.

This job recruitment process seems easy because you can take your time out to actually "Think" about the interview, and then "decide" whom to select out of the rest.

Imagine when you're under pressure of any kind? Imagine leading a team of employees in your organization, where effective communication is paramount to getting the job done? Imagine trying to have an interview under a fallen roof, or trying to handle customer complaints from one side of your desk?

Also, imagine during difficult times, trying to figure out how to stabilize your department, and the telephone rang from the other side of your desk? This time, from your deputy, vice, or assistant, stating that two of your most valued employees had dropped their resignation letters because of your leadership styles?

Because your staff could not cope with stress and workload, have you ever tried to work with them, and resolve certain emotional issues in their difficult times? Have you ever connected with them during the most derailing times of their employment? These are the kinds of leadership crises this book is talking about.

Exceptional leadership is about stepping above the norms, by tapping into another leadership territory that resides in the soul – your emotional boardroom. Controlling change in your environment, and helping your team to thrive shows your expertise in this department of leadership. By being proactive and responsive instead of reactive, you'll reconnect and understand other people's feelings, and use that exceptional knowledge to influence your daily decision-making processes.

The last position of dominion which the Creator of the universe promised mankind on the planet Earth takes various processes to accomplish. You can't just dominate your industry, your field or profession just by taking up a job or being offered your first management job. It takes years of hard work, self-discipline, resilience, and focus to train your mind and emotions on one vision, and become the expert in that field of life.

Here are the natural steps divinely laid out by the Creator of the universe, which business leaders must follow to succeed. Google uses these four principles for its global business. Facebook used it to create over US$933 Billion in revenue by September 2021. McDonald's, Microsoft, and other global business leaders also deploy these Four Biblical Business Strategies to remain successful.

No religion can claim ownership of these four strategies, except God, even though these four strategies are available in public domain (see the Hebrew Bible of the Old Testament or Tanakh). These strategies work for everyone who uses them to create automation.

#1: Multiply.
#2: Replenish.
#3: Subdue. And
#4 Dominion = Rulership.

Dominion Vs. Domain

The word "dominion" was taken from the word "domain." A domain is a territory, a country, a nation or an "area" controlled or "ruled over" by a king. With a Kingdom authority, the Creator of the universe made this public proclamation, "Let them take dominion over my resources – dominate the fish of the sea, dominate the beast of the field, dominate the birds of the air, and dominate every creeping thing that creeps on the surface of the land." Yet, he said to humans, 'I have a land flowing with Rivers and seas full of minerals – oil, gold, onyx stone, and bdellium." The sources of wealth on Earth are open secrets for anyone ready to tap into this wisdom to multiply, replenish, subdue, and take dominion.

Ownership vs. Rulership & Management

By nature, our Creator gave us the Kingship or RULERSHIP over his resources, but not Ownership. I believe that whatever we possess right now on Earth, is a gift to us to manage and safeguard. By management, it simply means to effectively and efficiently use resources available with the hope of producing results, fruits, or in multiples and much better conditions than we met them. In the words of King David,

> "The earth is the LORD's, and everything in it, the world, and all who live in it"
> (Psalms 24:1).

Through the Creative Property Rights, God owns everything on Earth, including us, while our principal job description remains the same: to govern; to rule, and to subdue His resources through the instrument of Management and Leadership.

Whatever You Fail to Manage, You'll Lose

If you fail to manage a thing, that thing will be taken away from you and given to those who can manage them effectively and efficiently in obedience to Natural laws - which is how the Kingdom of God operates. In one of his Leadership lectures on Financial Investment and Management (Matt. 25:14-30), Jesus taught his leadership students with illustrations on how God's Kingdom Business operates and is managed - so we can deploy the same strategy on Earth in our businesses or profession to guarantee success - just as it's done in Heaven.

The amount of money stated in this illustration is x 10 the amount used in the Matt. 25:14-30 of The Message Bible (MSG) are merely to represent a significant amount of money for business or investment in Great Britain as of December 2021. I have paraphrased Jesus' lectures from (Matt. 25:14, (MSG)). He started his morning lectures like this:

> In my Father's Kingdom business and investment, it is like a Leader, a wealthy businessman in Great Britain, going abroad on a long business trip. He gathered three of his leadership students together in the same lecture hall and delegated some business and wealth management responsibilities to them. To support them in their tasks, he shared eighty thousand British pounds (£80,000) among them in the ratio of 5:2:1 as follows:

- To the first leadership student, he gave him fifty thousand pounds (£50,000).

- To the second, he gave him twenty thousand pounds (£20,000).

- And to the third man, he gave him ten thousand pounds (£10,000), depending on their abilities.

Then he left them straight away to the airport and boarded his private jet to the US for his international business projects. Immediately as he had left the building, the first student "went to work and doubled the leader's investment, thus making £100,000 in revenue or shares in the stock market. The second did exactly the same, and doubled his revenue or shares, thus making £40,000 in revenue or shares in the stock market. However, the third man with £10,000 dug a hole in the ground, and meticulously "buried" the leader's money inside the ground in his back garden- to safeguard it from thieves. In other words, he never trusted his Bank Managers.

He continued with the story, that "after a long absence," maybe 1 or 2 years or more, the businessman returned to the UK to demand accountability. The one who was given £50,000 reported "how he had doubled his investment." The leader praised him and said: "Good work" my boy! "You did your job well. 'From now onward', he said 'you will be my business partner' and manage some of my Billion Pounds worth of investment portfolios.

The second man he gave £20,000 also narrated to his leader how he turned £20,000 into £40,000 in a short while through his business and investment. The Leader praised him and said: "Good work" my boy! "You did your job well. 'From now onward', he said 'you will be my business partner' and manage some of my Billion Pounds worth of investment portfolios.

The third person who was given ten thousand pounds (£10,000) had this to say to this wealthy man:

'Master, I know you have high standards and hate careless ways, that you demand the best and make no allowances for error. I was afraid I might disappoint you, so I found a good hiding place and secured your money. Here it is, safe and sound, down to the last cent.' (vs. 24-25).

We all know the outcome of the conversation, but I will reproduce it here for Kingdom investment lessons. The leader was very furious, and said to him:

"That's a terrible way to live! It's criminal to live cautiously like that! If you knew I was after the best, why did you do less than the least? The least you could have done would have been to invest the sum with the bankers, where at least I would have gotten a little interest (vs. 26-27).

The businessman was boiled inside with anger, and said to him:

'Take the ten thousand pounds and give it to the one who risked the most. And get rid of this "play-it-safe" who won't go out on a limb. Throw him out into utter darkness.'

This illustration above still occurs to this day. The internet is filled with men and women who were once millionaires, but later lost all from the height of "the 1%" of the population who are millionaires to the level of "the 99%" of the average, and became broke and homeless. Why? Because of bad management.

In the next chapter, I will discuss the five main Laws of Emotional Intelligence which if deployed in our life events, will catapult us into a higher level of leadership success.

Chapter Nine

Five Laws of Emotional Intelligence

"Excellence is a continuous process and not an accident."

- **A.P.J. Abdul Kalam**, the 11th President of India.

THIS CHAPTER is important for you if you want to succeed in any area of life, and to control your life circumstances. These FIVE LAWS of Emotional Intelligence are for you if you're a business owner, or someone planning to open a new business venture.

These LAWS are vital for your future success, if you're a leader in any form – political leaders, Head Teachers, and Entrepreneurs, CEOs, Religious Leaders, and Parents, or if you provide leadership, or you're in charge of businesses and non-profit organizations.

Understanding both principles and laws will set you apart from ordinary managers deficient in this knowledge. When you submit yourself to, and in obedience to these LAWS, you'll come out successfully in times of adversity.

If you're a team- leader in charge of a department in your organization, this chapter is also good for you.

Professor Daniel Goleman calls these laws, "Leadership Competencies." But I had chosen to call them Laws. Why? Because every product made by the manufacturer, including Effective Leadership, is made to function by Laws. These laws are universal and natural - hence "natural laws."

Whether you're in Africa, Asia, Europe, North or South America, and even if you dwell in Antarctica and Oceania, these laws function the same. To become wealthy or successful in business, you don't need to change your country of birth or relocate from one continent to another. Wherever you're right now, just apply these natural LAWS and you will achieve the same results anywhere on Earth. Why? Because all the natural laws have inherent results built-in. Both success and failures are embedded naturally into these Laws - but the results you obtain is dependent on which Laws you have chosen to submit to - obey or disobey.

Written versus unwritten Laws

There are two kinds of Laws – the Written Laws and the unwritten Laws. The unwritten laws are also known as Natural Laws.

On one hand, the written Laws (also known as Statutory Laws or statutes Laws) are Laws passed by a body of legislatures or lawmakers for Sovereign nations to help them "regulate" or "control" orderliness in their society. They call such written Laws "Constitution." However, when they are tired of you and want to target the opposition, the custodians of the law can decide to change that constitution to advance their political interest, in what is known as "Constitutional Change", "Constitutional Amendment", or "Constitutional Review."

On the other hand, Natural laws fall into the unwritten Laws category. Why? Because they are natural, divine, and truthful. They are created and passed by the Creator of the world = GOD, in the presence of the body of his heavenly legislatures (the Son and the Holy Spirit) who reigns supreme in His Kingdom. The Earth belongs to Him who created it through the Creative Property Rights. Because nobody knows how the Earth we live in functions at its best, except if that wisdom was given to them through a supernatural connection. He established these natural laws in His Constitution to show the world how to activate and follow certain laws to function maximally and govern itself – hence self-Government.

No government, therefore, has the right to change the laws of another government. Just like the UK cannot change the US Constitution, the EU Court of Justice also has no right to impose the supremacy of EU Laws over Polish and Romanian national Constitutional Laws. Likewise, humans who live temporarily on Earth, and who form their Governments and make their laws, should not attempt to amend God's natural laws to suit them. Why? Since these natural laws belong to another Government authority – the Kingdom Government of God – which had been in existence before the foundation of the world. Therefore, we need God's permission to change his Laws. He had created these Laws for His products to follow and function effectively – and those products include the Earth and humanity living therein.

Here are a few examples of God's Natural Laws and their inherent consequences when violated by humans.

- **The Human Body:** Our body – the brain, the heart, the lungs, the kidney, and every single part of the body – was designed by the Creator to function successfully by laws. From conception till death, each part is not competing with one another. Rather, they chose to work as a team to keep one body safe. We are never tired of inhaling Oxygen and exhaling CO_2, neither is your heart tired of beating in rhythms. They simply do their jobs by obeying the Laws of

Nature. On one hand, **SUCCESS** or **LIFE** was the main focus of each part. **Failure or Death**, on the other hand, was not part of that design, even though "failure" or "Death" was created first, followed by success superimposed on it. In other words, "failure" or "Death" was hidden beneath success or Life. For instance, this is a LAW: The minute you stopped inhaling Oxygen and letting go of CO_2, - the Lord says "You shall surely die! Although "failure" was sent to bed and in deep slumber when natural laws are activated legally or used righteously, but when wrongly activated, or activated as an ill act of rebellion to the Kingdom authority, failure or death wakes up and starts killing the body or destroying whoever is on its path.

- **Wealthy vs. Poverty:** These are the results of obedience versus disobedience to certain laws of financial management, investment vs. expenditure. The Laws of Money (currency) had divided the entire human race into four quadrants: the employees, self-employed individuals, business owners, and investors. The choice you pick out of this quadrant determines your future lifestyle: income or salary.

- **Marriage Vs. Divorce:** What we call "divorce" is simply the result of disobedience to the Laws or Covenant of Marriage. The Creator was very clear to humans when he established this sacred institution called Marriage, a covenant, for the assignment of *procreation*. His idea was rooted in His belief and principle that when two minds or opposite spirits are joined together in His presence, and his authority and approval, that sum becomes ONE (i.e., 1+ 1 = 1) and a complete powerful union. As we discussed previously in this book, since no man-made Government authority on Earth can change the legislature of another legitimate Government, in principle, the covenant of marriage defined by God can only derive its legitimacy from the same Government of Heaven that first established it on Earth. That covenant is enshrined in this statement by the Creator in the foundation of the world, "that is why a man leaves his father and mother and is united to his wife, and they become one flesh" (Gen. 2:24; Matt 19:5; Eph. 5:31-32, See also Gen 2:18, Prov. 31:10-31). Too many marriages had fallen apart due to our inability to control and respect our emotions and the feelings of our partners in crime. Some of the excuses given as the reasons for separation, and subsequently divorce include some of these statements, like " lack of preparation", "marrying too young", "infidelity, "domestic abuse", "alcoholic", and "violence", "grown apart", "lack of commitment", "unrealistic expectations", or "irreconcilable differences".

- **Crime vs. Parental Separation:** They are simply the result of the violation of the moral Law of character, values, and ethics. A broken family is the breeding ground for moral decay and crimes. In the absence of a clear direction of parental leadership, the children turn to alcohol, drug addiction, and sex just to make up for the absence of the guardians. They seek happiness and refuge from the wrong source - dried fruits, barks, and leaves - and allow plants and their metabolites to rule their spirits and their minds. Many have failed in life as a result of their emotional crises, but millions have failed to survive the stress due to the absence of fathers – the real Source. Therefore, fathers are not the head of the family, but the foundation or tail of the family. The real heads of the families are the mothers. Here is the reason for making the above statement. It is also a personal experience in my home and marriage to my wife here in Manchester. When the fathers (the foundations of the house) are away on a business trip, the mothers (the heads of the house) make sure that the house is "orderly" before the end of the day, and in preparation for the husband to return. But when the foundation of the house cracks, the roof and the walls fallow in obedience to the foundation. Nothing can prevent the roof from falling once the foundation is destroyed. Since I found this understanding, I am sticking to the head to look after the tail, and vice-versa.

- **The Fishes of the Sea:** The ability of the fishes of the sea to survive in the deep sea - swim, and breath - is governed by their obedience to the laws of water. You don't have to kill a fish by smashing its head against a stone. I have figured out that the easy way to kill a fish is to take it out of the water, and it's dead.

- **Accidents while on the phone, Unwanted Pregnancy,** and **Partying All Night** – the consequences are all due to disobedience to different natural laws - safety or abstinence, excessive indulgence on another spirit, disruptive imbalance of natural melatonin in the body or the circadian rhythm (sleep-wake cycle).

- **Birds of the sky:** Birds fly in the sky successfully without human support. Why? Because of their obedience to the laws of natural flight. Cut the wings and feathers, you have rendered the fish lifeless! Why? Because its life depends on its functions, and its functions depend on its ability to fly and escape from danger.

- **Aircraft:** To function and fly artificially like birds of the sky, aircraft must submit themselves to the laws of aerodynamics to function effectively.

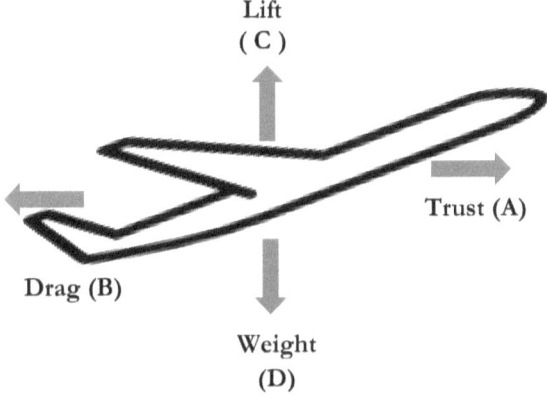

Figure 1: The Four Forces or Laws of Flight

All aircraft submit themselves to the various laws of flight, and the most prominent ones are as follows and illustrated in Figure 1: A, B, C, and D.

1. The law of Trust (A).

2. The Law of Drag (B)

3. The Law of Lift (C).

4. The Law of Weight (or gravity) (D).

5. Daniel Bernoulli's principles of Flight – states that as the air or fluid moves faster [past the wings], it produces less pressure, while slower moving air or fluid generates greater pressure.

6. Sir Isaac Newton's first and third laws of motion.

Let's have a look at an aircraft for a minute, and see how it follows the four laws or forces of flight to function, and fly across the continents of the world.

Consider the aircraft illustrated on the previously ready to take off.

- **The Thrust (A)**, also known as the Forward Propulsion is the mechanical force of the engine that pulls the aircraft forward. This Forward propulsion (Newton's first law at work here) functions following The Law of Inertia.

- **The Law of Inertia** states that if an object, including you, is at rest, it will remain at rest unless a net force acts on it. If an object is in motion, it will also stay in motion (with a constant velocity or speed), unless acted upon by a net external force.

- **The Drag (B)** is the opposing resistance (R), such as fluid (air or gas pressure) and force which the aircraft encounters to retard it from moving forward. Therefore, for the aircraft to move forward, the thrust force (A) must be greater than the Drag force (B), i.e., A>B.

- **The Law of lift (C)** is responsible for lifting the aircraft as the velocity increases (Newton's Third Law of Motion). Newton's third law of motion states that for every action, there is an equal and opposite reaction. As the aircraft is lifted, the air pressure below and above the wing changes. The air pressure under the wing is higher than the air pressure above the wings. These changes in air pressures allow the aircraft to lift with ease.

Principles and Laws: Are Leaders Ready to Fly?

As leaders in your organization, how do you apply the aerodynamic principles and laws to FLY and sustain your leadership when other pilots had failed? When our leadership aircraft stumbles in air turbulence in the sky, and your projects and leadership styles are thrown violently against the seat belts of your organization, how do stabilize that organization from crashing into pieces?

I believe that the keys to sustaining effective leadership under pressure are not hidden in the company's visions and business strategies, but are hidden in the Laws of Emotional Intelligence. To be successful as a leader in your organization, people in authority must obey certain laws which govern leadership, vision, values, and ethics and fly successfully just like the aircraft I have just illustrated previously.

The Predictability of Life

Success in business, marriage, or partnerships of any form also depends on obedience to or loyalty to the laws relevant to that partnership. If you're in business, there is a law governing revenue which you'll be are of: The Law of profit and loss. If you're in a relationship such as marriage, that union is governed by the natural laws of marriage. For instance, "Thou Shall Not Look at Another Man's Wife Twice." This is a natural Law. It is there to guarantee success and protect you from lust and infidelity (having sexual thoughts about her in your mind).

Since success and failures are predictable, consequences of "disorderliness" are also predictable. Knowledge of the Laws and Principles of leadership is more important than the office of the President deficient in the knowledge of the laws of the land or the country's constitution. Electricians and the students of electronics understand the laws of electricity to be successful – from Ohm's Law to Kirchhoff's Current, and Voltage Laws (KCL and KVL). These professionals are so valuable and expensive in the UK that they can demand up to £500 an jour just to fix an electronic device or the tumble dryer in your home.

Lawyers and the legislature must grasp the Constitutional Principle of the RULE OF LAW, and the administration of justice in such a way that maintains public trust and confidence in the Law profession. The solicitors and lawyers know the Laws and can charge you a premium just for a consultation. Consultant physicians know the laws of Health, and hold your heart in their hands, so are the mechanics in their garages near your home. They are successful experts in their job as a result of obedience to LAWS in the job.

I remember going for a £40 (forty pound) car M.O.T for my Range Rover Sports car during the Covid-19 pandemic lockdown, but I ended up paying over £1,200 to have some "unseen" faults fixed before I could drive it out of the garage. Why is leadership not the same? Why wouldn't leaders obey or submit to the Laws of emotional intelligence to succeed in their roles as LEADERS of our nations or businesses and companies?

The Hidden Law in the Vault of Your Mind

The question one can ask is, "where can I find these laws for exceptional leadership? Which planet or rocks or caves are these Laws hidden and locked up? The answer is simple. They are simply trapped inside the cave and rocks of your mind. You can find them in these special vaults which require special tools to unlock them. They are meant to help us survive difficult circumstances which are not readily accessible in our thinking brain.

Access to these Laws is reserved for a special kind of people with a different attitude, mindset or paradigm to life to maximize results for the organization. Entry into this gated vault requires an extra effort. But the problem is that not everyone wants to handle difficult executive matters!

Not everyone wants to become a leader even in normal circumstances when things are smooth. Difficulty accessing the vital vaults of wisdom is one of the reasons we have different kinds of leaders:

- bad leaders;
- good leaders; and
- exceptionally great leaders.

Right Keys Guarantee Right Access

Inability to access the keys to life, in the limbic system, could be why some leaders are far much better than others who are deficient in emotional rulership and wisdom. I strongly believe that the lack of the right keys for business, and deficiency in Emotional Intelligence could be the major reason why 50-60 per cent of the CEOs fail woefully within 18 months of being in leadership positions, especially in times of a crisis.

Access to the Emotional Quotient (EQ) in our limbic System requires having the right keys to unlock this important padlock. And these LAWS are the right keys you need for unlocking your leadership success. These laws and principles are not new, just that people are too busy with issues of life, that they have forgotten about them. Big corporations use these laws successfully for leadership training. Bill Gates of Microsoft, Elon Musk of SpaceX, and Google Inc. - all major companies have applied some of these laws to remain successful. McDonald's and other food companies deploy these laws to lead and manage their employees successfully.

Deploying them in your daily business activities as experts in your areas of expertise, these laws will protect your integrity and your function. In the absence of rules, laws, statutes, policies, or constitutions, what disorderliness and anarchy take over the leadership of the land. Therefore, principles and laws are there to create "orderliness" out of chaos in your organization.

The importance of Principles & Laws

Laws and Principles are important for the following reasons:

1. Laws and principles make our life easier.

2. Laws and principles bring peace and confidence.

3. Laws and principles terminate testing, trialling, or experimentation. They cancel any form of authentication.

4. Laws and principles safeguard us from failures.

Therefore, to maintain law and order, leaders and entrepreneurs create them.

LAW #1: The Law of Self-knowledge, Understanding, and Wisdom for Leadership

We live our entire lives studying other subjects at schools or colleges. We study all manner of subjects in the university, and practice them at the workplace, without first studying ourselves, our abilities, and inabilities. I will open this section with a quote from King Solomon: He says,

> "By WISDOM, a house is built, and through UNDERSTANDING it is established. Through KNOWLEDGE, its rooms are filled with rare and beautiful treasures."
> (Proverbs 24: 3-4).

Let's reverse the above statements as follows: "Through knowledge, our rooms are filled with rare and beautiful treasures.

Through understanding, it is founded, started, or initiated. And through Wisdom, the house we live in was built."

Therefore, THE THREE KEY messages for success in Life – whether in your business, marriage, or relationships, according to King Solomon, are not in your vision, but in your:

1. Knowledge.

2. Understanding, and

3. Wisdom.

Knowledge = information, learning new things. Understanding = dissection of information, assembling the components, and compressing them into a 3-dimensional format. It's about possessing the cognitive ability to relate to what you have learnt; the knowledge you seek and assimilate to make it appear real in your mind.

Understanding comes in three levels:

- **Level #1**: If you want to gain knowledge = information, learn it, or read about it.

- **Level #2**: If you want to understand it - become an author - and write about it.; and

- **Level #3**: If you want to master the subject – become a Tutor- an Instructor, and teach others about the subject. Talk about it as if the world was designed around you.

Wisdom is simply the application or combination of two things: Knowledge and understanding, i.e., Wisdom = Understanding + Knowledge. In layman's words, "wisdom" is simply the application of common sense – since common sense is not common. It's about making the right decisions, or the sagacity of our intellectual acuity.

Professor Daniel Goleman calls this first LAW "Self-Awareness." Businesspeople call it: Personal "SWOT Analysis" – strengths, weaknesses, opportunities, and threats. But God calls it IMAGE (Gen. 1:26). Your image is your Character, and your

Character is your Personality and what you stand for: Honesty versus dishonesty. Trust versus mistrust.

Therefore, having Self-Awareness is the foundation of effective Leadership. It's about self-discovery, which is the rediscovery of who we are. It's basically, the *re-introduction* of "ourselves" to "ourselves." It is the essence of the key drivers that keep us doing what we've got to do on daily basis.

Self-awareness is the "self-reflection" of your image, hence the word, "self-image" – the image of God you see or reflect in yourself. The knowledge gained studying yourself leads to 'Self-Confidence.' Emotional Self-Awareness is akin to 'looking at yourself in the mirror" each morning, and asking yourself these five rhetoric questions:

1. Who am I? – a question your identity, brand, image.

2. Where am I from? – a question of your Source - where you came from, and the materials you're made of.

3. Where am I going? – a question of your vision or destiny - which is your destination.

4. Why am I here/Why was I born? – a question of purpose, function, or the reason why you were born.

5. What am I supposed to do? - a question of action to answer the previous question.

Businesses and corporate organizations express their image through symbols or logos. A logo is simply a sign adopted by anyone to define their identity or branding. Nikki, PepsiCo, Adidas, Google, Tesla, and Microsoft, among others, are some of the World's big corporations whose self-images or logos speak volumes across the world.

Do you know about yourself or your image? In your career, your new job, or your new relationships, have you ever studied your weaknesses against your strengths to find potential opportunities in every threat or crisis you encounter?

In your relationship, have you ever devoted time to study what your partner likes most, or doesn't like, his food style, sleeping habit, or spending habit? When the issue of "Trust" creeps in, can you trust your partner when the two of you are in different locations?

Undertaking your SWOT is the key to understanding your natural gifts to improve upon your failures, limitations, or difficulties. It's about deploying the organization's assets - human and financial resources - into productive use. It's also about converting organizational threats or competition into business opportunities to improve your company's bottom line (profitability., net income, or EPS (earnings per share)).

When you're faced with crises, use them for your benefit. See them differently as opportunities, rather than challenges. When the real threats appear, view them as emerging opportunities to retool yourself, and find their solutions.

By being self-aware of our emotions and imminent changes, we can accurately assess our limitations and boundaries (Self-Assessment). Yes, although we have our weaknesses and vulnerabilities, great leaders turn them into strengths and see opportunities in every threat they face in life.

Great leaders see clouds of trouble and run into them. They don't run away from crises, rather they deal with them once and for all. They are like the Eagles. When Eagles see the storms coming, they fly into them and use the speed of the storms to fly hundreds of miles without flapping a wing. Great leaders are not known by the adversities they faced in their lifetime - in their jobs or personal lives, great leaders are known by the crises they overcame.

In the field of Theology, there are several leaders – both men and women – who are known for the problems they had solved.

- Moses was the slavery problem solver in Egypt. He took the Israelites out of the grip of the Pharaoh. The young Joseph – although sold into slavery to the household of Potiphar, the captain of the guard - an officer of Pharaoh in Egypt (Gen. 37:36; 39:1). He solved the economic crisis (famine) in Egypt and became an influential administrator under the leadership of Pharaoh – saving both his family and Egypt from the national economic crisis (famine).

• The young David, famed for his love of playing music, was a shepherd, a servant and amour bearer to King Saul. He too was a problem solver. He solved the problem of Goliath on his route to Kingship.

• Ruth - a Moabite woman - is the demonstration of a family's Loyalty to the Creator and His Laws (See the Book of Ruth 1&2). She was brought into the scene as a problem solver through the economic crises of famine in Israel. She was not an Israelite, and thus had worshipped mortal gods made by men in her country of birth! Rather, she turned her faith around to believe in the God of Israelites when her marriage to Mahlon, an Israelite, brought her into the land of God. Later married to Boaz – becoming the great-grandmother of King David, an ancestor of Jesus Christ.

• Esther – a Jewish by blood, but later a Persian Queen in Diaspora when she married the Persian King. She risked her own life to save the Jewish people living in the Persian Empire from a plan to decimate them.

• Jesus solved the problems of sin - through His sacrifice on the cross, and resurrection.

• Thomas Jefferson was a problem solver in his time – an American Founding father – is famously known as the author of the Declaration of Independence of the United States of America and the 3rd President of the USA.

• Andrew Carnegie – an industrialist - was known for the expansion of the steel industry in the US.

• Thomas Edison, Mother Theresa, Indira Gandhi, Martin Luther King Jr, Steve Jobs, Bill Gates, Elon Musk, and Jeff Bezos- were all problem solvers in their areas of life.

Self-awareness is backed by the skills, aptitude, or power of an individual to read one's emotions between the dotted lines. Understanding the impacts emotions have on people around you is the key to leadership development in your business, relationship, and how you handle difficult matters in the secret comfort of your homes. The knowledge gained from practising how to use these keys on daily basis increases our self-confidence and the way we handle difficult matters.

Finally, we started the First Law of Emotional Intelligence with a quote from the wisest man ever recorded in history - King Solomon. Therefore, let's see what King Solomon says in his book of wisdom (Proverbs) regarding The Law of Self-Knowledge, Understanding, and Wisdom For Leadership. He says:

> 21"Wrap yourself in them from head to foot;
> Wear them like a scarf around your neck.
> 22Wherever you walk, they will guide you;
> Whenever you rest, they will guard you;
> When You wake up,
> they'll tell you what's next."
> (Prov. 6:21-22, MSG).

LAW #2: Knowledge of Business or Leadership Environment

While it's imperative to understand yourself and where you stand right now in your family, or business, and the impacts your actions may have on others, it is also important to understand the macro-environment where you plan to exercise, establish, or unleash your leadership or business ventures.

The survival or growth of your business is dependent on the fertility of some external factors that neither you nor your organization has control of. That environment might be the industry or field where you want to rule over or dominate: medicine, painting, services, gardening, cleaning, trading, manufacturing, and so forth. It might also be a physical location

– city or country – depending on your plan or company's mission.

Although you don't have the power to stop these external factors from happening, rather great leaders tap into another territory of power and influence to control or stop the impacts from affecting the business. They do this by devising corporate plans or strategies to overcome or neutralize the impacts.

Theologians call this business environment, the "Garden" of Eden. Why? Because this piece of environment is the fertile ground where every business prospers. In the words of Moses – the mouthpiece of the Creator at the time, he said:

> "The Lord God took the man and put him in the Garden of Eden – to work it and to care for it" (Gen. 2:15, NIV).

Environmental Climates Affecting Businesses

Figure 2: STEEPLED Framework illustrating the Eight Environmental Factors affecting the business: You and your leadership.

Businesspeople use the PEST framework - a specific market tool that stands for Political, Economic, Social, and Technological factors – to analyze the extern business environment (Frue 2017). It also reveals how these factors impact equally on all businesses operating in the same market environment as yours.

However, market experts had figured out that PEST alone was incapable of capturing all relevant forces that affect the market, leading to various versions, such as PESTLED and STEEPLED.

Here in this Chapter, I would focus my interest on these eight STEEPLED business tools, because of their ability to capture more macro-environmental factors.

The **STEEPLED** outline:
Where:
S = Social; **T** = Technological; 1st **E** = Economics; 2nd **E** = Environmental; **P** = Political Leadership; **L** = Legal; 3rd **E** = Ethics/Ethical; and **D** = Demography.

- **Social Factors**: Similarly known as "The Socio-Cultural" factors, they are the epicentre of the people's shared values, such as beliefs, religion, tradition, behaviour, or attitude. In other words, it defines the population's culture or way of life. Changes in people's appetite, fashion, or luxury lifestyle increases the spending power of a particular group.

- **Technological Factors**: Relate to innovation, eCommerce, research and development, and the application of technology in almost everything in our lives - on a global scale. Typical examples include internet connectivity, business automation versus human labour, electronic communication, payments systems, healthcare, wireless charging, online banking, cryptocurrency, and virtual classrooms.

- **Economic Factors:** Involve the application of economic performance metrics (EPM) that impact the wealth of a large-

scale economy. They include trends in the country's gross domestic product (GDP), national income, growth rate, interest rate, taxation policy, VAT rates, a tariff on imports and exports, inflation versus unemployment levels, disposable incomes of both businesses and consumers, savings, and investments. They also affect business operations and the bottom line. Economic factors are subdivided into two:
- MicroEconomic factors, and
- MacroEconomic factors.

On one hand, the **Microeconomic Factors** refer to a smaller population of people, and how they expend their earnings. On the other hand, the **Macroeconomic factors** refer to the larger aspect of the economy rather than the economy of a particular population. They refer to how the Government of the ruling party manages the demands or needs of its citizens and uses this power to control the economy. For instance, the government uses tools such as taxes, interest rates, and expenditure as "instruments of control" to regulate economic growth and stability.

- **Environmental Factors:** The profitability of your business might be affected by the nature of the environment where it operates, such as pollution, waste, climate change, and weather conditions. These factors might impact your sales revenue or diversification into other business areas. The increased interests in "green energy, recycling of your products, and so forth are also factors to consider.

- **Political Factors**: These may include "Internal politics" within the organization that influence the corporate behaviour of your employees as well as their membership of the trade unions. "External Politics" outside the organization may include the influence of local politics within the community, city, or country politics – may impact either directly on indirectly on the economy, political stability, tax policies, minimum wage, professional regulations, government legislation, and trade restrictions.

- **Legal Factors:** include consumer rights and laws, health and safety, equality and inclusion, advertising standards, product labelling and safety. Understanding what is legal, and what is not, will allow companies to trade legally and ethically without compromise on the quality of their products and services.

- **Ethics:** Business Ethics refers to the moral principles and values of the company and its employees. In other words, it refers to how companies are committed to doing the right things in their business practices, such as cheap labour market, human rights and abuse, corporate governance, corporate social responsibility, inside trading, discrimination, bribery, and anti-corruption policies.

- **Demography:** Include population density, age distribution, career approaches, health awareness, and so forth. These factors help organizations diagnose who their customers are, segment the market, and understand the key drivers of success.

As the CEO in your organization, how familiar are you with your business environment (the STEEPLED framework) which if not mastered and certain laws obeyed, can kill off your profit or wipe your company out of the industry? These EIGHT macro-environments factors are very important because, as a leader in your organization, getting it right enables your organization to overcome all environmental challenges even before conceiving the idea of starting a new business venture in the industry you want to dominate.

Gaining *knowledge, understanding* and *wisdom* in this framework will help potential entrepreneurs or business executives PLAN strategically. This is because these EIGHT factors will affect anyone or businesses operating in the same environment equally, irrespective of their position in that country or business.

To apply these tools involves three crucial steps, such as:

1. Brainstorming.

2. Analysis of the severity of the impacts to your business – both Negative or Positive - and finally,

3. Designing robust strategies required to impediments in your STEEPLED and overcome business challenges.

LAW #3: The Law of Self-Management

Management was the first job title the Creator of the universe gave to mankind. Whether you're a titled, or non-titled leader in your organization, or you're just an employee with the "follower-mindset" and leaving your destiny to chance, everyone was born with the gift of management resting upon their shoulders.

The fact that you're a manager automatically means that you don't own the stuff you're managing. Self-management or self-control = managing yourself for the benefit of other people, which is service. It is the ability to switch yourself in tune - both in good times and bad times and get the desired results in times of CHANGE. You can also regulate automatic emotions, and align yourself with the changes in your business environment so that the invisible pet hiding in your closet doesn't metamorphose into the WILD tiger you cannot control.

For instance, you're the manager of a local store – managing the business of your organization. The Area Manager is constantly on your shoulders demanding performance figures, especially in your critical period when understaffed. Your sales figures are in a bad shape, and you know too well that you can't invent customers to improve sales.

Under pressure for high performance, it is not right to be reactive and aggressive without conscious thinking. Rather, it is better to be responsive in your thinking. It is about self-control and self-disciple, which leads us to transparency, honesty, and diligence in our leadership. Once you're aware of your emotions and their impacts, then you have the power of choice in your hands: either to control the emotions or you let the emotions control you. You can't control what you don't have.

The key solution to Self-Management is being aware that our emotions are embedded in the core of our DNA. It allows us to accommodate others into our leadership styles (adaptability), and the expectations we have of others to achieve their given targets or self-imposed targets in life. Planning is also a vital component of Self-control. It gives us the time to think and have a plan of action (initiative), become creative in our thinking, and finally believe (faith) that every problem in the organization has a solution (optimism).

As a leader in your institution, you're accountable for the actions of your team. Therefore, it is a joint responsibility – yours and your team whom you lead - to help you to find that solution – either from within or outside the organization.

LAW #4: The Law of Social Connection and Relationship Management

While the journey to becoming emotionally intelligent begins from understanding our own emotions - Emotional self-awareness, Self-management to social awareness/ empathy - our level of knowledge peaks with the people we connect with socially. Emotional connection with others is where true leadership comes to life. We are shaped by the people around us and the type of friends we keep. Remember that whom you see, determines whom you meet, and whom you meet determines your appetite. And your appetite determines your lifestyle.

In other words, the social circle you keep determines your financial status. Like I always tell my sons, the mindset of a child born and raised in a wealthy family is not the same mindset of a child born and raised in abject poverty. Children of wealthy parents, such as Bill Gates or Simon Cowell, only see millionaires in their homes as family friends, while the poor mix with children of the same kind. Children of wealthy families don't normally attend public schools, rather they attend private schools filled with children of aristocrats, the noble, and the movers and checkers of the society.

Your lifestyle is triggered by your emotions. The truth is that if we don't know what triggers CHANGE in our emotions, it would be impossible to know how to control the change, or develop effective communication strategies in response to the circumstances. Attuning or connecting effectively with others allows us to understand their perspective – their needs, and their wants.

Emotional connection, therefore, is vital to remain in resonance with a wide range of people if we want to increase efficiency and high performance in return. A great leader expresses emotional connection by listening to others: wearing the same shoes so you experience how the pain feels. It allows you to seek knowledge first, before giving your final verdict.

According to research by Gallup Organization:

> "The single most important variable in employee productivity and loyalty is not in the pay, or perks, or benefits, or workplace environment. Instead, it is the quality of the relationship between employees and their direct supervisors."

More precisely, people want to feel heard, seen, valued, and understood wherever and whomever they work with. They want to be inspired and motivated to maximize their ability by 100% - for the company's vision and mission.

LAW #5: The Law of Motivation

Leaders need "vision" to find their purpose in life for their organization, but we cannot really execute that vision in the absence of this element called "motivation." Our vision is the destination for our purpose. Unless we can see clearly where we are going, we might not really get there before the sunset.

Too often, many have failed to see their vision through the foggy clouds of life, and get motivated, they cling for opportunities created elsewhere through jobs. Their vision becomes dead, hibernated, or buried in the cemetery of their minds when we take up employment as employees from the employer - and forgo our mission and purpose on Earth.

When employers offer you a job in their business, they expect you to follow their doctrines, teachings, and directions, according to their established standard operating procedures (SOP). They also want you to add "additional value" on the job – above and beyond what they had offered you. Thus, if you work contrary to that SOP, that act of disobedience to their LAW is punishable by sacking.

Although you have the God-given vision you were born with, your employer expects you to simply bury that vision, and pursue their vision in your job. But you cannot really achieve much for your organization without first being motivated.

Increased sales are the results of the motivated employees who'd worked hard on the frontline to deliver fantastic services to the customers, service users, and members of the public.

Motivation, therefore, is the external force that pushes us forward to get the job done. It is the force that compels us to embrace the company's visions, missions, and culture but allows us to bury our vision in the safety of our minds in exchange for wage and salary.

Dr Amadi's Law of Motivation

As I was growing up in a little village in Eastern Nigeria, in the former Republic of Biafra, I had a lot of challenges in my life. In most cases, I was compelled to abandon my real vision and take up many other visions because they were popular paths.

When I moved to the UK in 2002 as a Scholar for my master's degree at Loughborough University, I struggled to find my balance in my first six years. I struggled to survive in a country where I had no immediate family to share my life challenges with – no father or mother, and no siblings to share my life experiences with. I felt like an orphan in a foreign land!

While my studies were intellectually hard, and mentally draining, the only way to get my mind back to normal was by working on odd jobs in addition to my studies in my free time to earn extra income. From kitchen pottery – watching plates in hotels – to working in Care Homes - serving the elderly residents and to working in the Leicester Royal Mail sorting centre at Christmas weeks - life was full of challenges. I also served drinks and meals at public and private events: weddings, cricket, and horse racing events at the Brighton Racecourse and Royal Ascot near London. But I never lost my focus.

While I suffered from the outside, I was strong from the inside. I knew within me where I was going, but the road took so long. I had wished that the world revolved around me, but I was wrong. I later found that the world system was not designed around me. Why? Because there are EXTERNAL, natural forces that impinge on the progress of every human being on Earth. I later found that these external forces had no boundaries as they affected everyone in the "world system" irrespective of their colour, country of birth, status or ranking in the society.

Immediately, I started searching for a solution to overcome my stressful situations. As a result, my efforts paid off. After 18 years of painful studies - day and night - I'd finally developed the "LAW of Motivation" and an "Empirical Equation" - which through my personal experience have helped me overcome many life challenges - through thick and thin.

I named this law, "DR AMADI'S LAW OF MOTIVATION" and the Equation, "DR AMADI'S EQUATION FOR MOTIVATION", respectively.

DR AMADI'S LAW OF MOTIVATION states that:

> "Motivation (M) is directly proportional to the products of Inspiration (I), Vision (V), Opportunity (O), and Passion (P), but inversely proportional to the product of Threats (T1), Time (T2), and acceleration due to gravity (g = 9.81 m/s2)."
> ~ Dr Emmanuel Eni Amadi

i.e., Motivation (M) = (I x V x O x P)/(T1x T2.g) ... (i)
But [I x V] is the equation for Electric Power = P.
i.e., Power = P ... (ii)
∴ M = Power (P) x (O x P)/(T1 x T2.g) ... (iii)
→ M = P x (O.P)/(T1.T2.g) ... (iv)

But POWER (P)= LEADER.
LEADER = INFLUENCE.
INFLUENCE = VALUE.
VALUE = Net worth (MONEY + WEALTH)

Thus, we can reverse these FOUR statements as follows:
Net worth (MONEY + WEALTH) = VALUE = INFLUENCE = LEADER = POWER.

Therefore, the more wealthy you're, the more VALUE you create with your wealth, through your gift, vision, business, leadership, and products and services. Your value attracts people to taste and feel your offering or services. This is the essence of Leadership.

When people or customers buy your products or services, it means they saw a value-added in your offering. Automatically, you become a person of influence. It's the influence that makes you a leader in that area of life.

How do you define "Leadership" without diluting its meaning? I have found that answer. In his book entitled, "The Spirit of Leadership," Dr. Myles Munroe defined leadership as:

> "The capacity to influence others through inspiration, motivated by passion, generated by vision, produced by a conviction, [and] ignited by a purpose."

Your leadership brings power to your bank account, or ROI through profits. The more powerful you are in your wallet the more you can reduce some perceived threats and see opportunities in every crisis.

- **Motivation (M).** Motivation is the external forces in our environment, the people in your team, the workplace atmosphere, and other events, which pull you forward from the front and push you forward from behind. The more the POWER (inspiration + vision), Opportunity and Passion, the more the motivation to accomplish your goal. A motivated man is never asleep. He's constantly awake, watching the 'Ts' (threats and time) without losing focus on the "g" - which is the natural force of gravity that gravitates downwards and push your business to failure.

- **Inspiration (I)**: Inspiration is the driver on the driving seat of leadership. Inspiration derives its energy from motivational forces to keep leadership on track to accomplish the vision. Inspiration and motivation help leaders to lead, and followers to bury their ideas and pursue the leader's vision.

- **Vision (I)**: Your vision is your destination while your eyes are for your sight. Your physical sight focuses on what you can see in the physical realm, but your vision sees differently from what the inner mind sees in the spiritual realm. It is the foundation built in your mindset before manifesting in the physical realm. Therefore, a man with sight without a vision is like a warlord on the highest mountains shooting at the moon as it passes by, hoping to bring it down to earth as a souvenir.

- **Opportunity (O)**: A crisis is the mother of inventions. It exposes hidden business opportunities amid uncertainties Every new thing that had ever surfaced on Earth, discovered on Earth, developed on Earth, or invented was established because of necessity or need. And that necessity is Crisis. Therefore, necessity is the womb of inventions. Wilson Churchill, the former British Prime Minister during World War II, is known for this famous quote: "Never let a good crisis go to waste." But how do you know when one crisis is good, and another a bad crisis? The answer lies in the "opportunity." Is it an opportunity cost or a missed or forgone opportunity? Whenever you see a crisis in your area, never ignore its presence - because you'll never know if that crisis is a good one or a bad one, unless you have tested it.

- **Passion (P)**: Passion is the inherent strong force from within you. It is the compelling emotional impetus, the intense desire and enthusiasm, which energizes you from within like a volcanic eruption to work on your vision. Passion is what makes you take risks, and start new businesses in the most challenging environments. It is the fuel that powers the visionary man and keeps him out of bed. You don't find passion hanging around on the outside, they are within you.

- **Threat (T1):** A threat is simply a crisis waiting to happen. When I encounter any threat or stress in my life, what comes to mind is an opportunity! opportunity!! In the Kanji characters used in writing in both Japanese and Chinese languages, it is extremely hard to disregard the word "Crisis" – written with two strokes: the first one meaning "danger" and the second meaning "opportunity." Aim to perceive your threat as an opportunity for innovative change.

- **Time (T2):** Time is one of the precious gifts ever given to mankind by the Creator. There are 24 hours a day. No more; no less. Everyone born on Earth was born within this TIME, but not everyone carries the same amount of TIME with them. That's why some people die young, others die old, and still more babies are on their way to this world in a matter of TIME. Whether you're poor or wealthy, TIME affects everyone equally. TIME doesn't discriminate. Your religion, culture, or country of birth doesn't increase or decrease TIME. Whether you're in Europe, Africa, Asia, or North America, you can never stop TIME from moving. The question is how do you manage your Time? The good news is that no matter how fast your time runs in your life, Time can be managed. Hence, TIME MANAGEMENT.

Time Management

Let's talk about time management for a little moment. TIME doesn't respect Royalty – the Kings and Queens. While I cannot guarantee that I will use my 24 – 100%, I can guarantee that TIME CHANGES all the Time.

What do you do with your TIME - my friend, if you don't mind me asking you? What do you do with these changes in TIME - you don't have control over? How you manage your TIME determines your future. It determines if you'll be poor forever, or if you'll be wealthy in your Lifetime. We spend two hours a day in a gym, training our muscles, toning our body and skin, and keeping our sizes in shape so that the boys or girls in the street will admire us. You can imagine, for 365 days, we had spent 730 hours training our body, hoping that someday, someone, somewhere would say, "WOW! What a pretty body he or she has." And so, what?

We spend one hour every night browsing our mobile phones for celebrity news and reading all sorts from Facebook, Instagram, and YouTube channels. We scavenge for fake news to feed our appetite. Imagine for 365 days a year, that's 365 hours wasted as an "opportunity cost" watching celebrity news, and Big Brother. Imagine devoting two hours a night, that's 730 hours a year crafting your new business ideas, writing your book manuscripts, or working on new projects that you couldn't have time to work on during the daytime. Why? Because our time during the day is tied to our job.

In my daily job personally, I'd spend 10 hours a day at work from 08:30 AM to 6:30 PM. By the time I get to my hotel room, I'd be so exhausted that I'd be tempted to jump to bed and forfeit my dinner. But I have "my project" which I must work on in my own time - which is writing new book manuscripts. The only time I had for myself was from the evening to the next morning. So, to get results, I had trained my body to think and work around my own TIME. I'd learned to maximize my 24 hours. I would load my body with 2 cups of Coffee to keep my engine running. From 8 PM to 1 AM or 2 AM i.e., 5 to 6 hours, I'd be on my desk at night writing a manuscript for a new book, only managing to rest my body in bed for 4 hours. That manuscript later turned into a book. And that book is the one you're reading right now: **EMOTIONAL RULERSHIP.**

- **Acceleration due to gravity (g):** I have included this gravitational force for a reason. Why? Because no one on the planet Earth is safe from the gravitational forces of nature. Standing at a value of 9.81 metres (32 feet) per second squared (9.8 m (32 feet) s^{-2}), that means that for every second in our life, mother nature is constantly dragging us away from our vision at the rate of approx. 10 metres per second. Everyone on Earth is pulled down to the Earth's surface. It cancels out your status, royalty, and might. Whether you are a millionaire wandering the streets of London or New York, or a poor man living in the Amazon forest, the force of gravity affects everyone equally. Therefore, to oppose this force every second, we must run in the opposite direction at the speed of 10 metres per second! But for how long? While we cannot stop it kicking us on the backside, we can find a way to work around it and standstill.

Chapter Ten

Interplay of Laws, Religion & Politics in Our Society

The Trinity of Life

"In politics, when reason and emotion collide, emotion invariably wins."

- **Drew Western**, The Political Brain: The Role of Emotion in Deciding the Fate of the Nation.

EVERY ECONOMY of the world system is controlled by either of these "Trinity of Life": Laws, Religion, and Politics. Religion and politics are the two dominant man-made, but opposing institutions that have continued to impact humanity around the world till today - either directly or indirectly. This includes threats of nuclear war between North Korea vs. the South/US, Israel vs. Iran; military tension between Russia and Ukraine /US, pandemic and inequality in vaccine distribution, terrorism and kidnapping in the name of religion, child sex abuse by the Clergy, and the unpredictability in the world's economy and healthcare.

The quest for orderliness or governance, which was lost at the beginning of creation, is inbuilt in the human spirit. Leadership was the original mandate given to mankind by our Creator to govern, rule and dominate the Earth on his behalf. In other words, humans were born naturally as leaders: rulers and governors. It is the desire to maintain "order" in society that led to the introduction of laws by the Creator. Religion and politics are the inventions of Man as the processes of introducing structures in the way he governs himself.

While religion was introduced by Man as an institution to re-establish himself spiritually to his Creator and bring orderliness in his world, Man also invented politics as a means to control this "orderliness" for group decision-making processes. Government, therefore, is that formal structure of leadership to keep Man organized in society. Laws take their positions in the affairs of leadership as the instrument to enforce governance in a Government.

The profession of Law is the common denominator, recurring between religion and politics. Both antagonize each other so deep that some people in the corridors of political leadership don't have high regard for their brothers in the world of Religion. As a result, some religious institutions in retaliation had banned their faithful adherents - the bishops, priests, pastors, and Imans - from participation in the running of the affairs of our countries' democracies through the instrument of politics. By doing so, our brothers in the Ministry have forgotten that the Creator 'rules' and governs His Kingdom as a real 'Sovereign Government authority' - with full military powers, citizens, currency, passport, and constitution.

Make no mistakes about this. There's always politics inside the altar of religion. Religion also brushes itself in the corridors of political leadership. Also, never confuse politics with the government.

Politics and Government are not the. Whether you belong to the faith of Christianity, Islam, Hinduism, Scientology, or a non-religious individual, you're either directly or indirectly influenced by a few people, the politicians, whose daily jobs are to change the laws that control humanity. They get paid in their jobs for controlling the affairs of the entire country through their private emotions. We are equally shaped by the influence of religion in our culture and societies. Both oppose each other, yet enslave us to follow their doctrines.

The religious people, however, are taught to avoid "politicking" altogether, even though our religious leaders play politics internally and secretly in the pulpit of the LORD. For instance, in the Catholic Church, the Pope is not appointed by the people or by the priests. The Pope is "elected" into POWER through the same voting system invented by politicians. He is voted into Power through ballot papers by the Papal Conclave consisting of only the "selected few" - a College of Cardinals - playing the key roles in the ecclesiastical government.

Whatever you don't control, therefore, someone else will. We live on Earth, we have our feelings, moral values, ethics, and character that define who we are. Yet, a handful of the "selected few" in politics control the majority of billions of people on Earth.

In 2021, the world population stood at 7.9 Billion. That means, only a handful of politicians control over 7.9 billion people. The real problem is that so many of our political leaders never studied Business Administration, Management or Leadership in their academic disciplines. Only a few managed to run successful businesses in their lifetime. The majority never owned a grocery store let alone starting new profitable businesses from scratch in the communities they live.

The people in politics are the group we had put our trust in their hands to manage the country's economy on our behalf. Our UK National Health Service was once led by a politician with no medical background to control the affairs of medical Professors and Consultant physicians just because he found himself in politics. Thank God he had a background in politics, philosophy, and politics.

The few classes of people we voted into power or government, had conceived their plans years before taking office. But once they step their feet in the corridors of power, sooner than later, they begin to hurt the feelings of the same people who had voted them in. They repeal the existing laws of the land, and replace them with new ones for their benefit or the benefit of their political sponsors. They simply control changes in our lives in time.

Our laws are also made by a selected group of people called Parliament (UK) or Congress (USA). They simply create new laws without even consulting the opinions of the people who had voted them in. These Laws will affect your life and the decisions you make in life personally in your entire life. They control everything including our educational system, healthcare system, transport system or technology we use at home and in our businesses.

The food we eat is controlled by our politicians. Even the fish and forests have "Ministers" to regulate them. The impacts will affect you privately, financially, economically, and down to the very last meal you put on your dining table. That's how powerful Laws, Politics and Religion are. That's why I encourage people to consider making careers in any of these three professions.

Our political leaders will impose their laws to influence our culture or way of life; change our belief system and dress code, and even change how people worship their God in their traditions. Washing your car at home, or watering your flowers in your back garden with a hosepipe, was once illegal in the UK once the water level was declared dangerously low – even though the UK as a nation is floating in, and surrounded by Seas – the Atlantic Ocean, the North Sea, and the English Channel.

Keeping silent means acceptance, and acceptance = sanction. Whenever we are silenced into approval, that Law remains a Law as long as the government is in power. Therefore, plan your life for yourself, and work on the plans until you get results. Why? Because if you don't plan your life, someone will plan it for you. If you don't plan for your destination, someone already has an idea where to keep you for a very long time.

Whoever Controls Your Life Controls Your Future

From conception to birth, and from cradle to the graveyard, your circumstances, your personal life, and your destiny are in the hands of one Instrument - the Government. Here are a few facts on why righteous people and the Ambassadors of God should join politics and influence positive changes in our community through the legitimate route of government, i.e., law enactment.

- **Birth:** As soon as your child is born, your child's birth will never be accepted in society until the politicians in government declare this birth through **Birth Certificate** and Registration.

- **Baptism:** When it's time to have your child baptized in your local Church and take up a Christian name, that baptism is classified as ILLEGAL, unless the child's name had been entered in the Parish Registers as directed by the Law of the Government by issuing a **Certificate of Baptism.**

- **College or University:** You had spent years studying your degree in medicine or diploma at a college or university, only to be refused recognition when your time has expired. Your academic achievements become pointless and worthless unless the government gives you a **School Certificate** or **Certificate of Graduation** as proof that you attended classes.

- **Job Offer:** No matter your academic qualification or job experience, your new job becomes questionable, unless you have been given "a Job Offer" or a legally binding "**contract of employment.**"

- **Buying a House with a Mortgaging:** That house you've just bought and paid a 20% deposit of your hard-earned income is not yours, unless your name and the amount you had paid for it are registered with the Land Registry title deeds in your city.

- **Marriage and Divorce:** You have fallen in love with your best-half, and want to marry in Church so you become husband and wife or separate from your partner through divorce Your marriage or divorce is invalid if the government doesn't issue you a Marriage Certificate; or Divorce Certificate (decree nisi or Decree Absolute).

- **Death:** Although you might be dead or resting in the morgue or buried in the cemetery. Yet, the Government says NO - you're dead yet. Why? Because a doctor approved by the same government to practice medicine in the country must first confirm you are dead, and then proceeds to issue a **Death Certificate.**

As I was about to conclude this chapter of the manuscript on 26th August 2021, when news from the U.S. started filtering into the UK online media through the US Mail Online newspaper with a headline captioned:

> "Italy to hold referendum on legalising euthanasia after 750,000 sign petition: Christian politicians condemn 'culture of death"
> (Baker 2021).

It is anticipated that in early 2022, Italian politicians will legislate on people's private lives by giving "life" to their legal system to start killing people - anyhow and wherever. They will hand over the legal "killing machine" to their fellow citizens to assist their relatives - brother or sisters, wives or husbands, grandparents or even neighbours – the power to kill themselves when they think they have had enough of you through the process of "assisted suicide."

The law is clear that nobody should destroy another man's property in vain. On that note, humans don't have the licence or right to intentionally kill fellow human beings they didn't assist God to create. No wonder Apostle Paul wrote about the thoughts of the human race when he said: "Indeed, humans are the only creatures on Earth, who are constantly devising innovative ways of doing evil (Rom.1:28-30).

With a minority of Christian politicians in Italy's small Christian political party, known as "Il Popolo della Famiglia" (The People of Family), unfortunately, they don't have the teeth to bite the legislation. Their collective efforts will be like raindrops falling into the deep Red Sea. Rather, the power rests on the shoulders of voters who had already signed the petition with over 750,000 signatories – which are more than 250,000 signatories over the usual 500,000 signatures required to trigger a referendum in Italy [1].

Therefore, since the Government controls almost every aspect of our lives, the righteous people should take part in the processes leading to Number 10 Downing Street, or 70 Whitehall, London – the seats of the Governments of the United Kingdom.

In the next chapter, I will walk you through the Brain Science of Human Emotions, and how the same chemicals we generate from our body are responsible for our present situations - from poverty to wealth, and from happiness to anxiety and depression - leading to other debilitating health conditions.

---

1. Source: https://www.businessinsider.com/italy-could-hold-euthanasia-referendum-vatican-says-its-an-evil-act-2021-8?r=US&IR=T

SECTION 4

SCIENTIFIC EXPLANATION *of* HUMAN EMOTIONS

"Companies' over-reliance solely on IQ and Technical skills during recruitment is one of the major reasons, according to the Corporate Executive Board (CEB), why '50-70% of business executives' failed to survive the storms of new Leadership roles and POWER within 18 months."

- Dr Emmanuel E. Amadi

Chapter Eleven

The Brain Science of Human Emotions

"If the highest aim of a captain were to preserve his ship, he would keep it in port forever."

~ Thomas Aquinas

EACH PERSON is constantly operating from one level of emotional state to another, ranging from happiness and excitement to anger, sadness or disappointment. Emotions are like water which exists in 3 states: solid ice, liquid, and gas when exposed to different temperatures and pressure. Below the freezing point and above the boiling point, liquid water turns itself into a solid ice cube and gaseous phase (vapour), respectively.

In neuropharmacology, during my undergraduate and postgraduate pharmacy education and a doctorate in nanotoxicology of nanomaterials, I came to understand that the body is simply a mobile, **Biological Chemical Reactor**, filled with various chemicals - acids, bases, and the body's telecommunication system - the neurotransmitters - whose functions determine or shape our daily lives. They function non-stop, from conception until we're "recalled" back to our Creator in Heaven. These chemicals are inherently built inside us – to protect us from harm. economically, our chemicals are also responsible for keeping the poor poorer for life, while making the rich richer depending on how they manage these neurotransmitters.

There are over 100 different neurotransmitters, but the prominent ones are responsible for keeping us safe well – including dopamine, serotonin, acetylcholine, gamma-aminobutyric (GABA), glutamine, and norepinephrine or adrenalin.

The problem is that no matter how smart humans are, we have no control of their production or synthesis. We also don't have control of the emotions they trigger. But what we do have control over is our minds. Yes, we do have control over what goes in and out of our mind - our thinking and our behaviour towards the trigger of stressful situations of life. We also do have control over how we respond to the CHANGE or message brought by the chemicals.

The basics to understanding ourselves lie in the re-discovery of the root cause of our emotions that drive our behaviour. We must also seek to understand why we react in certain ways throughout our daily responses to situations.

Every response to external stress is from within us. We are all familiar with the adage: "You cannot give what you don't have." In other words, you cannot manifest outwardly what you don't possess inwardly.

Therefore, we must strive to offer no excuses on why we behave in certain predicted ways which impact negatively on people around us or make statements such as "I'm too busy to get involved," "I'm too tired today," or "my mood is a private matter."

We must understand why we become judgemental or selective on the type of feedback we receive, and from whom we receive feedback depending on our emotions during times of crisis.

By seeking to study and understand our behaviour and reproducing a real-time scenario of emotional hijack, one can start to understand more about our habits and how they play out to disrupt our top efforts and achievements.

The true test of our Emotional Rulership and Emotional Intelligence is during a crisis. It is during the peak of thunder and storms of life that we can demonstrate our ability to apply the maximum level of IQ and technical skills to control those circumstances and achieve the desired results.

In the following paragraphs, I would discuss the Neuropharmacology of human Emotions, how emotions are generated through chemical messengers called Neurotransmitters, how they talk to each other, and how they warn us that CHANGE has arrived.

The Neuropharmacology of Human Emotions

The cells are in networks akin to being in relationships. They carry high voltage currents along live cables known as the "neurons." These cells equally talk to each other in a regulated fashion across a small gap or junction known as the synapse – from a zone of high voltage (the pre-synaptic neurons) to another zone of lower voltage (postsynaptic neurons) to accomplish a single mission leading to emotions and responses.

It is remarkable to understand that most of our emotional seconds are triggered by the electric signals we generate in our brain, provoking an enormous increase in certain chemical messengers, termed neurotransmitters, which in return initiate an immediate feeling of excitement, anger, or depression.

Our body is connected through a network of neurons. Each neuron comprises two major components: (A) the Sending

Neuron - with higher electrical potential, and (B) the Receiving Neuron - with a lower electrical potential. In between these two neurons (A and B) is a Cosmic Space, a gated zone called the "Synapse". This is the main gap - the building bridge - that connects the two super-powers responsible for information transmission. Without this cosmic space, the cells cannot talk to each other.

Neurotransmitters come in a lock-and-key model: shapes, and sizes. Some are rectangular, others are triangular or squared in nature. In our organizations, the employees also come from different backgrounds. Some are accountants, lawyers, electricians, while others are cleaners, technicians, or care support workers. Some are short, others are tall. With different faith, race or colour, everyone joins hands to get the task done. Everyone must put their differences away, and fit into the organizational structure. We gather to pursue a common goal of the organization we work for.

Each key must fit into the right padlock (the receptor) to trigger responses – open or lock it up. Each neurotransmitter from the sending neuron must pass through the "synapse" to fit into the right lock in the receiving neuron to generate a response.

Just like we are tested in our exams to prove, attest, or authenticate our knowledge, these chemicals are also 'tested' for authenticity inside the Synapse. This is to prove what they claim to be before fitting into the next role. Just as our Creator doesn't like wasting resources (see Gen 2:5), our neurons don't like waste either.

To recoup excess neurotransmitters present in the synapse, they undergo three major changes.

1. They are taken up through a process known as the "Re-uptake" Mechanism. Here, the chemicals are taken up or "recalled" into the presynaptic neuron (sending) through a specialized and customized "transporter" back to the warehouse for storage.

2. They are broken down through the process of **"metabolism."** Here, they are chopped into pieces as "metabolites" before being "recalled" into the sending neuron.

3. The useless ones – the ones without significant value to your body - are degraded or self-destroyed in the synaptic region in a process known as "autolysis", "cell-suicide," or "programmed cell death" known as **"apoptosis."**

How do you control waste and manage resources in your organization? For neurotransmitters, every penny matters. Holding inventory in your organization is the #1 killer in your business. It decreases cash flow and locks up working capital.

Below are some of the body's communication systems (neurotransmitters) that greatly influence our emotions and behaviour:

- **#1: Glutamate**

Glutamate is a natural amino acid. It is synthesized from glutamine in the central nervous system (CNS). It is found both in our body and externally from natural sources in our diet, such as mushrooms, cheese, tomatoes, and some sauces including Soy sauce or extracts, fish sauce, oyster sauce, hydrolyzed and autolyzed yeast. A typical example of commercial glutamate in our food is the Monosodium glutamate (MSG), the sodium salt of glutamic acid. It is commercially produced from fermented sugar or starch commonly used as a "food additive" to improve taste: soup, salad dressings, and spicy sauces (International Glutamate Information Service 2021).

This chemical is one of the tightly regulated neurotransmitters in the brain. It is the main excitatory neurotransmitter in the CNS. In other words, its job specification is to send, or fire high-voltage neurotransmitters from the pre-synaptic nerve to the post-synaptic nerve. It fires its cannon non-stop, that if it's not controlled could lead to nerve cell death, or cell suicide, or excitotoxicity.

The symptoms may appear as impaired brain function; shaky movements or restlessness; anxiety; or slurred speech. On the other hand, decreased amount or deficiency of this chemical is associated with low energy, mental fatigue, insomnia, or inattentiveness. In addition to this role, in normal circumstances, glutamate plays a vital role in learning (education, scholarship) and memory (retention, recall, or recollection).

The presence of a trace amount can activate, or recruit other neurons within its vicinity to join the drill, and fire orders the way a military commander does to his battalion. Like I stated before, the brain doesn't like waste at all. Excess glutamate, like other neurotransmitters in the synapse, is quickly sent back to the barracks – recalled or recycled for further service.

Just like we have our network of transport systems, the neurons have their in-built transport system! When excess glutamate is present, "transporter proteins" are recruited to sweep the synapse off excess debris to protect the brain from shutting itself down. However, there are instances where the brain cells could continue firing their cannons non-stop for more than 24 hours.

To safeguard the brain from the toxic impacts of over-excited neurons, the brain cells can lock themselves up and stop working, in what I describe as a *"self-imposed incarceration."*

- #2: GABA (Gamma-Aminobutyric Acid)

The good news is that the Creator of the universe also has a terminator for the firing squad of the glutamates. This is where the Team GABA comes in. They are the main opposition to Glutamate as Inhibitors. As an inhibitory neurotransmitter, its job is to diminish the firing effects of Glutamate in the CNS, and wedges several signals from the brain.

In the absence of GABA, the brain will be active all the time. GABA brings calm, tranquillity, or orderliness to the brain to slow you down. It protects you by simultaneously lowering your heart rate and blood pressure. It supports you to relax, reduce your stress for the day, and help you to go to sleep. But it doesn't do this job alone. Rather, it recruits other neurodermatitis such as Serotonin and Melatonin to help you enjoy a good night sleep.

- #3: Serotonin:

Serotonin is synthesized from the amino acid-base, L-tryptophan, in the brain neurons and stored in vesicles waiting to be released when activated. It regulates most bodily functions and allows the cells to speak and communicate one-on-one with each other. Although produced in the brain, distance is not an issue when it comes to serotonin. It has dual targets – the gut and the brain.

In the small intestine, serotonin boosts the feelings of satisfaction after each eating meal. It keeps your appetite in check and reduces the waste of food through excessive consumption. When you eat unpleasantly toxic food or nauseous food sub-stances, the serotonin quickens the removal of such materials from your intestine. It does this by activating the vomiting centre to purge them out or increase peristalsis and the urgency to use the lavatory/restroom.

Serotonin functions as the stabilizer of human emotions. It is the thermostat that controls the body's feelings: body temperature, libido, happiness or anxiety. Your sexual appetite towards your spouse is the impact of serotonin flooding your feeling centre. It is the key driver to what you do in your bedroom. The flaccidity of the male genitalia and subsequent arousal, are the results of the mere thoughts of sexual acts, which activates the feeling centre of the brain to release serotonin. Once released, the serotonin floods your system with oxygenated blood.

It is also implicated in many psychiatric, mood, or mental health disorders such as social anxiety disorder and depression. One prominent symptom of depression is known as "*Anhedonia.*" It is characterized by low mood, lack of or reduced motivation, lack of or reduced feelings of interest in activities, which in normal circumstances, would have brought you joy exceedingly.

The deficiency of serotonin or its reduced level in the brain can lead to unimaginable disorders, such as:
(1) Social anxiety disorders (SAD): anxiety disorders, mood disorders.
(2) Eating disorders:
(a) Binge eating - where people consume disproportionately high amounts of food within a short space of time.
(b) Anorexia nervosa – the fear of gaining weight leads to self-food restriction or over-exercising to lose weight.
(c) Bulimia nervosa – where people consume a lot of food, and then try effortlessly to purge the food themselves).
(d) Obsessive-compulsive disorder (OCD), and many other disorders including substance use disorders, and autistic spectrum disorders (Schneier et al. 2002).

OCD, as the name implies is a mental health condition where an individual has some kind of "intrusive" thoughts, ideas, beliefs, or opinions repeatedly. This habit is known as "obsessions". Therefore, to execute or work on these "feelings" to control their obsession, they carry out certain actions persistently and repeatedly (Helpguide.org 2013).

OCD falls in various forms and may lie in any of these classifications. For instance:
- The Hoarders pile up food, clothe, sanitary products, and even over the counter medicines (OTC) for fear of shortage.
- The Checkers routinely check stuff they feel may harm them or put them at risk. An example of the checkers might include checking the car and patio doors over and over again to see if they are secured.
- The same applies to "Washers" who wash their plates several times a day for fear of catching germs or infection.
- The "arrangers" are not let out in this scheme of disorder. They frequently re-arrange things to create a form of "perfection", "orderliness", and "tranquillity."

Medical Targets: Serotonin vs. Melatonin

The selective serotonin reuptake inhibitors or SSRI anti-depressants are the commonly prescribed medicines to target the serotonin and alter your brain's communication system. It does this by **_restoring or replenishing_** depleted levels by simply topping up its gasoline tank to a "near-normal" level. This approach stabilizes your mood. Medicines in this category are the **CFPS drugs**, my acronym for *Citalopram, Fluoxetine, Paroxetine*, and *Sertraline*.

It is vital to know that when your serotonin tank level is very low, it alters your emotional state from being positive to being negative in the spectrum of life. It throws all manner of bricks and pebbles to distract you from your job or sleeping pattern. If it throws bricks and pebbles on your face, the impacts will distort your ability to remain focused - from being attentive to being inattentive. This is followed by diminished concentration and disorderliness in your life. On the high spectrum, the impact could lead to attention deficit hyperactivity disorder (ADHD).

Serotonin is the precursor or mother of **Melatonin**. Melatonin is responsible for regulating our sleep-wake cycle or the circadian cycle. It serves as the body's natural internal clock relative to the Sunrise and Sunset, night-time and day-time. The cycle repeats itself every 24 hours. When the Sun goes to bed at night and darkness falls on the Earth, melatonin is the guy that keeps us well-wrapped up in bed under the duvet – so we can enjoy a long, good-night sleep.

As soon as we are all wrapped up in bed ready to doze off, the mother Serotonin sneaks into our bedroom to check on us – and help us sleep faster by taking charge of the battle from the non-REM Sleep (stages 1, 2, and 3) into the REM sleep (rapid eye movement) within 90 minutes after we had fallen asleep.

In a night of deep REM sleep, we begin to have vivid dreams – of flying in a mat from Africa to Europe without a visa or travelling documents. As the sun begins to wake up early in the morning, the Serotonin is the mother that comes with a smiley face to say "Good Morning"- and then kicks us out of bed. It keeps us awake and alert in the morning before we begin to flood the brain with early morning coffee or tea.

However, history shows that too much of anything - including too much petting of your children - is bad for their health. Likewise, too much oxygen above normal can harm the brain, and our lungs degenerate as victims of pulmonary toxicity. Therefore, excessive serotonin production in the brain leads to life-threatening disorders known as **Serotonin Syndrome** (SS).

The **SS** is characterized by emotional states such as overconfident (or arrogant), agitation (distress, anxiety, misery, upset, or worry), and aggressive behaviours. In physiological terms, the **SS** causes malignant hyperthermia (MHT) characterized by high fever, muscle rigidity, fast heart rate (cardiac arrest), abnormally increased breathing, rhabdomyolysis (collapse of muscle fibres), kidney failure, increased level of acid in the blood (acidosis), or blood clot (aka, disseminated intramuscular coagulation) (Genetics Home Reference 2020).

- **#4: Dopamine - The Pleasure hormone:**

This guy is a Catecholamine Neurotransmitter that acts on both the Central Nervous System (CNS) and the Sympathetic part of the Peripheral Nervous System (PNS). Dopaminergic activity (DA) is the most exciting neurotransmitter as it plays a part in the brain's **Reward System**, impulsivity, and motivation (Kolla and Wang 2019). It is responsible for different kinds of cognition (i.e., thoughts, reasoning, understanding, and perception), mostly "emotion-associated memory", reward decision-making, aggression, and alcohol abuse (Sun and Alkon 2012).

When activated by activities that normally give you feelings of joy, excitement, "accomplishment" or "success", dopamine is the guy which floods your synapse to stimulate the reward system and bring feelings of pleasure. It peaks during adolescence and is responsible for increased *drug use* and *abuse* in young children seeking excitement and high.

Overactivation of dopamine, either by drugs or addictive activities like gambling, video gaming or "shopping-addiction" creates "overexcitement" or "high." Thus, indulging in activities or habits that "over-activate" our dopamine over time become difficult challenges to change or remedy. Striatal responses by adolescents to images of food and sex stimulate the dopamine leading to overweight and sex drive.

In addition to the above paragraph, the overactivation of dopamine also boosts your wakefulness, appetite, and high sugar level. To combat the increased sugar levels in your system, the pancreas engages the services of Dopamine to release an adequate volume of insulin proportional to the amount of food you've consumed.

Dopamine also synchronizes your brain with your body to generate **voluntary activities**, such as driving your car and writing your name. All these voluntary activities are made possible due to dopamine.

- **#5: Adrenaline (Epinephrine)**

Although not domiciled in your brain, this guy is is released when the nerves connected to the adrenal glands are activated. Once released, adrenalin never returns empty-handed. It surges into the bloodstream where it holds the body to ransom when under stress. From the moment of panic when we first encounter emotional stress to the time of activation and release, this process occurs relatively fast - within a period of 2 to 3 minutes - to keep you alert just in case of any danger!

Here are some of the job descriptions of this guy in its portfolio:

- #1: Adrenalin is responsible for our body's fight-flight-freeze responses. This simple messenger increases the surge of oxygenated blood to all the entire muscles of the body, especially those of the heart and the lungs – supplying the energy we might need to fight off the danger, or flee from the danger, or stand in boldness to decide on the next action to take.
- #2: At the height of your emotional stress and pain, adrenalin becomes your pain killer, increasing your body's pain threshold, so that you feel little or no pains when injured while running for safety or fighting off the real threat head-on.
- #3: As the "energy booster" in times of crises, adrenalin plays the role of "non-anabolic steroids" as "stimulants" to

enhance your strength, reduce fatigue, improve aggressiveness, increase your endurance and performance. It intensifies your awareness to the maximum, so that you possess the willpower to survive the perceived threats. It does this by flooding your blood with Cortisol (a glucocorticoid) - the body's primary source of stress hormone - to improve your brains access to glucose and promote tissue repair damaged in times of stress.

Chapter Twelve

Two Kinds of Human Brain

"The human brain starts working the moment you are born and never stops until you stand up to speak in public."
~**George Jessel**, American actor, singer and songwriter.

THERE ARE two kinds of the brain when it comes to human intelligence: the Thinking Brain and the Emotional Brain (LeDoux 1998). The Thinking Brain is the Neocortex, or the Pre-frontal lobe of the brain, while The Emotional Brain is the limbic system, or most specifically, the "Amygdala."

The human brain is designed to function at its best in times of orderliness: good conditions and good times. Our body was never designed by our Creator to face excessive stress, such as anxiety, trauma, pressure, strain, or threats. Therefore, to safeguard people from threats – both assumed and real threats -

the amygdala is constantly active from birth to the graveyard to guard the body against such dangers or threats.

#1: The Thinking Brain

The Thinking Brain (i.e., the Neocortex, prefrontal cortex, or prefrontal lobe) is the largest part of the brain. It is about 76 % of the brain (approx. 80% of the entire brain) and approx. 90% of the entire Cerebral Cortex - aka the "Cerebral Mantle" (Strominger et al. 2012). The remaining 10 to 20% of the Cerebral Cortex makes up the *Allocortex*.

The best way to describe the Thinking Brain is like wearing a face cap. I also consider it as our "Thinking Cap." You can choose to wear this cap all the time, or you decide to take it off and go to bed. The choice to do both is all yours to control.

When the "thinking cap" is removed from the human brain, the entire human race ceases to think and reason. When this Neocortex is removed from us, mankind behaves like other primitive animals, just like the wild beasts of the animal kingdom. When this happens, we shout and scream on top of our voices like barking dogs when provoked, or encounter difficult challenges. We become *reactive* on impulses (in a reverse direction) rather than being *responsive* through thinking and reasoning.

The Neocortex is the Cognitive Centre of the human brain where our IQ, such as thinking, reasoning, remembering, and working memory resides (technical skills + business expertise). It processes complex, daily thoughts, feelings, ideas, such as:

- Sensory perception
- Language
- Spatial Reasoning
- Executive decisions
- Strategies

※ Delegation
※ Prioritizing
※ Traditional Intelligence (IQ)
※ Understanding future consequences.

For **Mild Threats**, the Neocortex overrides the amygdala. At this stage, we process the threat and respond rationally to resolve it. In the normal emotional state, the neocortex can process an emotional trigger by the factorial of four: 4! (1*2*3*4) = 24; i.e., there are 24 possible or variable ways to process a single emotion or function.

In Additional Mathematics, the factorial of a number, 'n' is the multiplication of that number (n) with every number till 1. n! = n x (n-1) x (n-2) x (n-3) x (n-4), etc.

#2: The Emotional Brain

(Feeling Centre)

Buried deep within the brain, just underneath the Cerebral Cortex (the Thinking Brain) lies the Limbic system of the Emotional Brain or the Feeling Brain. The limbic system itself is closely-controlled circuitry, or connection, comprising the Amygdala, Thalamus, Hypothalamus, Hippocampus (ATHH) and other leadership assistants involved in our behaviour formation, our emotions, and the responses we evoke for our survival.

While the components of the limbic system coordinate human emotions, such as rage, pleasure, sexual responses, etc., in this book, I would focus my interest on the tiny, almond-shaped body called the *Amygdala*.

The Amygdala

The amygdala plays an important role in unconscious, autonomic functions, learning, formation of new memories, and emotions. It also determines how strongly those memories are stored and retrieved depending on the severity of that emotion. Threats or daily life encounters, such as fear, or anxiety, which the mind thinks could be stressful to our body and make us feel highly emotional, are tightly stored.

Moreover, the amygdala attributes certain events to specific memories in the memory bank, and the last responses we had deployed to deal with them. When we face or perceive immediate danger, new events or old ones, the amygdala immediately recognises that event, and respond with a typical, predictable response.

The Amygdala is naturally active for crises, emergencies, or threats! During times of leadership crises, such as organizational challenges, pressures to achieve company targets, difficult relationships with our staff at the workplace, or in our homes with our spouses and children, our emotional centre takes control of our emotions, simply to protect us from danger (Goleman et al. 2013: pp. 28-29). Our feelings towards anything in life doesn't originate from the thinking brain but the feeling brain.

Like most of the components of the limbic system which occur in pairs, the Amygdala also occurs in pairs. It is located on both sides, Left and Right, of the cerebrum just above the ear regions.

The Amygdala is wired in a circuitry format in the limbic system. From there, the Emotional Brain is connected to the Thinking Brain, or Cerebral cortex through a high-speed route known as the Neural Highway (Goleman 1999: pp.74-75). This is akin to the UK's Smart Motor Ways or the German Autobahn. The Cerebral Cortex (the brain) is then connected, and wired to the Spinal Cord, beginning at the bottom of the brain stem called the Medulla oblongata. Thus, the brain + spinal cord = the Central Nervous System (CNS). The spinal cord stops in the lower back region as it mergers to itself forming a cone known as *conus medullaris*.

How the Amygdala Picks Up Stressful Events in Your Life circumstances

The Amygdala receives information from the following five sensory organs:
- A pair of eyes (sight vs. vision).
- A pair of ears (hearing).
- A pair of nostrils (for smell).
- A pair of mouthpieces (split into half)/tongue(taste) – with the upper and lower palate, and
- The skin (feeling) – the largest organ in the body, about 3.6 kg in weight in adults and 22 square feet (2 square meters) in dimension, making the skin the largest organ of the body (National Geographic 2017).

Although strategically located on the outside, all five sensory organs are uniquely wired to the limbic system to connect with the outside world. All these sensory systems are located on the head, except the skin which wraps the entire body like a suit shielding them from external aggression.

When we experience stressful events, our sensory organs such as the eyes take images or pictures of the crime scene, while the nostrils pick up smells, scents, or aroma from the source of threat. With its powerfully inbuilt auditory channels, the ears can pick up sound waves (noise or voices) from the scene of incidence and within the vicinities with slightly higher frequencies in the range of 20 Hz to 20,000 Hz. Human ears, however, are less efficient compared to our primitive counterparts like the elephants, which can pick up sounds 20 x lower than humans. The mouth, with the tongue, can sense the taste of the atmosphere, and confirm how we feel it in our gut – sweet, sour, or bitter - while the skin regulates all the senses of touch – feeling – smooth, hard, coarse - from the outside.

As all the 5 sensory organs pick up stressful, sensory information, they are immediately intercepted by the Amygdala as soon as they occur in the scene of events. The Amygdala also sends them immediately to the Hypothalamus (HPT) as distress signals. Being the highest level of "classified information," within seconds, the distress signals are are sent to the Human Control System - the *Autonomic Nervous System* (ANS).

The ANS primarily functions "unconsciously" to regulate bodily functions, such as heart rate, respiratory system, digestive system, pituitary response, sexual desire, and urination. The ANS is also accountable for the Fight-Flight-or-Flee responses.

The ANS comprises two components:

1. Sympathetic Nervous System (SNS); and

2. Parasympathetic Nervous System (PSNS).

While the SNS is the key driver of the Fight-or-Flight responses we take unconsciously, the PSNS drives the "Freeze" mode.

Like the CCTV cameras fitted to a building, their job is to "protect" the building against unauthorized intrusions. Remember that the camera does not prevent the crime from happening or intrusion taking place. The lenses scan the vicinity for intruders: detect movements, record images of objects across its paths, store images, pick up sounds, and can even alert the owner when unauthorized access occurs.

The Amygdala does the same job specifications as the standard CCTV cameras illustrated above. While the amygdala doesn't protect you from harm, what you do with the information or alert in your organization is what makes you stand out of the crowd in difficult times. The amygdala of the CEO, or the

Entrepreneur, is constantly scanning around your business environment for threats: threats in the form of businesses competitions, the introduction of new technologies, new legislation that would affect the industry, or new entrants that could impinge your business and its profitability.

Naturally, our body is "primed," or "built" to prepare us against danger – for survival with the primitive brain. It was built to succeed in life. The only way to warn us of the presence of danger is through the human fire alarm – the Amygdala. The Amygdala sounds the bell when it "perceives", "sees" or "feels" danger hanging around the corner. It tells the thinking brain to engage in logical thinking and response. It senses the external environment and relays what it "sees" through the power of "feeling" straight into the limbic system.

When we feel intense or severe threats, the *little* amygdala automatically takes over the entire brain functions and controls them. It immediately sends signals to the brain and floods the entire thinking brain with a stress hormone (cortisol). It shuts down the thinking brain – the part of our brain that makes us "human beings" - and reduces us to ordinary animals. At this stage, the immediate signal is sent to our vocal cavity and we begin to shout over our voices, and exchange swearing words to stay in control.

The Amygdala hijack reminds me of two dogs belonging to my two neighbours across my street in Crosslee Road, Manchester. One is bigger, about 3 years old, and the other is smaller, just about 5 months old. "They don't bark that much at home," said the two owners. But the dogs' attitude of rage, anger, and frightening behaviours when they see each other on the street always remind me of this tiny-shaped object called the *amygdala* and the situation called *Amygdala Hijack*. The puppies never attended a Barking School. Their ability to start barking once their eyes and ears are opened is strong proof that the a*mygdala* has its origin in primitivity.

When they see each other from a distance, the immediate response is danger. Each dog starts barking to ward off the dog.

The closer they are, the more the intensity of their barking. And the funny thing is that the smaller dog barks the most! The two dog owners understood their dogs' behaviour that they don't walk along the same lane in the same, rather they take different routes.

Amygdala Hijack:
Mild, Moderate & Strong Emotions

The *Amygdala Hijack* was first used by Daniel Goleman to describe our immediate and intense emotional response that's out of proportion to the real situation (Goleman 1995). In our responses to emotional threats – whether perceived or real – the *amygdala* hijacks the neocortex. The Amygdala is naturally active for Emergency responses resulting in either of the two kinds of responses:

1. Automatic physical Responses, and
2. Primitive Thinking.

- **Automatic Physical Responses**

When our body senses stressful events, the stress hormones (adrenaline + cortisol) flood the Amygdala. Our immediate response is *automatic*: fight-flee, or–freeze, sending vocal senses to the vocal cavity and we shout, scream, and swear. We behave this way as a mechanism to retain our sanity and control over those events.

Here, our blood pressure and cardiac output increase, and the heart rate leaps by 20-30 beats/min > normal (60-100) (Goleman et al. 2013: pp.22-28). More adrenaline is flooded into the bloodstream, increasing glucose and oxygen supplies to the muscles of our legs, lungs, and brain, but reducing supply to areas where immediate actions are not required.

- **Primitive Thinking Responses**

When emotionally hijacked, sometimes we attempt to think ourselves out of the situation to understand what's going on. But in acute cases of emergency, our complex thoughts are diminished, and the only thinking available becomes *primitive* – just anything to end the encounter very fast.

The consequences of our primitive thinking become detrimental - and we **automatically** default to *self-protection*. We become *fixated* on the perceived threat with the strong need to respond by engaging or disengaging. Our immediate thinking is to create a barrier: an emotional/physical distance (stonewall).

If the emotional hijack is left unattended, the impacts of prolonged stress hormones released during a toxic workday could last for many hours later (Dolf Zillma 1993). When the Thinking Brain fails to veto our emotions or becomes compromised, the Amygdala Hijack takes over our body and "rules" over it.

The amygdala, therefore, is the "defensive drone" or "survival centre" of all animals, including humans.

Your Perception Determines your Life

At the point of amygdala hijack, whatsoever you call *a threat* – mild, moderate, or strong - it becomes. For instance, if you call a sugar *a threat*, it becomes - and that sweet thing turns itself into a diabetic-inducing agent. If you call a pen *a threat* - so it becomes. And when you call a family mere dispute *a threat*, so it becomes.

But when this threat is "perceived" to be "Strong," the amygdala quickly overpowers the prefrontal lobes, the thinking brain, and triggers the "fight-flee or freeze" responses. It is an automatic response in the absence of thinking.

All the external five senses are connected as a conduit to the limbic system – the nose (smell), eye (sight), mouth/tongue (taste), ear (hearing), and skin (touch). Therefore, every sense of stress is sent automatically into this computing centre. The speed of the amygdala's response to threat is ~ 100 x faster than the frontal lobe. The problem with the Amygdala is its deficiency in discriminating between the real versus the perceived threats.

The Neocortex is located far away on the front of the head, while the amygdala is deeply tucked away below in the limbic system. The two communicate with each other in good times through an emotional bridge. However, under a perceived threat, the connection, marriage, relationship or bond between the two is automatically broken. The emotional brain quickly usurps your thinking brain by force in a process akin to "colonization." This is Amygdala Hijack. At this stage, the information about the threat is not yet processed or "thought about" in the neocortex. No willful thinking.

I remember when I was playing a draft with my son – Michael. I told him that my goal is to watch his amygdala hijack throughout the game. I had wanted him to win, but he made a wrong step, and his King was killed. He lost confidence. I heard him say, "I am not going to play." I asked him "why?" His response was, "Because ... I am a loser." I said "No, Son! You aren't supposed to say that! This is just a game. You'll win if you put your mind on it!" And in the next game, he nearly won!

Well, the truth is that we all experience 'amygdala hijack' on daily basis, but having the ability to know how to manage the hijack – and manage our emotions - is the key to thriving when things are not working in our terms.

When the Amygdala hijack takes over, one is filled with negative bias such as: "Oh! They said that I'm a failure. It's true because ... today is definitely going to be a bad day!

Size does Matter, but Small Sizes Matter Most

Big sizes, indeed, do matter, but small sizes matter greatly. When it comes to size, the amygdala is not near in competition with the cerebral cortex. The amygdala is very tiny relative to the neocortex. Like the Lions - the King of the Jungle - relative to the elephants, the amygdala can colonize "the mind" of the Lion to behave differently. When the Lion sees other animals - elephants or giraffes, – his amygdala controls his attitude - his thoughts and his emotions. The only perception he has is "food." Food is ready. And the last question on his mind is the time – when?

When other animals see the lions, they too are terrified, and the amygdala hijack takes over their minds. Their only perception of the lion is *"flesh-eater"*. The next thing on their mind is "escape." Why? Because the *meat-eater* is around.

Despite its tiny size, the amygdala can usurp the logical thinking of War Lords, Kings and Presidents, CEOs of businesses, Government officials, parents, friends, thieves, armed gangs, notorious criminals, and daytime robbers - and renders them useless.

Impacts of Amygdala Hijack on World Leaders

Our libraries are filled with history books concerning World Leaders who had been impacted by emotions and the amygdala hijack. Emotions can drive the great leaders into the corridors of sad histories that had remained documented in the sand of history.

Below are some examples of the impacts of emotion and amygdala hijacks in the history of leadership.

- It was Amygdala hijack that led King Henry VIII (1506-47) to annual his two marriages and had two of his six wives and many concubines – Anne Boleyn (c. 1501-1536) and Catherine Howard (1523-1542)- beheaded in his quest to have a healthy male child.

- It was the same amygdala hijack that led the same King Henry to change his foreign policies and broke up with Rome (the Roman Catholic Church) when the Pope – Pope Clement VII - at the time refused the King's request to annul his first marriage to Catherine of Aragon (1485-1536) so he could marry Anne Boleyn. It was this refusal that led the King to the "Reformation" agenda to establish his own church - the *Church of England*. Instead of reading history, he created a history that changed religion till today and divided the Church.

- We are all familiar with the history of the *Boston Tea Party* (16th Dec. 1773) and *Massachusetts massacre* that precipitated the "American Revolutionary War" also known as the "American War of Independence" (1775-1783), leading to colonial independence and the birthing of the United States of America.

- King George III, the King of the former British Empire imposed taxation policies on the 13 North American colonies without colonial representation of Americans in the British Government in London. All acts of legislation to increase revenues were for the benefit of one man – The King – so he could pay back the huge debts incurred in "The French and Indian War" or "The Seven Year's War" (1754-1763).

- Colonies of Kingdoms and Empires are "supposed" to be protected and provided for by their Colonial Masters. The wealth of the colonies should be like those who colonized them, but it was not so in all the world's Kingdoms and

Empires. Rather, the British Empire introduced the Tea Act (10th May 1773), a new act of Parliament, to heavily collect taxes from its colonists and protect one of England's own companies – The East India Company – from economic collapses, and The Intolerable Acts as a punitive measure to the American people for destroying thousands of pounds worth of British-taxed teas and the 13 American colonies in Congress immediately objected to, and many sought for independence.

- It was amygdala hijack that led to the emergence of wartime presidents of the United States of America (Martin Kelly 2020). It was amygdala hijack when President Gorge W. Bush (Jr) and the former British Prime Minister – Mr Tony Blair - perceived the unreal threats of the existence of unverified Weapons of Mass Destruction (WMD) (chemical, biological, and atomic weapons) in the Iraqi regime of Saddam Hussein. They sent troops into into the war on 20th March 2003 in Iraq and deposed him and his government. Between 20th March 2003 and December 2020, the Iraqi nation has never had a peaceful leadership and governance.

- It was the same amygdala hijack in action that on May 2, 2011, President Obama's US administration determined to eliminate global terrorism - leading to the killing of Osama Bin Laden – the founder of the Islamic militant group, al-Qaeda - by the US Navy Seals. Because you don't kill an ideology, his death gave birth to other proscribed violent extremist groups (Boko Haram, ISIS, or Al-Shabaab).

- It was also the amygdala hijack in the minds of President Donald J. Trump's administration, that on 3 January 2020, they deployed drones as *"weapons of assassination"* to eliminate some prominent military generals of the Iranian regime - General Qassim Soleimani.

- Finally, I imagined that *amygdala hijack* was also on display on the 27th November 2020 in the emotional state of the former leader of the Israeli regime - Prime Minister Benjamin Netanyahu - leading to the "alleged" approval of the killing of the Iranian nuclear scientist – Brigadier General Mohsen Fakhri Zadeh.

Chapter Thirteen

Domains of Success Competences
IQ versus Skills & EQ

"Mediocrity is never a desirable destination ... At least, not when practice might transform mediocrity to competence, or even skill.'
~ Napoleon Bonaparte

FOR THE past three or four decades before the coining of Emotional Intelligence or before its application to businesses and every life endeavours, humans had operated under the two abilities (fig. 3): Intelligent (IQ) and technical skills (e.g., job experience).

Figure 3: Intelligence Quotient (IQ) vs. Technical Skills

- **Academic Institutions**

For academic institutions, being "intelligence" is the most "desirable" competency required to gain admission to high schools, colleges, or the citadel of learning. For professional courses such as Law, Pharmacy, Medicine & Surgery, Dentistry, and Engineering, one must have a high intellectual quotient (IQ) of between 98 and 128, which is 13.0 more than the average candidates (85-115) to succeed in the classroom.

Most candidates with high IQ are likely to proceed into research through master's degrees, Executive MBAs, and PhDs, while only the selected few with a different mindset go on to become innovative entrepreneurs in the likes of Elon Musk and Jeff Bezos. This fraction of the population in the likes Mr Musk and Bezos take the highest financial risks in business. They venture into the untapped territories such as *Space Exploration* and *Tourism.* They achieved extraordinary ROI far better than the ordinary individual working in the London or New York financial markets, or people searching for job vacancies created by someone else. Musk becoming the first person to ever be valued at more than $300billion [1].

- **Employment**

For employers, the "desirable" requirements to secure your next job are "experience" and "technical skills." They are classified as the "essential" and "desirable" competencies". But you will discover that the more you're into the job system and climb higher in your role, you will begin to drop your technical skills and focus more on other areas of value and significance such as team management to departmental management and as the CEO.

The hiring managers or the agencies used by corporate organizations make the greatest mistakes using the same template in the selection criteria for hiring new candidates: "Job skills" and "recent work experience." Unfortunately, if you don't possess any of these criteria, you and your CV/resume are on your way to the shredder. See you in the bin.

They "judge" you based on your old CV/resume. They decide who you are, and the maximum value you could bring to the organization. They rely on your old junk CV to judge your future potential. What a life we live in! In other words, they have made their "conclusions" about you, that because you don't have the required experience, your potential in life is limited to your old CV.

This is why many hiring managers had failed consistently to hire the right candidates with the right potential for future success. This is what potential is all about. What you have achieved in the past, as listed in your CVs/resumes are no longer your potentials, but a history gone and buried in the cemetery. Hiring managers, therefore, should look into the future to see your potentials: which is your future, the untapped capabilities which cannot be decided in a split second.

Like the base of the Iceberg Model as previously discussed, your potentials are the hidden talents in you that are not yet manifested. Some hiring managers don't see hidden talents because they are under pressure to fulfil the employer's desires: experience. Thus, they see only the visible, tiny tip of the iceberg and miss out on your huge potentials hidden underneath the base of your brain.

Sometimes, the environment we find ourselves or our emotions of previous events before the interview may play crucial roles in shielding our true potentials from job recruiters. Therefore, never judge a man or woman by the colour of their skin, their religion, their height (short or tall), their size (chubby or slim), belief systems, or past experiences, rather judge them by their future potentials.

Harvard Research Predictors of Success

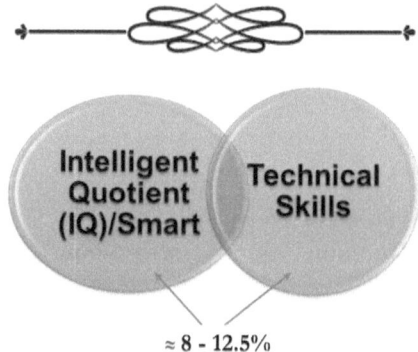

Figure 4: Prediction of success using the Harvard University Success predictors (Anchor 2011).

According to Harvard University's predictor of success, your success or failure in life-based on your academic qualifications and job experiences is predictable. The data is an eye-opener and very astonishing. The authors found that the sum of your natural intelligence (IQ) and your technical skills (TS) is equal to 25%. Since success is predictable, that means your failure in life is also predictable. Why is this true? This is because success and failure are both governed by natural laws and principles.

Whichever one you chose or failed to choose is a matter of your choice. Some people choose to study science while others choose to study business degrees. However, your success in any of them is based on your ability to master the relevant laws and principles within them and the secrets to wealth creation. To be smart in Mathematics, you must be grounded in the laws of calculations, calculus, or projectiles, and their application using relevant equations. For instance, can you solve this simple mathematics: $2+(4+6) +2 \times 9 \div 3-17$?[2] It is not magic! You can't simply guess the answer without following a certain "Law" of mathematics called "BODMAS."

In Figure 4, the value of an employee's IQ is predicted to fall between 8.0 to 12.5%, the same value for technical skills according to Harvard University's predictor of success. That means, for an average CEO, the maximum value for success is 25%, which is the sum of IQ + technical skills i.e. (IQ +TS) ≈ 25%. The question one would ask is this: "What happens to the rest of the 75% of success unaccounted for?" There is a vacuum here. That means, there is much more to IQ and Technical skills combined to become successful in life. This is where the third domain of success, Emotional Intelligence, comes in to fill the vacuum.

Companies' over-reliance solely on IQ and Technical skills during recruitment is one of the major reasons, according to the Corporate Executive Board (CEB) why "50-70% of business executives" had failed to survive the storms of new Leadership roles and POWER within the first 18 months of being hired or positioned to a position of power - whether sourced internally or externally from other organizations[3]. Out of these statistics, about three per cent failed dramatically, while fifty per cent battled silently to survive.

Daniel Goleman's Domains of Success Competencies

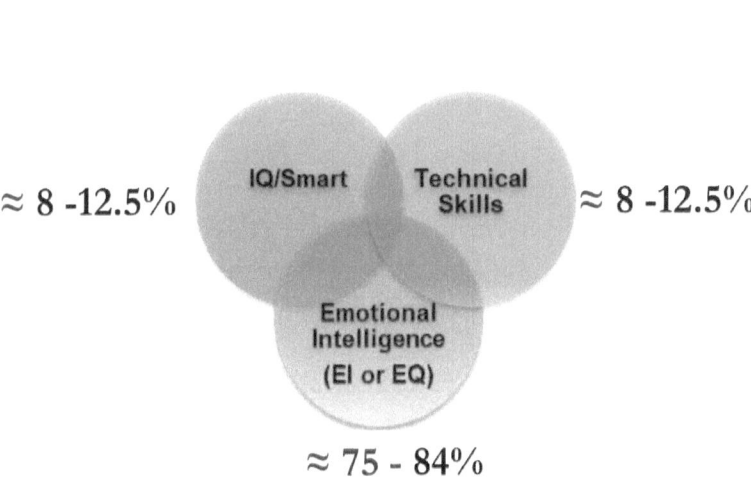

Figure 5: Illustrations of Daniel Goleman's 3 domains of success and Leadership Competencies under pressure

In addition to the two domains of success identified by the authors of the Harvard university predictor of success, Daniel Goleman had identified Emotional Intelligence as the third domain (See Fig. 5) which plays a significant role in effective leadership in times of crises:

- IQ/Smart.
- Technical Skills, PLUS
- EI/EQ.

When top senior managers or CEOs are locked up in the same boardroom to discuss all those important business strategies, research shows that all of them possess equal or almost identical IQ and technical skills at the executive level. They might have the same work experience and technical skills to perform their roles.

However, what really differentiates one executive from another doesn't lie in their academic qualifications nor in their skills to do the job. This is because, senior executives are primarily focused on the "external" – devising strategies for the organization to drive the business forward. They are in fact, less competent in the technical skills they possessed at the time of recruitment. That is the truth when the CEOs are concerned.

Therefore, the only thing that differentiates a supervisor, a senior manager or a CEO from another manager of the same rank lies in a higher level of intelligence, called Emotional Intelligence. We all have emotions, but not everyone is high in emotional intelligence. It is not available on the frontal lobe, the Thinking Brain, where we make our daily business decisions. Rather, the key drivers of our emotions are hidden and locked up in the limbic system (Emotional Brain) where Amygdala and Hippocampus reside.

Under intense high emotions, we fail to connect the dots between our emotional brain and the thinking brain leading to emotional disaster under pressure. To be a great leader in your organization with an outstanding performance in times of pressure, when other managers of the same ranking are crumbling under pressure to achieve financial targets, great leaders don't rely on experiences and technical skills alone. Rather, they step ahead of the competition by connecting the wisdom and power embedded in the limbic system (emotional feeling brain) with the neocortex or frontal lobe to thrive.

Whatever difficult relationship you are in, Communication crisis, remember that every difficult environment is a crisis. Please check my other books where I had written about emotional intelligence and leadership. A crisis is there for a reason. It is seasonal, and as such, leaders don't bring long-term solutions to solve temporary or seasonal problems.

A crisis throws storms and stones at you – in the form of fear, stress, anger, conflicts – eroding your confidence to lead and manage under pressure. Therefore, a crisis can be defined as any circumstance that triggers CHANGES in your current situation, which takes you from your comfort zone to an unknown territory you have no control over.

In difficult times, we need Superheroes, champions or superhumans with extraordinary powers or supernatural skills to overcome earthly problems. Those superheroes are those with high Emotional Intelligence.

---

1. Lepore, M. Stephen (2021), "Elon Musk becomes first person EVER to be worth more than $300billion thanks to Tesla shares spike – as Microsoft regains title of world's most valuable company after Apple's stock slumped." Dailymail.com. Access date: 16 Dec. 2021 https://www.dailymail.co.uk/news/article-10145385/Elon-Musk-person-worth-300-BILLION-fortune-surges.html
2. The answer is = 1.
3. Ettore, Mike (2020), 'Why Most New Executives Fail - And Four Things Companies Can Do About It', Available: https://www.forbes.com/sites/forbescoachescouncil/2020/03/13/why-most-new-executives-fail-and-four-things-companies-can-do-about-it/?sh=4a00dbab7673; Accessed: January 1, 2022.

Chapter Fourteen

ANGER: The Perfect Gift from the Manufacturer

"Slowness to anger makes for deep understating; a quick-tempered person stockpiles stupidity."
- **King Solomon** (Prov. 14:29, MSG)

THE MOST important gift ever given to mankind by the Creator is not Happiness, even though we need daily therapeutic doses of happiness as a safety enclave to guard against stress, strengthen our immune system, increase our business performance. We also need happiness to commit to our marriage and relationships in life.

The greatest gift is not in innovative thinking, even though our innovative thinking has produced new ideas, theories, philosophies, music, symphony harmonica, entertainment, or modern technologies that govern and control humanity, including Medicine, an exploration into space and other planets as well as remote surgical operations through the internet.

The greatest gift to humans is not Life. Why? Because life itself is a risk. The opposite of Life is Death. Every human on the planet Earth holds two passports: a temporary passport to Life on the right hand, and a hidden passport to death on the left hand. That "Death Passport" is tucked behind our back that guarantees exit from this world anytime, any day, any hour, irrespective of our status in the society. Therefore, the greatest gift from God, the Manufacturer of heavens and Earth, is the gift of ANGER.

The first gift our Creator gave to Mankind was his IMAGE – character, and personality. First, we were created as a dead body – statue, sculpture, monument, or lifeless body. Next, He breathed His breath of life, and that dead body, made from the dirt of the ground became a living soul – comprising the MIND, the WILL, and the EMOTIONS. And ANGER was one of them. Anger is a special attribute that occurs for specific reasons. It puts us closer to the pedestal of our Creator. When He gave us His IMAGE, anger was the POWERFUL force to help us survive in our leadership troubles.

Humanity has been consumed by the emotional states of anger, anxiety, frustration, and depression since the Fall of Mankind from the presence of His Creator – in the Garden of Eden. Mankind lost the Kingdom of Heaven on Earth (Genesis 3) – the loss of true leadership and rulership position of the Earth to Lucifer – the enemy of God – who temporarily took authority of the Kingdoms of the World (Matt 4:8-9). Hence, Jesus was reminded by Satan who controls the World "just in case" Jesus had forgotten his history lessons, saying:

> 'I will give you all their authority and splendour; it has been given to me, and I can give it to anyone I want to. If you worship me, it will all be yours."
> (Luke 4:6-7; NIV).

Most people have failed to understand ANGER as an emotional trigger for CHANGE Management. Temporary feelings of anger or sadness are normal, but this normality changes to abnormality when anger is prolonged over a 24 hours. Millions have failed to interpret its meaning. And the few reading this book are still grappling to find out what to do with extreme anger when it hits them on the blindside.

The good news is that ANGER did not originate from the Fall of Mankind, but the Creator of the universe. Anger is a component of the human spirit and existed in the heart of the Creator even before the foundation of the world.

God is a victim of anger. Although He is perfect and pure, He is not FREE from ANGER as an inherent instrument in leadership. It was God Himself, who once admitted that His Kingdom Government is not pure and perfect. He made this revelation after the disastrous, and rebellious First World War in Heaven between God's Kingdom and the Kingdom of Lucifer - when two Spiritual Powers collided in the realm of the spirit (heaven) (Rev. 12:7-10). This was the first-ever recorded World War in history between the forces of Light (Good) and darkness (evil) (not the Earthly First WW of 1914-1918).

In the words of Prophet Ezekiel the priest, he revealed that: "God places no trust in His holy ones [the angels]" (Ezekiel 28:17, emphasis added), let alone on humans "who are [*inherently*] vile and corrupt, who drink up evil like water!" (Job 15: 15-16, emphasis added).

Apostle Paul, best known as one of the early founders of the Christian Ministry is famed as the author of most parts of the New Testament Bible (Romans, 1 and 2 Corinthians, Galatians, Ephesians, Philippians, Colossians, 1 and 2 Thessalonians, 1 and 2 Timothy, Titus, and Philemon) - he, too, was a victim of anger.

Before his arrest and subsequent conversion from Soul to Paul by the Holy Spirit, Soul was an oppressor, persecutor, and a terror of the early Jewish followers of Jesus and the "Way of Salvation" (the early name for Christianity; Acts 26:10-22). People were stoned violently to death by his orders! In the eyes of the present-day governments of the US and the UK, *Soul of*

Tarsus at the time could have been "proscribed" as a global "terrorist" in the minds of the Christians.

In one of his letters to the Ephesians, while locked up in prison, Paul issued this warning to the leaders and ministers of the Kingdom of Heaven on Earth concerning anger:

> "Go ahead and be angry, you do well to be angry – but don't use your anger as a fuel for revenge. And don't stay angry. Don't go to bed angry. [And] don't give the Devil that kind of foothold in your life" (Eph. 4:26-27), MSG).

The New International Version (NIV) approached Paul's warning differently, thus:

> "In your anger do not sin: Do not let the sun go down while you are still angry."

In other words, you can be angry temporarily. When you're angry in the morning, never carry over your anger till the evening or into the night, let alone the next day. Why? Because prolonged strong anger is the yeast that raises the dough. It is the precursor and culture of hidden crises.

The first family acts of violence ever recorded in the history book of life were envy, jealousy, and murder. They were the results of prolonged ANGER between Cain and his younger brother, Abel, leading to the former killing the latter.

Although Cain the murderer, was forewarned by the Creator about the danger of unguided ANGER, the Creator did not attempt to stop Cain from following his strong emotions' blueprint. This is how the Lord engaged Cain in a leadership debate about hot temper, emotional self-discipline, management, and the repercussion of the failure to control thyself:

> "Why are you angry?" He spoke to him gently. "Why is your face downcast?" He paused, and continued thus: "If you do what is right, will you not be accepted? But if you do not do what is right, sin is crouching at your door; it *desires* to have you, but you MUST *rule over* it" [*or else it will rule over you*] (Gen. 4:6-7; *emphasis* added).

The problem is this. God knew that Cain will kill his brother after seeing his heart, hence the warning was issued. Still, the Lord God could not stop Cain from killing his younger brother. Why? Because God cannot intervene on the Earth if we don't first consult Him – even though He is omnipotent (possessing unlimited power). He believes that He had given us ALL the power to resolve any challenges we face on Earth.

The Creator is angry with humans when we're ignorant of the inherent ability we were born with. Despite the murder incident, the Creator did not kill Cain physically. Rather Cain suffered from self-destruction and rotted from the inside as a murderer and wonderer till he was recalled.

Why Heaven Doesn't Answer Your Prayers

When we pray to the Creator for help, on many occasions, it appears He's silent and doesn't answer prayers. Rather, he's watching our patience. Sometimes, It appears that the Creator doesn't even exist, even though He's omnipresence (ubiquitous or simultaneously present anywhere, and anytime).

When this happens, doubts take over our thoughts and emotions. We begin to question Him on violence or adversities we suffer in the hands of our fellow men: "If God really exists, why should He allow my spouse or child suffer from diseases or difficult life experiences?" "If God really exists", they would ask, "why does He 'allow' nations to wage war against other nations?" "Why can't I find a job?" "God, I need money." "God, I need this, and I need that" - and the requests go on continuously.

Still, when He doesn't respond, we resort to fasting and invoking fire to consume our enemies. We pray for everything to happen miraculously, while the Lord is whispering to us to invoke our divine kingdom power and authority. Why is this so? Because although we are in the world (Cosmos), temporarily, we are indeed not of this world. Originally, we are all citizens of another Government superior to the world's Governments.

Anger is not a SIN

God uses legal terms to describe events as a King. The word "sin" bears a legal connotation. Sin can be described as an offence or action that 'violates' moral law or the divine Laws of God (1 John 3:4). Divine laws, per se, are natural laws with inbuilt penalties hidden inside them. In other words, natural laws inherently attract heavy consequences when violated.

Some deaths are activated immediately when certain natural laws are violated. This includes jumping from the cliff, skydiving or jumping from a plane without a parachute. Death is automatically built-in and activated in response to rebellious activities against the force of gravity.

The word 'Sin' covers evil and lawlessness. It also means acting the opposite of what is right, hence righteousness (Gal.

5:17). This includes transgression (willful trespassing, intentionally disobedient), crime, immorality (depravity, decadence, corruption), scandal, disgrace, fall from grace, sacrilege, and iniquity (from the word, Adikos: a Greek lexicon when translated means guilty of punishment or injustice. It is the worst sin ever in the hierarchy of divine law (pride, and All communicate the same idea.

The royal insignia of ANGER was stamped on the human DNA by the Creator - our manufacturer – so we can function effectively just like Him. If Anger is a SIN, then the Creator of the universe is a SINNER! But the Scripture did not tell us this. Rather, it tells us that SIN (iniquity) entered into the world through one man, and death through SIN (Romans 5:12).

It went further to prophesy about the person who holds the solution to sin. And that solution will come from the seed of a woman and crush the heals of death caused by the accuser of the brethren (Gen. 3:15, Rev. 12:9-10).

Apostle Paul went further to educate us further that the "wages" of SIN is death (Romans 6:23). The creator created everything that ever existed – including Life and Death. Since the Creator has never died, therefore, He has never sinned.

Traditionally, our religious leaders of Christianity, Islam, Judaism, Buddhism, Hinduism, Chinese Traditional religion, Scientologists, and non-religious sects had thought us, either formally or informally, through theological doctrines that anger is a SIN.

People across the world had questioned the existence of God, blaming Him for not coming down from Heaven to help them out of their crises - when such crises were purposely or artificially created by other humans and nations who claim to have superior power over other people under their charge.

If everyone was taught in the classroom how we can manage our anger, the world would've been a much better place to live. Murder and wars could have been eradicated. Many marriages could have been saved. There are more Christian divorces than Christian marriages in the UK. According to the divorce statistics in 2019, about 42 % of marriages end in divorce (ONS 2021). Child abuse could have been a thing of the past. If our Anger is managed, economic terrorism in the name of religion, kidnapping for ransom, homicide, or racism of any form could have been stopped right from its foundation.

The keys to solving the world's problems are not far from us, they are within us. They are not hidden in rocks, or caves, they are hidden in your mind.

Anger is The Emotional Currency for Leadership

When I state that "anger is the emotional currency for leadership", I'm not referring to physical violence or aggression. I'm not referring to the legislative violence of political leaders or Members of Parliament in Nepal, Turkey, Nigeria, South Africa or Georgia fighting over reform bills or drafts of new constitutions.

I'm referring to anger as the emotional currency to influence positive changes in our society. Satisfaction is the boardroom for stagnation. When you're satisfied with the leadership you've inherited or the poor projects that are yet to be completed, you'll have no drive for change or R&D.

Anger in leadership is the emotional key driver that tells you that your organization is in dire need of progress. But anger is a neutral emotion. Not everyone can express it with wisdom publicly. It doesn't have a character of its own. Anger is like Money. Its character is determined and labelled by the people who hold it. It's a tool, a resource, or an instrument to cause a change in our life. People have negative and positive attitudes, but whichever attitude you choose to express with your wisdom it's a matter of choice. But don't blame anger for your bad choices and attitudes to life.

Money is good, but it is the state of pleasure and lust (emotion) attached to it that makes money the root of all evil. Why? Because you cannot serve the creature and the Creator simultaneously.

Money is the currency for transactions. It is very innocent and has the mind of a little child. When money goes into the wrong hands, the innocent currency changes its brand name – becoming proceeds of crime, money laundering, financial terrorism, drug dealing money, blood money, prostitute money, cyber-fraud, wire fraud, bank fraud, scam, and so forth. How you label your emotions and manage them positively is what keeps you apart from others.

Poor Anger Management is linked to many irreversible cardiovascular diseases, such as high blood pressure, cardiomyopathy, stroke, congestive heart failure (CHF), tachycardia, bradycardia, and so forth, and the consequences could be more damaging than the damages caused by cigarette smoking.

Therefore, ANGER by itself is not a SIN, because it was never the invention of Mankind. Anger is triggered by your chemicals (epinephrine/adrenalin, or cortisone stress hormone) made in your own body – to protect you, so you can defend yourself from external aggressors under extreme stress.

Although, anger doesn't have the *locus standi* in any known court of law - a legal term that refers to the right or capacity to bring an action against you, or compel you to appear in a court for judgement by any court of the land, nor in the court of the Lord God. However, the consequences of its misconception leading to misinterpretation, or misjudgement and mismanagement manifesting in the form of harm, damage to properties, assaults or abuse of other people - either mental or physical - has the *locus standi* in the appropriate court of law. Therefore, you're responsible for your actions or inactions (verbal and non-verbal) leading to crises, inside crises, or post-crises situations.

The Power of the Human Spirit to Control Circumstances

Humans have the power to control their destructive emotions, and to use them positively for the benefit of everyone in society. Ironically, Mankind has deployed this single element of leadership as a catalyst for self-destruction that has taken over the entire world like wildfire.

A reminder of how powerful the human spirit is, is demonstrated by the instruction Jesus gave to his leadership students and delegates. While sending out the 72 appointed delegates to lead the "Healing Campaign" of His Ministry, Jesus reminded them of the huge powers embedded in the human spirit to overcome adversity, irrespective of its dimension: form, or size; the seen or the unseen.

He said to them:

> "I have given you AUTHORITY to trample on snakes and scorpions and overcome ALL the power of the enemy; nothing will harm you" (Luke 10:19).

The snakes and scorpions in this Scriptural passage represent all manner of leadership challenges, crises, or difficulties we face on daily basis, such as failed relationships; divorce cases; deaths of loved ones; wrongful accusations; poor health conditions; accidents; financial crises; house repossession; career disappointments: joblessness or lack of promotions, redundancies; bankruptcy proceedings; victims of robberies, and murder.

Therefore, when you become angry due to any of the above temporary events, you're simply manifesting a Divine Character of God. Be known for your self-discipline or self-control. Bring your thoughts and plans in conformity with the plans of your Creator for your life. Never use future permanent solutions to solve immediate, temporary problems.

When you start facing leadership challenges in your organization, remember the words of your Creator that you're not alone in the struggle. Although you have the power to control some of your life events, you still need to tap into another Kingdom influence to assist you in your journey as an ambassador of Heaven to achieve success here on Earth.

Your earthly physicians or psychologists are there to support you in this journey to make your life easier, overcoming the crises you're facing right now.

If anger is misguided, it becomes the pathological foundation for other vile emotions to emerge. This includes greed, violence, bitterness, aggressiveness, jealousy, or selfishness.

These other POWERFUL emotions stand in the corridors of anger waiting for their recruitment and deployment. Anger is the employer, while "over vile emotions" are the employees. Once anger is triggered, it never returns empty-handed. It recruits other emotions along its path, depending on the state of your body – your mind, your will, and your other emotions.

Your mind dictates the next action your body takes to survive your crises. Therefore, how you perceive threats at the time determines the responses you deploy to overcome them.

There are various options available for you at the time to solve any emerging threats in life:

1. The Fight option.

2. The Flight option.

3. Freeze Option.

- **#1: The Fight Response:** You can nip it in the bud before it morphs from an unseen and unreal perception into the seen, real, and destructive elephants and tigers you can't control. Here, you've got the power to "rule over" your emotions at the outset before they become the bread makers' yeast. Failure to control this catalyst of change is characterised by destructive events which can be regretted thereafter.

- **#2: The Flight Response:** When you see a crisis coming, and you know you can't handle that stressful event, there is no need to stay and yell. The right advice is to FLEE. Flee the scene, and make your judgements later. It is only trees that remain calm and relaxed in the same dangerous place when they perceive harm. Other creatures – birds, fish, animals, and humans. Only the living can face charges while alive. A dead man can't give accounts of his activities from the grave.

- **#3: The Freeze Response:** This happens when you're caught unaware of the immediate presence of danger. Because you're undecided, you stay during the storm and do nothing (freeze mode). It doesn't matter your position in the world, the problem with this solution is that if you stand in the way of anger and do nothing, it will consume and enslave you.

There's Nothing Like Bad Emotions

Since I started writing this manuscript, I have found that there is nothing like bad emotions. Rather, it is the human perception of the trigger (cause-and-effects) and how we label and interpret an emotion that changes its meaning. It is the meaning we attach to it that gives it the POWER to function as Anger.

When your adrenaline and cortisol stress hormones are released in your body, they are not there to destroy you. Rather, these chemicals came to warn you of an impending event that needs attention.

They are released in your cells to protect you from harm - both internally and externally. They are just messengers! You don't kill the messenger that delivers the message. It is our misconception of the message by the recipient that leads to tensions, disruptions, and wars in our society and countries around the world.

If ANGER was so bad for our health and in our relationships like the way cancer is to our body, neurosurgeons around the world could have adopted new technology, such as split-brain surgery to dissect the brain and surgically remove the Amygdala from the limbic system which is the root source of anger.

Pharmaceutical drug companies had tried but failed to find the permanent cure for anger. Up to date, at the time of writing this manuscript in November 2021, no vaccine has ever been discovered to obliterate this great component of emotions called ANGER.

Physicians are too busy prescribing cocktails of antidepressants – treating the symptoms on the surface, to help you improve your mood, keep your bipolar disorder in checks-and-balances, but they have failed to medically treat the anger from its root sources inside.

Even our clinical psychologists who could help you overcome problems like mental health, drug addiction, anxiety, behavioural issues, and so forth also have their limitations in knowledge. They are ring-fenced on what they can do, and what they can't do. They, too, have tried and failed, but only succeeded in scratching the surface with no immediate solution to obliterate anger.

Therefore, although anger cannot be treated medically, the good news is that it can be "ruled over," or "managed" – hence Anger Management.

The Characters of Anger in Leadership

I believe that ANGER is here with us forever and it's going nowhere. It will stay with us forever. This powerful agent is here to serve us for many reasons, but not to kill us.

Anger has unique characters or characteristics that distinguish it from other emotions. Although ANGER is so powerful that it has the natural ability to cause destructions in our society and transform a harmless dove into a scary lion, it is different from other natural forces, such as a tornado, hurricane, or earthquake. Why? Because Anger is positively beneficial and is the AGENT OF CHANGE.

Below are some of the points, which I believe, justify my thinking that ANGER is an important catalyst for CHANGE in Leadership.

Let us begin from the Scriptures in the Hebrew Bible or Torah, to see how the Creator of the universe and human beings had positioned themselves within emotions, and adopted this important element called ANGER as an instrument to fulfil their purposes and desires.

- #1: God adopts Anger to Effect Changes:

In the realm of Leadership, Anger is historically an instrument of CHANGE. Let me show you that controlled anger is more powerful for change than excessive happiness or joy which keeps you satisfied with what you have. Over satisfaction doesn't allow growth or diversification. It keeps you from thinking BIG.

When I searched for the worlds "ANGER" and "Happy" in the entire Hebrew Torah or Holy Bible (NIV), "anger" was mentioned 268 times, i.e., 256 in Old Testament, and 12 in the New Testament, while "Happy" generated 20 times, i.e.,

16 in the Old Testament, and 4 in the New Testament. We know that any statement or word repeated in the Torah or Bible by God is a sign of its importance or seriousness.

Therefore, anger is more important than happiness for a simple reason. Happy people are just okay with the status quo, while a leader with anger is an indicator that change has arrived. Anger is the litmus paper that changes its colour when change is needed. Even God, who created the Heavens and Earth, the Lord of lords, and the King of kings, has a reputation for ANGER.

Although theologians had used these three words to describe God:

- Omniscience (ever knowing).
- Omnipotent (all-powerful, unstoppable), and
- Omnibenevolence (exceedingly good).

Yet the Creator uses ANGER for his advantage even though He knows that uncontrolled anger is a killer of the human Spirit. Moses once quoted the Creator in His statement that the Creator is fiercely over-protective of His rights and possessions when He said to him:

> "For I, the Lord your God, am a jealous God,
> punishing the children for the sin of the parents to
> the third and fourth generation of those who hate
> me."
> (Exodus 20:5).

- **#2: The Creator Withheld Rain on Earth:**

I believe that the Creator had a crisis moment during the time of creation, but He never let the circumstances he faced deter him from achieving His purpose for creation. Here is one of God's crises monuments.

The Creator refused to allow rain to fall on the Earth even though rain was part of his business strategy to cause growth. He withheld any drop of rain from falling to the dry, arid ground of the earth (Gen 2:5). Whether it was dew, drizzle, frost, moisture, mist, tears, precipitation or whosoever that could trigger rainfall was stopped from happening.

This single act of power demonstration stopped anything from growth, succeeding, or manifesting. Even the shrubs, trees, seeds, fruits, the birds of the sky, ants, mosquitos, the beasts of the wild, and the fish of the seas – everything was stagnant, dormant, quiet, undeveloped, or underdeveloped. All these creatures made by the Creator of the Universe were subdued from manifesting themselves. Yet, it was the Creator that once proclaimed: "they were good!

The Creator was disappointed with Himself that there was nobody on Earth to till the ground and maintain "orderliness" in the world system. In other words, there were no "managers" to "work" the ground, or "manage" His resources on Earth. The land was good and filled with mineral resources, oil and gas, bdellium and onyx stone, gold, silver, and rivers, but lacked leaders who are competent to supervise the project.

So, what did the Creator do in response to His crisis? A job vacancy was created for the role of the "Earth's Resources Manager." An advert was placed on the Earth's popular news media at the time. If it was in our generation, the advert could have appeared in various media, including Indeed, LinkedIn, Facebook, or YouTube videos as well as through popular newspapers and magazines.

But do you know who applied for the job? It was Satan. His application form for the job could not make it through to the desk of Jesus who was, and is still, the Head of the recruitment team. In the absence of no applicant, the Creator went back to work in His lab. He decided to create two applicants - Man and Woman - from the pieces of Lego He and His business partners had carefully assembled to function in sync – the head, the eyes, nose, mouth, arms, legs, and so forth. And that person is you.

That's why Prophet Jeremiah reminds us of God's mindset, his original intent or purpose for human creation before we were conceived. This is what he said:

> "Before I formed you in the womb I knew you [*from the beginning*], before you were born I set you apart, I appointed you as a prophet to the nations."
> (Jeremiah 1:5; *emphasis* added).

- **#3 Mankind Shall Not Live (in Sin) Forever:**
God couldn't hold His anger for a single minute when our first parents sinned against Him - a crime known legally as Disobedience. In the kingdom of Heaven, disobedience to the King is a criminal offence akin to a military coup to overthrow a legitimate government. It can also be referred to as "an act of rebellion" against the Monarchy of the Kingdom of Heavens. It is also a treasonable felony.

In a recognized government, 'disobedience' to a governing authority, or a King, is a sign of disloyalty, or misdemeanour to the King. The Creator simply activated punishment that was legally embedded in that single act of breaking Natural Law.

First, our ancestors (Adam and Eve) were scolded. Secondly, the Creator read a "witness statement" for each person according to the degree of their punishments. And thirdly, He delivered His judgement, part of which was to have them ostracized. They were banished from His presence (the garden of Eden) to wander in the East of Eden as independent ex-Royals.

For me, I think that what had happened to Adam and Eve of old is exactly what was repeated in the life of the Duke and Duchess of Sussex, Harry, and Megan Markel, of the United Kingdom, versus The British Monarchy - Queen Elizabeth II. When Harry and Megan declared "Mexit" from the monarch as independent ex-Royals, they thought their decision was good for the monarchy and the United Kingdom.

Although they were members of the royal family, they didn't really have a deep understanding of how Kingdom Rulership is governed in a similar pattern to the Kingdom of Heaven. Even though Harry was born in the monarchy as a Prince, the British public thought that he could have understood the Kingdom style of God which mortal beings adopted as an imitation of the real Kingdom.

What they didn't understand, and never understood, was that at a member of a Kingdom authority, seeking to work and make a living or billions without recourse to the Sovereign Grant, but using the Kingdom's image for their purpose was akin to Adam and Eve who committed treasonable felony or rebellion in the sight of the Queen.

Just as Adam and Eve lost the Kingdom of Heaven on Earth to Satan, so will Harry and Meghan lose access to the throne of the UK Monarchy and their offices will be given to other agents. God didn't want to break His commandments when

He declared to Adam, saying: "The moment you eat from that tree, you're dead" (Gen. 2:17, The MSG). He had to fulfil His promises, through His statements which become Laws as soon as they are pronounced. Those Laws were activated resulting in their expulsion.

Although they were driven out of His presence – The Garden of Eden - He never let them go naked into the cold weather. Again, He became creative and made Coats of Leather, tunics of skin from animals, and clothed them (Gen. 3:21). In ANGER, on the last hour of their departure, the Lord God raised his voice with Sovereignty and said:

> "The man has now become like one of us,
> knowing good and evil."

He raged with anger, and continued:

> "He must NOT be allowed to reach out of his hand
> and TAKE also from the TREE OF LIFE and eat,
> and live FOREVER" (Gen 3:22).

While it was assumed that expelling them into the wild was cruel, it was a Plan B from the Creator to protect them and their generations from living a sinful life forever if they had also eaten the fruit of life.

- **#3: The Creator Used Pharaoh For His Glory:** It was Anger that compelled Pharaoh, a former King of Egypt to appear stubborn and strong on the outside, but help-less from the inside (induced by God) (Exodus 3 -12).

After Moses, a former Prince in the household of Pharaoh, a Shephard, a Lawgiver, and People Deliverer who helped his fellow citizens escape the tyrannical regime of King, had requested that Pharaoh should let his people go: "Let my people go."

This tragic story showed how the human mind, society, or authoritarian governments could turn their power and values over other people or society. Pride was the root of all these events that culminated in his downfall and reputation.

- **#4: A hardened Mins is s House Built on Rocks and Steel:**

When people's mindsets are hardened with anger, it's practically impossible to soften and tame them from the outside. This is because the mind is the most dangerous, but fertile part of the human body. No one can change your mind under duress, except you.

The scripture tells us that the Creator could not change the mindset of over two million Hebrews (the Israelite tribes) in the desert after leaving Egypt. With 600,000 male soldiers, excluding women and children ready for war (Exodus 12:37), they were hungry for food, and simply forgot the power of their saviour.

Stranded in the hot, barren Sinai desert, the former slaves held captive for 430 years in servitude in the hands of Pharaoh in Egypt (Exodus 12:40), had accepted slavery, oppression, and subjugation as a new lifestyle in the land of Egypt. Through Moses, the Creator brought them out of the Kingdom of Pharaoh, but could not change their slavery mindset which had been conditioned as hard as the steel for more than ten generations.

They felt it necessary to go back to Egypt, where it was guaranteed they would find some bread for food, and meat for protein rather than remain in the desert with an unseen King living in His unseen Kingdom of Heaven, controlling to seen world. They deployed Aaron to create an imitation god they could see to help them move back to Egypt.

In a journey to the Promised Land that could have lasted for one month, the Creator had a different business strategy, PLAN B, to fulfil His purpose.

"God did not lead them on the road through the Philistines country, though that was shorter." Why? Because "If they face war, they might change their minds and return to Egypt" (Exodus 13:17-18, NIV).

For 40 years in the desert, God fed them with various kinds of fresh meals (Manner – the bread of heaven and Spiritual meat) on daily basis with no leftovers; their clothes didn't wear out, neither did the sandals of their feet wear out. Their articles of clothing were as fresh as new for 40 years. He made them live a healthy life by withholding bread and alcohol (wine and beer) from them (Deut. 29:5, Nehemiah 9:20-21).

He preserved them from death, self-destruction, and implosion due to excessive consumption of FREE food and alcohol, with consequences such as diabetes, obesity, high blood pressure, congestive heart failure (CHF), strove, hypercholesteremia, kidney failure, liver disease. Rather, The Creator allowed all the old people born in the land of Egypt with the Egyptian slavery mentality and servitude to die off gradually.

- **#5: Joshua – The Appointed Successor of Moses:**
Joshua was the business partner of Moses (Joshua 1:1-9). They were appointed into leadership by the Creator with a responsibility: to lead the Israelite tribes from the land of Egypt to the promised land which YAHWEH promised to their forefather – Abraham.

With no military training, Joshua assembled the first armed forces as the Commander-in-Chief, and successfully won the war against the Amalekites in Rephidim for the independent nation of Israel since leaving Egypt. Despite the deaths of Moses, and other Israelites, and his age as a result of living in the desert for 40 years, Joshua consistently followed the common dream, hope, and aspiration to reach the promised land.

- #6: Mother Theresa of Calcutta:

It was anger and selflessness that birthed Mother Theresa. She was angry about the way society and the government treated the poor and street beggars. She gathered uneducated children from the slums and streets of India and used her last wage to feed them.

- #7: Rosa Parks and Martin Luther King Jr.

It was the anger of racial segregation in Montgomery, that Rosa Parks, being the only woman of colour in a bus refused to give up her bus seat to a white man because of her race. Her arrest on 1 December 1955 caused 381-days of a state-wide boycott of the Montgomery Bus System which was led by a young pastor and civil rights activist - Martin Luther King Jr. The governing authorities intervened through the Supreme Court and segregation on public transportation was BANNED. To solve the racial problem.

It was an ANGER that compelled King Jr to abandon his vocation from the pulpit, as a Baptist Minister, into the streets of the United States of America to pursue his vision of exposing the evils of racism through his Civil rights activism.

It was the same forces of ANGER that compelled the government of the day to create equality in the USA - end racial dis-crimination of African-Americans, and create economic justice for the poor Americans giving birth to various civil disobedience, including the Civil Rights Act of 1964 (banned discrimination in employment, and public accommodation based on race, colour of your skin, religion, and country of origin); and the Voting Rights of 1965.

In 1968, he was assassinated, a confirmation of how hu-mans have placed more love over the animals – cats and dogs –than their fellow humans who agitate against the injustice meted on their race, ethnicity or religious affiliations.

- **#8: Black Lives Matter (BLM) Movement:**

Police brutalities against the black race in the U.S. gave birth to the evolution of the BLM Movement. From the #EndSARS protect in Nigeria due to police brutality of her citizens, the killings of black people in the UK, the death of black American, George Floyd on 25th May 2020 at the hands of the Minneapolis Police officer, Derek Chauvin, who snuffed life out of the young man.

Racism against the people of colour is a continued reminder of the human slavery of Africans the Colonial British and American Slave owners who traded on innocent Africans to enrich their pockets.

On 23 May 2021, a UK prominent BLM activist, Sasha Johnson was shot on the head at a property in Peckham, London, but survived. Do you know who shot her? Her people – a group of four black men whose thinking had been corrupted to think and behave like their great-great-grand parents' colonial masters.

Unless you've been personally, and racially abused, just like me, you can't imagine the magnitude of the impact it would have on you throughout the remaining years of your life.

- **#9: Racism in Sports:**

Sports, which are meant as an avenue to unite people irrespective of their colour, religion, or ethnicity has become a melting point for racism. A recent nationally acknowledged racial incident in 2021 was the abhorrent racism inflicted against the three black England Football players - Marcus Rashford, Jadon Sancho, and Bukayo Saka - who missed penalties in the final defeat of England by Italy in the Euro 2020 match on Sunday, 11 July 2021 at the Wembley Stadium, London. They were abused on social media platforms leading to global condemnation.

As if the above incidence was not enough, a week later, on 18th July 2021, Sir Lewis Hamilton, a 7-time world champion in Formula 1 was subjected to racist abuse online – from 31 Instagram accounts owned by Facebook, including sending him monkey emojis after winning the Silverstone Grand Prix. Why? For being involved in a car crash with an opponent – Max Verstappen.

Even though this young man at the time was a massive advocate of racial equality and diversity in the motorsport industry, he was never safe from being the target of other racial attacks. It goes to demonstrate that no matter who you are in society and what you stand for, humans are as safe as their emotions and their thinking.

- **#10: Invasion of the US Capitol:**

The storming and violent attacks against the U.S Congress in Capitol, Washington, D.C., by the supporters of the former US president, Donald J. Trump on 7 January 2021 was the result of accumulated ANGER over falsehood that their votes were manipulated in favour of the new president, Joe Biden.

According to the Democrats, it was reported in the Evening

Standard that the US Capitol rioters believed in their minds that they were acting on Donald Trump's orders"(Edmonds 2021).

- **#11: The Concept of Product Recall:**

Every manufacturer has copied the Kingdom of Heaven's strategy of recalling a failed product, a term we know as Product Recall. God was angry with himself when His Spirits in Human bodily form was used to commit deplorable evil in his sight. God defied His laws with the instrument of ANGER.

In His worst moment of ANGER, rage, depression, and frustration, God once "regretted ever creating humans" – His products - that He decided to wipe the first human race out of His sight with a flood (Genesis 6: 1-8).

Have you ever asked yourself this question? "Why did God permit the storms to wipe away humanity - sons and daughters, children and adults, infants, and babies, pregnant women and nursing mothers even though He decreed; 'Thou Shall Not murder?" (Exodus 20:13 NIV).

I believe that the Creator did so to accomplish his purpose on earth. He cleared off the filthy human race for a reason - and that reason was for His REPUTATION. Why? Because the human race at the time of the flood was deemed incapable of rulership or self-governing. They were judged as experts who were good at devising strategies for evil thoughts. Violence, rape, murder, crime, prostitution, and all forms of immorality had no limits in the minds of the human race. Both educated and the uneducated - everyone had thought that immorality was the pathway to wisdom.

God was ANGRY with Himself that humans were following the path of moral decay, self-destruction, and internal deterioration. In the face of the Creator, nothing good was ever left of his products in His earthly territory. The only option left in God's mind was one thing: Product Recall! Product Recall !! Product Recall!!

Here is what Moses had to say regarding God's Anger and the product recall of his Creatures:

> *"The Lord saw how great the wickedness of the human race had become on the earth, and that every inclination of the thoughts of the human heart was only evil all the time. The Lord regretted that He had made human beings on the earth, and his heart was deeply troubled."* (Genesis 6:5-6, NIV)

Product Recall versus Reputation

A product recall occurs when the manufacturer of a product finds that their product – which is already in the market - has a *defect* in any of its functions. They immediately withdraw them from the market, back to the factory, to save their face = Reputation. And that reputation is their IMAGE.

Imagine the economic impact and the strong emotional states of the CEOs of luxury cars and planes - such as Tesla, Mercedes Benz, Jaguar, Rolls-Royce, or Bentley, Airbus and Boeing - when they realize that their products meant to offer luxury and opulence had turned themselves into weapons of mass destruction and as pollutants leading to lung cancer and death!

No company will ever like their "reputation" destroyed or tarnished by their products. Therefore, their "image" is more important than you – the user of the product. And there is an urgent need to protect that IMAGE and Character.

The only option left for such manufacturers is to imitate God by sending a mandatory "recall" for all products involved. They don't do so for your own sake, or safety, rather for their own "REPUTATION."

And the Lord God said to himself,

> "I will wipe from the face of the earth the human race I have created—and with them, the animals, the birds and the creatures that move along the ground—for I regret that I have made them."
> (Gen. 6:7)

This illustration is exactly what the Creator did to the first human race - a product recall to protect His IMAGE and CHARACTER. He recalled all men and women back to heaven. He cursed the rain to destroy every living thing on the face of the planet Earth, except Noah and his immediate families, plus a pair of each species of other creatures to start a new life, thereafter. Why? For His name's sake – His REPUTATION. His name was at stake.

Chapter Fifteen

The Benefits of Anger in Leadership

"Bitterness is like cancer. It eats upon the host. But anger is like fire. It burns it all clean."

- Maya Angelou

SINCE 2009, I have had the opportunity to study human behaviours and how our emotions, such as anger, frustration, envy, and so forth influence our daily activities. I have specifically devoted the past 3 years studying the minds and emotions of some of the world leaders including:

1. Business leaders, CEOs, and Entrepreneurs.

2. Some political officeholders - past and present.

3. Former US Presidents – Barack Obama vs. Donald Trump.

4. Some African Presidents.

5. Princes and Princesses of the British Royal Families.

6. Rulers of Kingdoms and Monarchies, such as the Queen Elizabeth of the United Kingdom, Sultan Bolkiah of Brunei, King Norodom Sihamoni of Cambodia; Queen Margarethe of Denmark; and Emperor Akihito of Japan.

I have also studied the state of mind of some Religious Leaders such as Pope Francis of the Roman Catholic Church, Dalai Lama of the Buddhism faith. And most importantly, I have managed to tap into the minds of parents with children and the mindset of ordinary people. I had taken this painstaking journey to discover why they behave the way they do and compose themselves before making public statements.

In this research, I've found one powerful element they all share in common. And that element is ANGER - Emotional Crises. They are all products of their emotions: The way they feel and think is the way they act.

I had found that their impressive public appearances for the press are merely public stunts to hide their emotions conceived in the privacy of their own homes, palaces and Kingdoms. The actions they take, both personal and in the public domain are ruled by their thoughts, their mind, and their emotions. Therefore, after this research, I can conclude that without emotions, humans cannot achieve anything of significant value.

What do I mean by the above statement? Here is the explanation. When our plans are going on well on daily basis, anybody can be in charge. We function on natural defaults – customs and traditions – and executive business and government policies without further thoughts of technical problems.

However, when a crisis comes, a problem that shifts our current paradigm or status quo to another level we don't have control over, we begin to "stumble" and "crumble" under enormous pressure. We become angry or frustrated when circumstances around us aren't working as normal. Anger and frustration are the triggers of our emotions that compel us to think and act differently.

I have studied so many books about leadership, crisis, and emotions, and I have figured out that hard times are in fact, good for humanity for new concepts to emerge. I had found that there's nothing like bad emotions, rather it is our perception and attitude towards specific and well-known traditions, or events, that make us assume that anger is bad. Anger is good for growth.

Here are the 15 benefits of Anger to help you improve as a Leader in your organization.

- **#1: Anger Is the Incubator of Change:**

When people feel comfortable in their present conditions, nothing will ever convince them to change their minds. They will continue to do the same job over and over again, and get the same predictable results repeatedly. And for 20 years, they'll remain contented in their state of poverty.

But when you are not happy with yourself, the chances are that you might begin to search for solutions to improve your life, and provide for your family - spouse, and children. When companies introduce changes – new technologies, new ways of working, and changes in wages - resistance is always anticipated through anger.

- **#2: Anger Is The Reason Why We Do What We Do:**

The losses or successes you recorded in your businesses today were the results of your anger yesterday, and how wisely or unwisely you responded to the circumstances before your actions. Even in your relationships – business and private – its stability is partly due to how you've managed to deal with your daily emotions.

According to Darwin's Theory of Natural Selection, as published in the National Geographic, Washington DC, it says that creatures evolve over many generations through the inheritance of physical or behavioural traits better suited to the environment than others, and thus are more likely to survive and reproduce (Society 2019). In other words, animals, or creatures such as lions, tigers, wolves, dogs, cats, etc., outgrow parts of the body that are not vital for their survival. The Amygdala, where emotional anger is domiciled in both humans and beasts is retained as a tool for survival. Therefore, in the absence of the thinking brain, humans will behave just like the dangerous beasts of the wild.

- **#3: Anger Comes to Test Your Authenticity:**

Whatever you claim to be; and whomever you claim to be at this very point in time, you're truly not that person you had claimed his or her identity unless you have been tested for authenticity. You must be certified for validity, truth, evidence, or proof of whom you claimed to be. Look at all the products in the market! The cars you drive to work every day, the wristwatch, and your mobile phones. Everything!

Before any product is released into the market by the manufacturer, those products would have been sent for testing by the manufacturer, to ensure that the products deliver the functions which the manufacturer had in mind, and thus packaged inside the products. And when they are satisfied with the results of product testing, they would put a stamp of their "name; image; logo; character" on the products.

In other words, in terms of leadership, you're not truly "that leader" you think you are in your organization unless your leadership capabilities have been tested in challenging times. This is because anybody can claim to be like you - the best leader in the world. My experience of studying the emotions of leaders around the world has shown that most leaders rate their perception of leadership up to 80%, but in challenging times, the ability to deal with real crises diminishes to as low as 10%.

Therefore, when you have anger issues, it has come to test

you. A crisis comes to test if you're fit enough to lead your country, your organization, and your relationship. A crisis comes to test if you're the real head of the household or the tail.

There is no great leader who had not had one form of crisis or another during their times in office. Great leaders such as Martin Luther King Jr and Nelson Mandela are not known for the good things their achieved, but are remembered for the crisis they overcame.

Nobody is immune to challenges. There was a certain Jewish Rabbi born in Bethlehem in Judea, who later grew up in Nazareth, and lived about 2,000 years ago in present-day Palestine. Famous for His teachings and natural laws, such as "Love your neighbours as yourself," "I am the Way, the Truth, and the Life. No one comes to the Father except through me."

History has that this man was tested for authenticity. He was tested for His claims, one of which was that He was, and still is the Son of the living God. He was led by The Holy Spirit into the rough country and subjected to cross-examination by Satan - the tester, tempter, or examiner (Matt 4:1-11).

He was not just tested once or twice, this man was tested three times with irresistible, mouth-watering offers in the face of starvation having spent forty days and forty nights without food or drink.

Before He took the tests, He was prepared for the crisis. He knew that trouble would be coming his way, someday. So, how did He do that? By fasting for forty days and forty nights.

As a leader in your organization, how prepared are you to face crises of any form? How prepared are you with your Senior Management teams to tackle any uprising, customer complaints, poor financial performances, absenteeism, and mass resignation due to emotional stress at work? The answer to all these questions lies in your knowledge: Whom you know; What you know about yourself and the leadership team you had surrounded yourself to.

Times of adversity come to test their loyalty to you, and your loyalty to your organization. It is also here to test how you communicate and engage with the employees under your leadership when your company hits rock bottom. If you say that you have a degree in Economics or MBAs from one of the top universities around the world, a crisis is a time to prove to the Shareholders that you're an economist and a business expert to solve the financial crisis.

- **#4: Anger Comes to Restore Your Sanity:**
Governments come, and Governments go. Leaders come in different shapes and sizes, no matter how big or small you're, crises will attack each one equally. Can you imagine the world leaders doing the same thing over and over again, and expecting different results?

Can you imagine the World's Banking systems conducting the same transactions the same way, year on year, and expecting the same results? What do you think when our scientists continue to work on the same project with the same adjuvant year-on year-out and expect different results? I call such activity "in-sanity".

Insanity, therefore, is the opposite of sanity. When you add 2+2 and expect to get 10, that's insane – right! Therefore, Crises comes to restore you to your original senses.

- **#5: Anger Accelerates Growth**

Many business executives are aware that achieving top in profit margin, year-on-year in their stores could be a tough challenge like slamming the rock with a big hammer and expecting water to gush out. They are not the Mosses of our time. Body movement doesn't mean progress. Because you are busy moving around the organization, and devising strategies to shrink short-term overheads for short-term profits, it doesn't guarantee long-term financial growth.

Anger and hunger for growth are the only activators to accelerate your pedal power. CEOs of corporate organizations may attempt to boost double-digit sales and revenue without empowering the team, they "seem" profitable by adopting various short-term measures – including cutting down on costs of sales, turning every full-time staff into part-timers; diversifying into other businesses without adequate resources, delay paying out cheques or slashing down management wages to compensate for big-time losses.

The question we have to ask ourselves is this: "Are these temporary measures sustainable?" If they aren't, that means the tactics for temporary growth should not be applied at all.

Business crisis doesn't come to kill you, rather they come to stop you from moving backwards. When the leadership of your organization starts conducting any of the above measures in what is termed "restructuring," that is a big-time traffic indicator that something is not working well somewhere.

A leadership crisis is the #1 single factor that triggers you to think out alternative and sustainable ways to grow your business at an incremental rate. Anger for growth doesn't come to kill you; it comes to stop you from moving backwards.

- **#6: Anger is the Incubator of Innovative Thinking:**

Innovative thinking is a new way of thinking. Innovation itself is nothing other than a new way of doing things to solve modern problems. When problems begin to show up in your organization, it is an indicator for the senior leaders that the old ways of doing things are now obsolete. The old ways of solving global crises are no longer needed, or sustainable in the long term. The truth is that there is nothing new under the face of the earth. Innovative technology is the man-made combination of old software differently to resolve new problems.

Therefore, innovation is simply a unique application or the unique "assembly" of old materials in a different way, form, shape, or size to solve a new problem or immediate need. For instance, when the COVID-19 pandemic arrived in March 2020, scientists all over the world couldn't find a new solution. No new vaccines for the virus were ever discovered.

What the whole world didn't know is that the research companies used old stuff called "adjuvants" unto an "existing base" to create a new virus-specific target that produces the required immunity. What they called "new vaccines" are old vaccines or adjuvants combined differently to produce different immunity.

- **#7: Anger Comes to "Forge" You:**

Anger comes to make you great again. How many of you are wearing rings right now – wedding or engagement? Some are original gold, very expensive ones, while others were made from ordinary metal – knots or bolts – and gold-plated. Those rings didn't come easily. They were forged with fire and sweat! Black-smiths use high forges as high as 3,000 to 4,000 degrees Fahrenheit to heat these metals, before slamming harmers, anvils, and chisels to forge the new products from rusted, old metals into the desired shape – with his thoughts, feelings, and emotions working as a single entity.

As a leader, CEO, or entrepreneur, when situations get hotter than normal or when a crisis rocks your organization in any form, use it to create the "new you" and new organization. Use it to train, and transform your employees into future leaders when you're gone. You become "forged" to better face future challenging problems. This is how anger comes to forge leaders in molten steel!

- **#8: Anger Brings You Back to Your Original purpose in life – To become a leader:**
Without encountering difficulty in your life, mankind cannot discover who they are, and whom they were born to be. In times of difficulty, that moment brings you back to humility by asking yourself some rhetorical questions such as: "Who Am I?" and "Why was I born? Anger makes us realise that we are born to lead – and to lead effectively in our domain of expertise – job or profession.

- **#9: Anger Cancels the World's Expertise and Skills:**
Whatever we call our emotion, so it becomes. Every life problem is designed with a solution in mind. But when we encounter circumstances that are beyond our control, that means our expertise and skills are neutralized to zero, and our weaknesses exposed. Whether you're a professor, a surgeon, or a cleaner, when bad circumstances catch us unawares, we suck. This is where an innovative mindset becomes crucially important.

- **#10: Your today's Problems = Tomorrow's Businesses Opportunities for Others:**
It's ironic to know that all the world's market research is not working, and the tools for finding business opportunities had

failed to identify new business opportunities compared to the personal problems we face in our lives. The Covid-19 pandemic has just done the opposite. Thousands of lives had gone with it, but ten thousand jobs had been created as a result of the pandemic.

While the lockdown had confined people to their homes and local communities, thousands of businesses were forced to close down and some aircraft companies went bust. What many forgot is that tragedy create real, new opportunities. Such new opportunities are the new normal of wearing Face-Masks in public and the new normal ways of business operations such as increased online GP consultations and viewing properties by virtual appointments. The rate of internet romance and ways to reach out to new friends online gained momentum during the pandemic.

Let's talk about wearing face masks in public 10 years ago: Between January 2000 and March 2020, as a black man or just anyone, walking the streets of Manchester or London, or boarding a plane at Heathrow Airport, London wearing a face-mask, a head cap, and clutching a handbag containing an umbrella – this appearance could have made that black guy a potential flight risk and a "terrorist" suspect.

Anyone wearing masks in public in those years could have been arrested or shot dead. But, with the advent of Covid-19, the old ways of life, doing business, or meeting people face-to-face are classified as "abnormal." Some of the "New Normal" life codes between 2020 and 2021 include wearing face masks, not visiting friends except if they are your loved ones; and keeping a distance of at least 2 meters apart from each other while in public. Hugging or kissing loved ones in the public domain were out-lawed – and people were fined for gathering in public.

These scenarios I have just painted above simply reminded me of my emotions on 22 July 2005 when the news broke, that a young man, known as Jean Charles de Menezes, a Brazilian-Portuguese electrician living in London, was mistakenly killed by the London Metropolitan Police Service at the Stockwell Tube Station, South London, as a suicide suspect. At that time, I was a student of the Postgraduate Diploma in Pharmacy programme at the University of Brighton, East Sussex, UK.

We were still in shock over the four coordinated London suicide attacks two weeks before, on 7th July 2005, targeting commuters travelling on the London transport systems, which claimed 52 lives. As if those incidences were not sufficient for the enemies, another four attempted bomb attacks happened on 22 July 2005. So, the authorities were desperate and poised at fishing out the Islamist extremists responsible for the heinous attacks. But the Metropolitan Police targeted the wrong man – an innocent and unarmed Mr Menezes.

Do you know his offence? Not face covering, but "racial ambiguity", they said. They described him as a "Mongolian" – a man with "dark hair" and "Mongolian" "dark eyes." These two characteristics were used to link him mistakenly to the previous day's failed bomber suspect – Osman Hussein.

A sign of fundamental intelligence failures and seriousness of ineffective leadership from both the government and the MET for their "shoot-and-kill" policy at the time.

The word, "Mongolian," used to describe him is akin to racial profiling connotation. That means, my two bi-racial boys – from a Polish mother and a Nigerian father - are in serious trouble of identity crisis in the UK when institutions like this are woven with a fabric of racial profiling. My boys are neither black nor white, so the society I live in has already profiled them as "MIXED" even before they were born.

According to the Merriam-Webster Dictionary, a "Mongolian" is "a member of a group of people formerly considered to constitute a race of humans having Asian ancestry and classified according to physical traits" (Merriam-Webster (n.d.)).

So the 27-year-old, young man, Menezes, was shot at close range 8 times: seven times in the head and once in the shoulder (BBC 2005). He died at the scene as a suspected terrorist of "foreign Middle Eastern heritage." In the words of Tony Blair, who was the UK Prime Minister at the time, as quoted by the BBC News stated that 'he was "desperately sorry" that an innocent man had lost his life.'

- **#11: Anger helps to Manage Resources:**

Resources Management is very critical in times of crises, such as in M&A, repossession, marriage breakdown, or any form of difficulties that impact our normal experiences. Allocation of resources for immediate crises solution should be the priority than planning future solutions for future crises.

Whatever you mismanage, you'll lose it. If you fail to manage your business, you will lose it through bankruptcy. You've just created a new business opportunity for insolvency practitioners who'd take over your assets.

If you fail to manage your marriage, you'll not only lose your marriage through divorce, but you might also lose your house, your money, the entire assets you'd worked for throughout your life. If you're not careful enough, you might equally lose the custody of your children to the ex-husband or wife you hate.

- **#12: Anger brings People and Businesses together:**
Anger, depression, or disaster bring people and businesses together. In the UK during the Covid-19 pandemic around the world, people of great minds came together to help in any form they could. Some registered with the NHS Volunteer Programme to assist the health service where it mattered most. Ranging from retired doctors to Nurses, and delivery drivers to individuals – these people came together in solidarity to beat the pandemic.

Some companies sent free PPE (personal protection equipment). Drivers delivered prescription medicines to patients' homes who were isolated, for free, and were not paid for their service. Other companies gave out food and water, plus discounts to NHS staff across the UK. It was a wake-up call for people to engage with local organizations. Leaders from both profit and non-profit organizations such as Churches and Mosques brought out the best from their worshippers.

- **#13: Violence through anger Means You've run out of Ideas:**
Using violence as the expression of anger is an indicator that leaders have run out of ideas. Next to every problem is a hidden solution waiting to be discovered. Becoming hostile and toxic about your present circumstances, or being submissive to the perceived threat (violence and aggression) is an automatic sign of your incapacity to lead as a leader and handle difficult matters In other words, you have simply run out of practical ideas for that problem.

The problems we face on daily basis want us to go back to the boardroom. It's sending us back to the drawing board to review our business model, re-equip ourselves, and then decide on the best solution for the problem.

- **#14: Anger = Self-Preservation and Self-Protection for others:**

Whatever actions or inactions we take or refuse to take are for our preservation and protection. Even though we never planned it to be, these actions can influence others within our territory.

Humans and nonhumans alike have the instinct to behave in such a way as to protect themselves from harm and maximize their chances of survival. Whether in business, jobs, leadership, or relationships (marriage or divorce), what motivates us to get involved in what we do currently is due to self-protection.

Here are examples of how Self-preservation and Self-protection work. The car you commute to work with or take your children to school instead of public transport is not primarily for the benefit of other people, but for your self-care - even though you might use the same car to offer lifts to others.

Likewise, this book you're reading right now is not by accident. The truth is that you're not reading it to impress other people right now. Rather you're reading it to learn something different for your personal development. but may impact others in your world.

I can therefore make this bold statement, that:

> "Self-preservation does not lead to self-benefit,
> rather it is the preservation of self for others."

In other words, good trees yield good, quality fruits, yet they don't eat their fruits. The porous rocks that dish out pure spring water for people to scoop from don't drink their waters; rather they pour out their waters for others.

Are You an Eagle or a Vulture?

Crises of any kind bring in opportunities for corporate businesses to come together, and think-out new business operations or strategies going forward. Therefore, your today's problems create business opportunities for a certain kind of people - the Bald and Gold Eagles.

While vultures have an appetite for carrion (old and dead meat unsuitable for human consumption), the menu for the bald and Golden Eagles is fresh – new concepts and new business opportunities. The Eagles are the class of people who aren't afraid of danger. When they see danger in a cloud, they simply jump into it and use its package to thrive and fly. In their lifetime, the bald Eagles practise their skills mid-air to thrive and manage their situations.

The divorce lawyers are waiting at the door with open hands and bank details. The death of a family member is even the worst to ever happen to anyone. It's painful and emotionally suicidal to lose someone dearest to you. While you're groaning in pain for your loss, the funeral directors are smiling their ways to the banks.

Opportunity! Opportunity!! Opportunity!!! They are going on expensive vacation overseas at your own expense. Therefore, take heart. Life was not designed around you. Life was designed to function this way – which makes life and death appear mysterious.

SECTION 5

STRATEGIES FOR MANAGING CHANGE

EMOTIONAL CHANGE:
Anger, Anxiety & Depression

PERSONAL CHANGE:
Bereavement, Dispute & Divorce

ORGANIZATIONAL CHANGE:
Corporate Transformation, Mergers & Acquisition

"If you don't have the head for planning CHANGE, CHANGE may happen in your LIFE and force itself on your head to CHANGE you as a Man or a Woman with a broken head."

- Dr Emmanuel E. Amadi

Chapter Sixteen

Introduction to Change Management

Anger Management. Crises Management. Managing Organizational Change

> "Life is 10 per cent what you experience and 90 per cent how you respond to it."
>
> ~Dorothy M. Neddermeyer, PhD

CHANGE COMES in different forms. **Emotional Change** might be anger, depression, or anxiety. This change affects everybody equally. There will be CHANGE in your **Personal Life** (marriage vs. divorce, pregnancy (wanted vs. unwanted), birth vs. bereavement, gaining vs. losing weight; financial circumstances or personal disputes of any nature). CHANGE will also affect you in your **Social Life** (friends vs. relatives). While there will be CHANGE in your Public Life (Politics vs. politicians), CHANGE will also affect your **Economic Life** (job market vs. earning power). We also have **Organizational Change** in the form of corporate transformation, rebranding, unplanned change, and Mergers & Acquisition

However, from all these CHANGES listed above, it is evident that human emotions are involved. Some are scared of losing their jobs while others are struggling to put food on the table for their children.

How do you lead people, the employees, and the institution in times of organizational CHANGE? How do you manage the thoughts of uncertainty going on in the minds of ex-couples undergoing marital CHANGE in the name of divorce, or separation?

What do you do, when your body is ravaged by diseases – diabetes, high blood pressure, or sepsis, and you don't have access to the doctors? How do you manage the mental health of crime suspects facing criminal court charges or life sentences for murder, manslaughter, or homicide they never committed? How do you deal with CEOs of businesses charged with stealing from their own companies – the same companies they had sworn to protect and grow?

The worst still. What do you say about our religious leaders - Bishops and Priests in the Catholic Church or Pastors of other institutions who currently face charges of rape of young male altar boys they had professed to protect? Where can we find the best solutions when councillors have lost the capacity to provide evidence-based counselling to families who are bereaved?

Every crime or a crisis conceived or dispensed was once the suspect's idea, thoughts, or emotions before it was committed. The sales or revenue in your organization was once an idea of the leaders. Planning your company's vision, strategy, targets, and implementation were once conceived through emotions in the minds of a few, highly-ranked officials in your organization.

What do you do, when life throws stones on you, and you have no hiding place to run for safety? What do you do, when the rains of animosity begin to fall on you, that you have no shelter to run for cover? And what do you do, when circumstances you don't have control over, begin to throw pebbles and granites on your face, shattering your head and leaving you with a broken heart?

Here's my take on these questions. First, it doesn't matter what had happened to you previously, or the challenges you're facing right now. What matters is how you responded to those challenges and manage them without giving up hope.

Secondly, when life throws stones on you, and the rains of animosity begin to fall in your home and you begin to feel that there's no hiding place to run for safety, collect the stones, gather the rain and pebbles, and the granites. Mix them up, and use them to mould bricks for your safety. Use the bricks to build the next mansion you had always dreamt about. Start the businesses you'd always wanted to own or the quarry company you'd wanted to establish, and use the proceeds (profit) to pay for the private jet or luxury car you'd dreamt about as a child.

Therefore, the solution to every problem should start at the root cause of the problem, the foundation of the crisis, rather than chasing shadows treating the symptoms. That foundation for solving the problems of life is **MANAGEMENT**: Emotional **CHANGE** Management. If you don't have the head for planning change, **CHANGE** may happen in your life and force itself on your head to Change you as a man or a woman with a broken head.

Whether we conform with the idea of change or not, **CHANGE** must always continue to change, where there is stagnation, constant, or where tradition is the new normal.

This section of the book will help you in managing change if:

1. You're undergoing pressure in your family, relationship, friends, or having a crisis in your marriage with lawyers waiting to serve you the divorce papers.

2. You're a student preparing for Change in your studies, exams, jobs, or moving into a new property.

3. You're a Manager, managing people or resources underdoing Change, merger/acquisition.

4. And you're a Corporate organization – profit or non-profit - undergoing Transformational Change, in the form of restructuring and repositioning to remain competitive in the business environment.

How Do You Manage Change?

At the beginning of this section, I started with a quote from Dorothy M. Neddermeyer, PhD, a Metaphysician, influencer, and transformational coach:

> "life is 10 % what you experience and 90 % how you respond to it."

In that statement, she means people spend hours resolving a minor case that should have otherwise taken less time. In other words, life events and the emotional experiences we face can take approx. 2.5 hr. of our day, but most people spend approx. 9 x that period (21.6 hr.) to figure out how to manage those problems.

When I returned to my home in Manchester England, United Kingdom from the U.S. after attending the Harvard University, Extension School's leadership programmes in September 2019, I immediately started work on several projects, including a series of books, and leadership company registration. At the same time, I commenced academic research on Emotional Intelligence and Leadership. Some of the crucial questions I was asked by participants who attended some of my leadership programmes were these:

- "How do you manage emotions, and control the negative outcome when you're in the midst of a crisis?"

- "How do you control yourself when arguments occur at home, between you and your spouses, or between you and your children, where nobody accepts the blame?

These questions triggered a high level of thoughts and research that most nights, I had gone to bed with books, and converted some as pillows just to make sure I am deeply soaked in the contents. As a result, I was able to figure out the keys to managing changes in all areas of life.

I find the strategies personally useful, leading to the writing of this chapter of my book. I have also tested these foundational strategies for their authenticity, or proof-worthiness, especially when I encountered challenging times in my life during the Covid-19 lockdown. These solutions are perfect for you when you're locked head-on, right in the middle of a Crisis – when the Fire Alarm goes on!

Here are the four key steps which, I believe, could help senior business executives understand the nature of CHANGE which is anticipated to happen in their leadership roles. They will aid you to manage change when under pressure, as well as engage the entire organization to overcome any employee-related reservations which might occur in times of CHANGE.

- **Step #1:** Step away from the Source – To activate the **S.O.W.S.** strategies (see the next chapter).

- **Step #2:** Invoke the Five fundamental Principles of Emotional Intelligence - The "RULER" (see next Chapter) to help you Recognize emotions you've just experienced – a sign that CHANGE is imminent. This principle will also help you to careful study and understand the change that needs changing, label them precisely, and express them communicatively in the most efficient manner. By following this strategy, you'll be able to master and regulate change (auto-regulation) for the benefit of the organization.

- **Step #3:** Hack into the emotional brain to observe the emotional contents of what might have just happened.

- **Step #4:** Deploy specialized emotional tools to separate Emotions according to their intensity:

  1. Emotional Wheel.

  2. Emotional Scatter Diagram.

In the following THREE Chapters, I will walk you through the THREE Change Management Strategies to help you can deploy succeed in any life circumstance fully when CHANGE becomes imminent in your life.

Chapter Seventeen

S.O.W.S. Strategies for Managing Change

"Change is painful, but nothing is as painful as staying stuck somewhere you don't belong."
~ **Mandy Hale**, blogger speaker, and New York Times best-selling author.

WHEN CIRCUMSTANCES, situations, or events don't work in our favour, we suck. We become slaves to our emotions. These private emotions become our Master and rule over us as slaves. They take charge of us and control our thinking and our decisions. But should this be right?

Although you cannot control certain circumstances before they happen, but I promise you that you can control your mind – your thinking and reasoning. When leaders in high places are emotionally hijacked, their rational thinking is cancelled by their emotions. No wonder our leaders and institutions who operate in this level of irrational thinking in our society are now embracing the modern style of ostracism known as *"cancel culture"* as an instrument to be "cancelled" when your freedom of expression in public conflicts with the accuser's emotions.

When *emotional hijack* takes over the brain, humans automatically transform into beasts of the forest. We become equal to pigs, cows, dogs, sheep or lions and behave just like them. Has this ever happened to you in the past?

Depending on the situation, they take up the case publicly online or social media platform as an "accuser of the brethren" to express their disgust and condemn the offending party and black list them in the minds of the "public court" without first understanding the perception of the 'accused.' By boycotting "the accused" and imposing ourselves as "online judges" without qualification in the public's mindset, we are gradually re-introducing the hands of capitalism in the 21st Century.

If an *emotional hijack* occurs between people who are close to each other, it is common to hear them shout over their voices to express their disbelief and disgust. They'll swear with every conversation, and on extreme occasions, engage in a physical altercation – fist fighting and kicking one another. They lose their perspectives and become more judgmental. They end up making hasty and nasty conclusions. Finally, they give reasons to support our actions: "I am right. You are wrong. End of the story."

The **S.O.W.S.** Strategies are vital to helping us disrupt our brain from being judgmental.

Where:

S = Stop.

O = Oxygenate.

W = withdraw from the scene; and

S = Seek knowledge; seek the right information.

I believe that these four steps – **S.O.W.S** – which I coined in late 2020 can help you gain access to the neocortex under pressure. It will also help you restore rational thoughts and get back on track immediately without losing your senses.

These strategies have helped me to deal with my life cases, as well as manage other people's emotions in the workplace. It is for this reason that I have decided to reproduce them in this book, hoping that they may assist you in planning and dealing with your everyday emotional life situations.

Here's the best way to train your mindset into adopting these strategies as part of your normal routine: When you hear the fire alarm in your building, the next thing in your mind is to rush out of the building and gather in the designated fire point for your safety. We have trained our minds to follow this pattern without prompting. Thus, we habitually step away from the perceived source of fire and run for safety. We do this before the Fire Marshals step in to check the source of the alarm.

This simple illustration above should be applied to our lives when we face challenges that trigger anger, and stressful emotions. When stressful emotions creep into our lives, the best way is to keep ourselves safe from harm by stepping away from the scene of events and deploying the following Four **S.O.W.S Strategies** as described below.

- **STEP 1: S.O.W.S - STOP**

The first "S" stands for **STOP**. It is a physical action that presses the brake pedal or "pauses" the emotional hijacks (negative words, tone of voice, shouts, body language, etc.) and creates Self-Awareness. It permits us to disengage from the trigger using the pattern-interrupt approach (PIA).

Patterns allow creating habits or auto-pilot mode. For instance, when people wake up in the morning, the next thing in their mind is to rush to the bathroom to tidy up themselves, brush their teeth, apply their perfume, and so forth without even thinking about them. Patterns enable allow us to navigate the same old habit or behaviour, again and again, even when we know that that habit is unproductive. But we can actively break up our thoughts, behaviour, or emotions using the pattern-interrupt techniques to engage the neocortex and disengage automatic responses.

STOP Coping Strategies

The following coping strategies are vital to helping you overcome the amygdala hijack – either when you are alone or in a one-to-one meeting with a colleague or with a family member. You do not have to follow the steps in sequence. You can always personalize them according to your needs.

When You're Alone

1. Move away from the scene as quickly as you can. Take deep breathes. ERASE your mind from the obstacle, and then return to it later.

2. Twist your body and your head gently to your right and left.

3. Decide not to say negative comments – tame the tiger! Whether you are right, and the other person is wrong, do not say anything; make no further comments or offer suggestions at this stage as any utterances could trigger the other person's amygdala.

4. Swap your current task – take up a different project, send an email, call a friend, family member, etc. Do not discuss the topic right now over the phone, until you are mentally strong to do so, and that you have engaged your thinking brain (neocortex) with the emotional brain (amygdala) to work in sync.

When in One-2-One Meetings

1. Take a deep breath.

2. Sip a glass of water.

3. Relax your mind.

4. Think of your favourite sporting activities, e.g., gaming, football.

5. Sit upright with your palms resting freely on your thighs.

6. Take a piece of paper and sketch what you see around you.

7. Say to yourself, "Yes, I can" – to resolve the problem.

- **STEP 2: S.O.W.S - OXYGENATE**
Letter "O" stands for OXYGENATE. While you're under pressure, the adrenalin surge increases your heart rate, and your breathing becomes shallow, shorter, but faster. In normal daily activities, the brain of an average man weighing 70 Kg consumes about 49 ml of Oxygen (O_2) per minute, which is approx. 20% of the total body O_2 we breathe (approx. 250 mL) (Rink and Khanna 2011).

During intensive, stressful times, the brain can consume up to 50% (approx. 125 mL) of the total volume of O_2 we breathe in per minute, which is 2.5 x that normal. Thus, in one minute of emotional dealing with issues - such as stress managing operations in your organization, managing staff redundancies, dealing with stubborn children at home, talking about your finances, debt collection, marital breakdown, or the bereavement of a loved one – the brain needs 125 mL of O_2 to function rationally, equivalent to half a bottle of 500 mL of Highland water.

For one hour (60 minutes) of intensive work under pressure, the amount of O_2 required by the brain to function rationally is equivalent to 7,500 mL (approx. 1.65 UK Gallons of water). If that situation is not resolved within one day, and for 24 hours, your brain needs a total of at least 180,000 mL = 180 Litres of O_2 or approx. 40 UK Gallons of Oxygen to function effectively.

Lack of O2 can shut down the brain through hypoxia. I have watched many people around the world, including politicians, government officials, and so forth who suffered from hypoxia during stressful, and intensive cross-examinations involving money laundering cases and questions about their integrity and character committed during their leadership.

Clear symptoms to watch when someone is under intense emotional stress include confusion, intermittent cough, shortness of breath, high blood pressure, and blackout. By actively breathing SLOWLY and Deeply, we consciously flood the brain cells with OXYGEN to eliminate the cortisol stress hormone.

Steps to avoid Hypoxia when under pressure

After withdrawing from the scene of emotional stress to oxygenate, the best way to increase oxygen flow to the brain during pressure situations is to follow the 3-2-4 Breathing Strategies as discussed below

1. Ventilate the area - By opening the windows, switching on the fan, or going to an open field with no atmospheric air obstruction.

2. Using the 3-2-4 Breathing Strategies, inhale quietly through your nose and then count to THREE.

3. Pause: Hold your breath for the count of TWO.

4. Exhale completely through your mouth, making a 'whoosh' audible sound as you count to four.

By counting, we actively recruit the neocortex. The longer you wait in the presence of the crises, not STOPPING and getting away to OXYGENATE – the further the trigger will continue to control our emotions.

- **STEP 3: S.O.W.S. – Withdraw:**

The letter "**W**" stands for WITHDRAW from the scene. Here, you have to move out of the fire zone and disengage yourself from the scene with high emotions for the following reasons:

1. Your physical presence alone could be an additional source of the trigger. Two unfriendly lions cannot survive in the same cage.

2. Your words, actions or inactions may continue to flare up the trigger. In this situation, you aim to find the best way to Reconnect with others, understand their perspectives – their feelings, and the impact your actions have had on them. This is not the right time to make political statements or give reasons to justify the threats.

- **S.O.W.S. – SEEK Knowledge or Right Information:**

The final stage of the S.O.W.S strategies '**S**', is to SEEK KNOWLEDGE from the right source and at the right time. Knowledge is information. Lack of knowledge about people's calling in life is the simple reason why billions of people are in their present bad situations.

Where do you get your information? Who is the source of your information? How authentic is this source? Is the information coming from the CEO, the Head of Department in your Institution, or someone with authority and influence in your business? Or are you sourcing your information from strangers – from random people on the streets? Also, be aware of misinformation.

Knowledge is the key to understating what went wrong, how to accept other people's views, as well as finding a suitable strategy to solve the problems. Every problem is unique in its own right and should, therefore, be solved with different and innovative solutions.

When you deploy these four basic strategies STOP – OXYGENATE – WITHDRAW – SEEK KNOWLEDGE – while under intense pressure, you're invoking the POWER of your thinking brain to establish a strong relationship with your emotional brain. Once the relationship is established, any solution conceived in the subconscious mind becomes the real deal – the answer.

You might as well begin to probe yourself with several questions like these:

- Was the threat real or perceived?
- How does this change impact me right now?
- What impact will it have on the employees?
- In what ways will it impact the organization?
- What are the consequences of CHANGE in the next hour, next day, next month, 1 year, or the next 5 years?
- How could my mentors or those we call "exceptional leaders" have handled this CHANGE?
- What could have been their good intentions versus bad intentions?

Chapter Eighteen

Five Principles of Emotional Intelligence

"An army of principles can penetrate where an army of soldiers cannot."
~ **Thomas Paine**, political activist, philosopher, political theorist.

I HAD spent over three years studying, researching, and working on Emotional Intelligence across various sectors of the economy: leadership, business, government, politics vs. religion, and leadership in families. I also focused my interest on how leaders communicated their messages, team building, and decision-making processes that align their thinking with their emotional states in times of turbulence or adversity.

During this intensive research, I had found the secrets that successful CEOs deploy in their organizations, especially those leading people. Those secrets are coded by FIVE natural Principles which must be obeyed and implemented to achieve maximum impact.

These Five Principles are also known as Principles of Laws. The Principles of LAW are not Laws themselves, rather, they are the "*precept*" that provides the foundation for the development of LAWS. The Principles of Emotional Intelligence are themselves built into itself in the "RULER-definition" of Emotional Intelligence, which is:

- Recognizing emotions - which is accepting or admitting that change is imminent.
- Understanding emotions through thinking.
- Labelling or naming emotions, by giving the right name to the Change happening in your organization.
- Expressing or communicating emotional change appropriately.
- Regulating emotions, which is controlling change, orderliness, and standardization of the Change across the organization.

These FIVE Principles of Emotional Intelligence are so basic that they can't be contradicted or invalidated. These FIVE Principles are so true and universally acknowledged as Axion or Maxim incorporate business and leadership. As principles of Law, they have already existed by themselves, and in the minds of everyone born in this world before being expressed in the form of RULES. Let's dive into each of these Five principles.

- **Principle #1: Recognizing Emotions as Evidence for Organizational CHANGE**

The foundation to grasping Emotional Intelligence is your ability to recognize when change is required in your family or organization. Whether we like it or not, that change will impact the emotions of others, and influence their attitude towards work.

By acknowledging the fact that CHANGE is imminent, it allows you to arm yourself to the tooth with diligence and humility. It prepares you to respect other people's opinions without asking for reasons. It also allows you to void being judgemental, but to accept that CHANGE is mandatory. When this happens, the best step is to embrace it and seek an understanding of the extent of CHANGE that is needed for growth.

Recognizing emotional change is like recognizing medicines based on the diseases they treat. For instance, when your doctor prescribes your medication, you will automatically recognize the type of disease it's meant to treat. For instance, when you see insulin, you don't need a doctor or a specialist consultant to tell you that it's for diabetes. When you see acetaminophen or paracetamol tablets, what comes to your mind automatically is "painkiller." Hence, the key emotional intelligence principles are built into its definition.

- **Principle #2: Understanding Emotions as Organizational CHANGE**

The question one might ask is this: "How do I understand CHANGE when it happens – in my relationships and the business? Our emotions are our informants. The chemicals we generate give us information about what's going on within or outside the body.

For emotions, the best way to understand them is simple: Feel it in your pulse, chew it like an apple, regurgitate it if you like, and digest it in your gut, then, and only then, you're on your route to understating that emotional change has arrived.

If you cannot understand the message, is likely you may not understand the hard times your junior staff is undergoing privately. In most cases, even if our emotions pass across your path, you might still be clueless about what it is. That's why most people cannot control or deal with their prolonged situations on daily basis.

- **Principle #3: Labelling Emotions Correctly for Organizational Change**

This is what I call, the Declaration of Corporate Intent. Whatever you fail to give a name, you will fail to control. Naturally, our emotions are neutral. They don't have names but are willing to take up names you adopt to describe them. They don't have teeth to bite you. Emotions are "emotionless", harmless, and "useless," unless we give them "name-tags," such as 'anger,' 'hate', 'depression', or saying such words like 'this job is 'killing' me'.

When you tell yourself that "this job is killing me", what your mind understands are some keywords in that sentence: "this job = my job," "killing," or "killing me." So, who's being killed by the job? You. That job would eventually kill you when you consciously keep repeating the same words over and over in your subconscious mind for just one month! You will turn yourself into a walking corpse because your subconscious mind had already registered you dead in his DEATH RECORD. Thus, your job is now registered like this: "my job is a killer" because whatsoever you tag an emotion so it becomes.

The CEOs must assign responsibilities to selected leaders or the wise men tag a name to the transformation agenda. Labelling corporate change correctly according to its character ensures there's clarity at every level of the organization.

- **Principle #4: Communicating Government Strategies:**

I have figured out that the Fall of Man in the Creation story was not due to Adam and Eve eating the forbidden fruit. Rather, The Fall was due to revealing leadership secrets to the opposition party or government.

Many governments and political leaders have fallen as victims of their strategies and Policies which had kept them in power for decades. When the government's secret strategy is declared publicly by a Minister of a ruling party or government, that Minister has simply armed the opposition with weapons (the same information) to attack and derail the Government. This is exactly the outcome of the "political debate" between Eve and Satan in the Parliament of the garden -

Like in a democracy, the government vs public interests are well served by rugged public argument on the floor of the House of Commons. This was the case when a debate on the "political correctness" of God's statement was pitted between Even and Satan in the parliament of Garden of Eden.

The accuser was prepared in advance. He arrived at the scene with a notepad written with God's original instruction. However, he rephrased the question as a decoy to distort Eve's rhetoric, sway her opinion of her government, and steal their rightful position of leadership. And it worked in favour of the opposition:

"Did God really say, 'You must not eat from any tree in the garden'?" (Gen. 3:1).

Therefore, the Fall of Man in the Garden was the Fall of Leadership communication strategy. Your communication strategy is the tool that would give trust to the people under your charge. We do what we say, and say what we do. Sometimes, the message might be over-communicated through various means leading to misinformation or information overload.

Your good intentions might be misinterpreted by others in different contexts. This message is composed of our feelings and emotions but can be expressed in various ways, in different times, and seasons. That means, emotions are seasonal so are crises.

Expressing emotions is a way of connecting with someone, and the way this message is expressed determines the mood of the atmosphere. It can be verbal or non-verbal.

Non-verbal emotional communication:
- Facial expressions: widening our eyes, pulling back our chin.
- Body language: hand gestures or action (running away or hiding from threats).
- Composure.
- Physiological reactions: Breathing rapidly, increased heartbeat, speaking fast with flurry under pressure.
- Cultural representation, e.g., attire, dress code, traditional dressings, food, body tattoos, etc.

Verbal (Communication):
- Word of mouth. Your words can be more powerful than a sword. It is a double-edged sword. It can make a baby smile but can become a powerful tool to curse your foes.
- Vocal tones: The frequency and latitude of the tone of your voice have different connotations. Just like the words, their use can determine the level of anger, frustration, excitement and joy at any given conversation.
- Effective communication (Expression) of the transformation agenda to all parties and stakeholders both orally and written could increasingly motivate the team spirit.

- **Principle #5: Regulating Organizational CHANGE:**

The word 'REGULATE' can be described in many ways. It can mean 'control over,' 'subdue', 'overcome,' 'manage', 'leadership', 'influence', 'power', or 'mastery'. Remember that whatever you give a name to, you also have the power to control it. The names you give to your children, in most cases, are the names they are known in life, with some exceptions such as marriage.

By first naming your children when they are your, you can actually control their minds or "paradigm" as teenagers to follow you and your tradition or culture, religion, food, or dress code. They'll listen to you and probably submit to your instructions as they grow into adulthood. When they become 'matured' mentally and emotionally to make their decisions, then they to chose the right from the wrong without your regulation.

In your organization, it's not just enough to understand people's emotions, but being able to understand the impacts of work on their personal and social emotions is the key to motivating them to achieve company targets.

Remember these two important statements:

#1: Whatever you fail to control, WILL CONTROL YOU.
#2: Whatever you fail to manage, YOU WILL LOSE.

The bottled Spirit vs. the Human Spirit

How many of you like drinking wine, beer, or whisky? Although they have different names, what they have in common is alcohol (ethanol). Alcohol is a spirit. Once consumed, its first target is the human spirit. Once your spirit is held bondage, the next stage is your soul- the mind, the will, and your emotions.

Once your soul is caged, your body will cave in. If you fail to control the influence of this external spirit, it will turn back to control you. That's how powerful the spirit of any form is – Holy Spirit versus the evil spirit

Excessive consumption of alcohol might render your kidney dead with kidney stones, and control your ability to control your life circumstances. When you regulate circumstances in your organization or family, you'll have a rulership influence over those circumstances and excel where others have crumbled in similar conditions.

Finally, taking ownership of the CHANGE process is vital to guarantee success. Being ready to take control or regulate the transformation is vital for the benefit of the organization. You cannot control what you don't have or own.

Chapter Nineteen

Emotional Hacking

"Your mind can be either your prison or your palace. What you make it is yours to decide."
~Bernard Kelvin Clive

WHEN SURGEONS take you to the theatre to repair or replace heart valves, in a procedure known as open-heart surgery, they do so to increase blood flow through the heart. What they do is surgically rip your heart open and hack into it to access the damaged valves.

When it comes to emotions, the procedure is almost the same: taking emotions out of context, dissecting them into bits to understand each chunk of the message. Applying the key RULER Principles to understand them: Recognizing, understanding, labelling, expressing, and regulating them, followed by Synaesthesia – will help you to integrate all senses and establish the intensity of each emotion and its true meaning.

To understand and interpret other people's emotions, one must first step into the minds of other people through a process of "emotional hacking." Once you're inside, Emotional hacking leads to Creative Thinking – where you remain on the fence, without bias. If you have a personal relationship with the individual, it is vital to stay neutral or find someone unrelated to the individual in any form to deal with the problem. In this way, the element of bias in the outcome may be avoided. The essence of taking this step is to ensure that you generate creativity in your mind-playing field without manipulating other people's emotions.

Our body houses over 34,00 different emotions. In our hectic days as leaders in our organizations, parents with children, and many difficulties of life that hit us front and back, left, and right, it is extremely difficult to navigate safely across all the thousands of emotions we encounter in life.

There are various tools to help you separate emotions into many layers such as:

1. Plutchik's Wheel of Emotions – where emotions are codified in the form of Colours and Colour Intensity, and

2. Emotional Scatter Diagram – where the intensities of different emotions are plotted in a diagram according to their force, power, or energy.

Tool #1: Plutchik's Emotional Wheel

Dr Robert Plutchik (1927-2006) developed an emotional wheel to demonstrate how colours can be combined – manipulated and decoded – to give different meanings to emotions. For instance, the eight basic emotions – Joy, Trust, Fear, Surprise, Sadness, Disgust, Anger, and Anticipation – were coded with different colours, but linked to human psychological signals required for survival. In other words, emotions are our psychological (spiritual, or mental) defence mechanisms designed for human survival.

These emotions were further arranged in a bipolar or opposite way to each other:
- Joy vs. Sadness.
- Trust vs. Disgust.
- Fear vs. Anger, and
- Surprise vs. Anticipation.

These emotions were represented with various colours of different intensities and arousal. Humans are the same as other animals because we share the same basic emotions as the beasts. For instance, the midbrain or the limbic system in humans is the same in other animals – pigs, cows, cats, dogs, and so on. The only difference between the brain of humans and animals is the Thinking brain or Neocortex, otherwise known as The Thinking Cap.

The use of the Emotional Wheel involves a series of processes of dissecting emotions into several components:

1. The source of the emotions.

2. The presentation or manifestation at the time – low mood or hyperactivity.

3. The wisdom, or application of other cues around the person to juggle.

4. Approach emotions with due diligence, and

5. Discernment.

Therefore, we cannot just judge people's emotions at face value. By combining our basic emotions using Dr Plutchik's Emotional Wheel, we can generate new emotions. For instance:
- Joy + Trust = Love.
- Trust + Fear = Submission.
- Anger + Disgust = Contempt, etcetera, etcetera.

Emotional Wheel in Practice

How do you apply this wheel in real terms? There are two best ways I have used in this book to describe the Wheel.

1. The Lego City.
2. The Planetary 4-Ring System.

The Lego City

Consider a Colour-gated Lego City with Eight Main Houses – which represent the Eight Main Emotions in the grid of the Emotional Wheel. Each house has Four bedrooms – each bedroom representing the intensities of each emotion on a single grid. Each house has one shade of colour on the exterior - Deep Red, Yellow, Orange, Green, Dark Green, Blue, Magenta, and Oxblood – to distinguish them from one another.

However, as you approach each Main House and enter the cloakroom, or landing, and walk straight along the corridor, the first thing you'll notice is that each room has varying colour intensities than the exterior. If you walk further away from the entrance and move closer to the end of each home, or the centre of the wheel, the colour of the room in the centre becomes very intense. When you move back towards the entrance, the intensity decreases.

This method of visualizing information, data, statistics, or figure (one colour intensity) represents can stimulate other changes (varying colour intensity) in our life through the process of *Synaesthesia*. Visualizing colours allows us to grasp each emotion, plus its sub-components - which collectively impact us either positively or negatively. That's why people who are gifted in this department of Synaesthesia are a special type of people. Why? Because they are capable of converting colours into images or voice, and the sound of music or hearing into sight. In other words, they "see" music as colour patterns once they hear it. They "feel", and "visualize" the texture, or shape of their appetite – food and drink - through the power of their taste bud.

The Planetary 4-Ring System

Studying Plutchik's Emotional Wheel is not that easy. The wheel can be described like this: The wheel is made up of four circles, which I termed "Planetary 4-Ring-System" from the centre towards the boundary. The main eight emotions - Joy, Trust, Fear, Surprise, Sadness, Disgust, Anger, and Anticipation - are organized with colours like the Houses in the Lego City as previously described. These eight emotions are sandwiched in grids between the first ring (#1) and the second ring (#2) in a clockwise direction The closer the colours are to each other, the more similar the emotions are to the one next to it.

For instance, Anger and Rage are identical in colour. If you slide your eyes across the grid or the Main House and gaze towards the centre of the circle, the emotions become very stronger, hence the intensity of the colours of each grid. Since Rage is nearer the centre of the circle, the colour intensifies. Therefore, the intense oxblood colour of rage is greater than the emotion of annoyance which is lighter in colour.

By hacking the limbic system, you have full access to other people's emotional package: recognize those emotions, understand them, label them correctly, and then express them effectively, to redirect them for the benefit of the parties involved.

Bearing in mind that our emotions have impacts on us and those around us, hacking into emotions should be done with the hope of using the information harvested to improve performance outcomes for the organization. It would also assist other people in developing themselves, improving their well-being, emotional connection, and building strong relationships.

Tool #2: Emotional Scatter Diagram

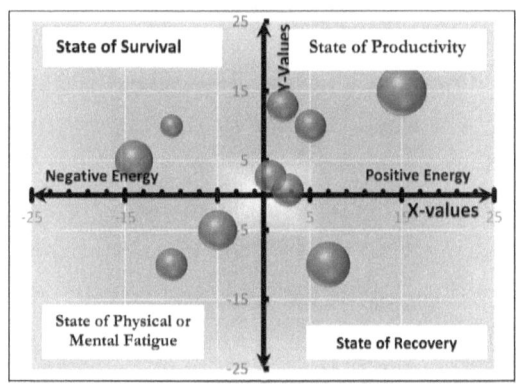

Figure 6: An illustration of an Emotional Scatter Diagram using energy potentials versus impacts.

The Emotional Scatter Diagram involves plotting the power, energy, or force of emotions in a quadrant relative to their intensity or nature versus the impacts (positive or negative). In the above illustration, the Y-axis represents the power, energy, or emotional force – High vs. Low Energy potentials.

The X-axis, on the other hand, represents the Impacts of emotions – Negative (-) on the left hand, and positive (+) on the Right hand of the axis.

- **State of Productivity or Execution** = High Energy + Positive Emotions: The Top-Right Quadrant represents emotions of high impactful, positive emotions that get positive responses, such as joy, and trust. You feel connected, passionate, hopeful, challenged, and energized for high performance.

- **State of Survival** = High Energy + Negative Energy: The Top-Left Quadrant consists of highly powerful, negative emotions whose role is to provide emotional safety for your survival. Such emotions include fear, anger, anxiety (worry, concern, nervousness), defensive, tension, or frustration.

- **State of Recovery** = Low Energy + Positive Emotions: The Lower-Right Quadrant represents an area of mental and physical recovery, such as relaxing, mind-wandering or autopilot, quiet, or laid back.

- **State of Physical or Mental Fatigue** = Low Energy + Negative Energy, represents an area where leaders are depleted, empty, worn out, overwhelmed, despondent, miserable, or devastated.

Human activities - such as wants and needs – are the results of personal, or individual emotions. Your state of poverty or wealth is the result of how you gauge, map, or manage those emotions. Emotions, therefore, are chunks of high voltage, Energy or Power source. Emotions are like a high grid electrical power supply with a high impactful electrical current. It carries electrical energy along a particular wire in one direction. Thus, the current of emotions flows from an area of a high voltage potential to an area of low voltage potential. It flows through whoever is on its path.

How to Apply the Emotional Scatter Diagram

Match the intensity of your desire with the intensity of your emotions and plot them inside any of the quadrants. You write them on the walls, on papers, or your ceiling. In the bathroom or your kitchen, say them loud and speak to yourself through the reflection of the mirror. Repeat this regularly and consistently for 7 days - one week - one month - or even one year.

Having matched the frequencies of your thoughts, emotions, or feelings with the desires you want, you cannot help but achieve that desire. That's the impact of mapping emotions against their intensity.

Conclusion

Applying these Lessons to Good use

> "At the end of the day, it's important to know what really matters most in life ... your sanity, your health, your family, and the ability to start anew."
>
> ~Les Brown

STUDYING THIS book alone without reflection and taking action on what you've read cannot make you a great Leader. Using the contents of this book will not protect you from a crisis or criticism, either privately or in public domain. But what I can assure you is this: the only person who can help you influence CHANGE in your life circumstances, so you live a life you'd once dreamt of is not in your parents, friends or work colleagues. The person is hidden in YOU.

By applying the knowledge, understanding, and wisdom contained in this book can help you simplify your life, and keep you in shape in times of opposition. and change.

As previously discussed in this book, the presence of Emotion simply means CHANGE has arrived. And that change means changing from an area of a known territory or tradition, to an unknown territory where life might be different and most challenging.

Experiencing and expressing anger, frustration, excitement, pleasure, or other forms of emotions are strategic signals our body uses to remind us that change management has arrived. Ability to control your emotions and events effectively in the presence of challenges is the number one natural gift that differentiates a leader from a follower.

How do you deal with a crisis when they happen? How do you deal with the death of a close relative, financial crisis, or loss of a job, breakdown of relationships, separation versus divorce, accidents or diseases?

How do you deal with these storms when they hit you on the blindside? Your solution, therefore, is not in the hands of the politicians or the government in power. You cannot prevent Hurricane Ida or Tornado from happening through prayers and fasting. But you you can reduce their impacts through **Emotional Rulership.**

Once you have mastered emotional rulership, principles, laws, and emotional intelligence, you can use the knowledge to achieve high level of reasoning and exceptional leadership under pressure. You can achieve it by building a **Mental System of Function**, whereby you integrate or sync your emotions (the amygdala) with your thoughts (prefrontal lobe) as a single entity. Don't react to events, but become proactive to change the events for your benefit. By doing this, you can convert your unconscious, emotional responses into conscious, physical emotional experiences (LeDoux 1998: p. 296).

When you begin to sense any emotional disaster happening to you, or someone within your responsibility, accept them as just any other change that is imminent. Register them in your memory databank, and your body will attune to that **Mental System Of Function** to influence subjective experiences into objective solutions.

The greatest killer of effective leadership is our inability to control change through the power of emotional feelings. The visibility of a leader makes him or her more prone to, or more vulnerable to attacks. A leader will always be misunderstood. His or her vision or manifesto might be rejected. His character might come under threat – with many accusations, both real and unreal. Unfortunately, these are parts of the human nature.

Those in public leadership positions, whether in the police force, military, government, academia, and religion are familiar with this illustration. When the opposition is envious of your status, or jealous of your success through CHANGE, but see that you've risen from **nobody** to **somebody**, it becomes human for them to gossip about you. When they can't find any deficiencies to accuse you of any wrongdoing, they will become creative in their mind. They will invent stories, or allegations against you, just to destroy your character.

When the news against you starts filtering in, embrace it with smiles, and with shoulders high. Don't let bad news distract you from chasing your dreams to impact the world positively.

Never be angry about what people say about you, but be angry to tell them what they don't know about you. Always thrive to be in the news about your belief system and vision, than being out of the news. Why? Because people who take pages of Newspapers to gloat and criticize your vision and your business are, indeed, giving you FREE publicity in the media for your vision.

Criticisms invoke anger, depression, or anxiety. It is normal to be criticized because criticism is the normal way humans deploy in response to CHANGE. Never work with people who don't have the balls to criticize you, because absence of critique is the absence of growth.

If you respond to Bad news by getting angry or being mad at them, that means, you've given them the power to control your emotions and your life. You'll soon become a victim of your own emotions. Remember that whoever controls your emotions, controls your mind. And whoever controls your mind controls your life.

Emotional are the cells telecommunications methods bringing you "News alerts" that CHANGE has come. If you don't want to be a leader, please remain invincible. But, if you want to be an effective leader, accept Emotions as the CHANGE agent and be ready to be criticized for the visions you're willing to die for.

Leaders don't pursue projects they can live for - become millionaires, live in mansions, enjoy a life of luxury, and retire with a great pension at 60, 66, 67, or 68. Rather, great leaders pursue projects for which they can die.

Control your environment, and influence it by taking responsibility for the changes you've caused. But never let change happen in your environment without your permission and influence.

Finally, I will conclude this book with a quote about emotions and criticisms from my leadership mentor, motivational speaker, educator, best-selling author, consultant for government and business, and the Founder and former President of Bahamas Faith Ministries International (BFMI), Dr. Myles Munroe (1954-2014):

> "If you do not want to be criticized, then decide to do nothing in life. It is better to be criticized for taking action than to be ignored for inaction."
> - Dr. Myles Munroe, "Becoming a Leader," Whitaker House, Kensington (USA), 2018, p.220)

I rest my case.

Reference

Adams, J. and Adams, A. (1996-2021) *King George III*. PBS.org website: WGBH Educational Foundation.
https://www.pbs.org/wgbh/americanexperience/features/adams-king-george-III/ Accessed May 9, 2021.

Anchor, S. (2011) *The Happiness Advantage: The Seven Principles that Fuel Success and Performance at Work*. UK: Virgin Books.

Baker, S. (2021) Italy to hold referendum on legalising euthanasia after 750,000 sign petition: Christian politicians condemn 'culture of death'. *Mail Online*, *https://www.dailymail.co.uk/news/article-9929607/Italy-hold-referendum-legalising-euthanasia-750-000-sign-petition.html* Accessed 26 Aug. 2021

BBC (2005) *Police shot Brazilian eight times*. BBC News: BBC.
http://news.bbc.co.uk/1/hi/uk/4713753.stm Accessed 21 July 2021.

BBC News (2021) Boris Johnson outlines new 1.25% health and social care tax to pay for reforms. *BBC News*, *https://www.bbc.co.uk/news/uk-politics-58476632* Accessed 12 Sept. 2021

Cowen, A. S. and Keltner, D. (2017) Self-report captures 27 distinct categories of emotion bridged by continuous gradients. *PNAS* 114 (38).

Davidson, H. (2020) First Covid-19 case happened in November, China government records show- report. *The Guardian Newspapers*, *https://www.theguardian.com/world/2020/mar/13/first-covid-19-case-happened-in-november-china-government-records-show-report*

Dolf Zillma (1993) Mental Control of Angry Aggression. In Wegner, D. and Pennebaker, J. S. (editors) *Handbook of Mental Control*. Englewood Cliffs, N.J.: Prentice Hall.

Dr Myles Munroe (2018) *Becoming a Leader*. U.S.: Whitaker House.

Edmonds, L. (2021) US Capitol rioters believed they were acting on Donald Trump's orders, Democrats say. *Evening Standard*, 11 Feb. 2021, *https://www.standard.co.uk/news/us-politics/democrats-u-s-capitol-rioters-trump-impeachment-b919500.html* Accessed 18 July 2021

Frue, K. (2017) *PESTLE ANALYSIS: SWOT and Business Analysis Tools*. Pestanalysis.com website: Pestanalysis.com.
https://pestleanalysis.com/who-invented-pest-analysis/ Accessed July 9, 2021.

Gallup (2015) *Sate of American Managers: Analytics and Advice for Leaders*. Washington DC: Gallup. Accessed May 1, 2021.

Genetics Home Reference (2020) *Malignant Hyperthermia*. [Online]:MedlinePlus.
https://medlineplus.gov/genetics/condition/malignant-hyperthermia/ Accessed May 22, 2021.

Goleman, D. (1995) *Emotional Intelligence: Why It Can Matter More than IQ.* London: Bloomsbury.

Goleman, D. (1999) *Working with emotional intelligence.* London: Bloomsbury.

Goleman, D., Boyatzis, R. and McKee, A. (2013) *Primal Leadership: Unleashing The Power of Emotional Intelligence.* Boston, MA: Harvard Business Review Press.

Guinness World Records (2021) *Largest rocket.* Retrieved from the Guinness World Records' Website: https://www.guinnessworldrecords.com/world-records/largest-rocket Accessed 29 July 2021.

Heath, M. and Hays, K. (2020) Top World Bank Economist Says Financial Crisis Could Emerge From Pandemic. *Economist Bloomberg,* https://www.bloomberg.com/news/articles/2020-10-16/carmen-reinhart-sees-risk-financial-crisis-emerges-from-pandemic

Helpguide.org (2013) *Obsessive-Compulsive Disorder (OCD): Symptoms and Treatment of Compulsive Behavior and Obsessive Thoughts.* Helpguide.org website: HelpGuide.org. http://www.helpguide.org/mental/obsessive_compulsive_disorder_ocd.htm Accessed May 22, 2021.

History.com Editors (2009) *King George III speaks to Parliament of American rebellion.* History.com website: A&E Television Networks. https://www.history.com/this-day-in-history/king-george-iii-speaks-to-parliament-of-american-rebellion Accessed May 8, 2021.

House of Commons (2021) *The UK's contribution to the EU budget.* House of Commons Library website: UK Parliament. https://commonslibrary.parliament.uk/research-briefings/cbp-7886/ Accessed July 13, 2021.

IGS (2021) *Gemstone Encyclopedia.* Gemsociety.org Website: Internal Germ Society LLC. https://www.gemsociety.org/gemstone-encyclopedia/ Accessed June 13, 2021.

International Glutamate Information Service (2021) *Glutamate: A Natural Part of Our Food.* IGIS website: IGIS. https://glutamate.org/nutrition/a-natural-part-of-our-food/ Accessed May 23, 2021.

Kelner, S., Rivers, C. and O'Connell, K. (1996) *Managerial Styles as a Behavioural Predictor of Organizational Climate.* Boston: McBer & Company.

Kolla, N. J. and Wang, C. C. (editors) (2019) *Chapter 29 - Alcohol and Violence in Psychopathy and Antisocial Personality Disorder: Neural Mechanisms.* Academic Press.

LeDoux, J. (1998) *The Emotional Brain: The Mysterious Underpinnings of Emotional Life.* London: Orion Books Ltd.

Martin Kelly (2020) *American Involvement in Wars from Colonial Times to the Present.* Online: ThoughtCo Website.
https://www.thoughtco.com/american-involvement-wars-colonial-times-present-4059761 Accessed April 11, 2021.

Merriam-Webster ((n.d.)) *Mongolian.* In Merriam-Webster.com dictionary: https://www.merriam-webster.com/dictionary/Mongolian Accessed 31 July 2021.

Miller, M. (2015) *Emotions, Feelings and Moods: What's the Difference?* Six Seconds Website: Six Seconds.
https://www.6seconds.org/2017/05/15/emotion-feeling-mood/ Accessed June 2021.

National Geographic (2017) *Skin: Skin is the human body's largest organ.* from the National Geographic.com website:
https://www.nationalgeographic.com/science/article/skin-1 Accessed 31 July 2021.

O'Neill, A. (2021) *Gross domestic product (GDP) of the United Kingdom 2026 Statista (in U.S. dollars).* from Statista Website: Statista.
https://www.statista.com/statistics/263590/gross-domestic-product-gdp-of-the-united-kingdom/ Accessed 29 Aug. 2021.

Office for National Statistics (2021) *Employment in the UK: August 2021.* Office for National Statistics: ONS.
https://www.ons.gov.uk/employmentandlabourmarket/peopleinwork/employmentandemployeetypes/bulletins/employmentintheuk/latest Accessed 29 Aug. 2021.

ONS (2021) *Divorces in England and Wales.* ONS.
https://www.ons.gov.uk/peoplepopulationandcommunity/birthsdeathsandmarriages/divorce/datasets/divorcesinenglandandwales Accessed 30 July 2021.

Pressman, L. ([2011-Present (2017)]) How Evolution was used to support Scientific Racism.
https://digitalrepository.trincoll.edu/cgi/viewcontent.cgi?article=1058&context=trinitypapers Accessed 24 July 2021

Rink, C. and Khanna, S. (2011) Significance of Brain Tissue Oxygenation and the Arachidonic Acid Cascade in Stroke. *Antioxidants & Redox Signaling* 14 (10), 1889-1903.

Ritchie, S. J. and Tucker-Drob, E. M. (2018) How Much Does Education Improve Intelligence? A Meta-Analysis. *Psychological Science* 29 (8), 1358-1369.

Schneier, F. R. B., Carlos, Anita, S. X. and Liebowitz, M. R. (2002) The social anxiety spectrum. *Psychiatric Clinics of North America* 25 (4), 757-774.

Sheerin, J. (2019) The mental rigours of being US president. *BBC News*, https://www.bbc.co.uk/news/world-us-canada-47671986 Accessed May 3, 2021

Society, N. G. (2019) *Natural Selection*. Washington DC: National Geographic. https://www.nationalgeographic.org/encyclopedia/natural-selection/ Accessed July 17, 2021.

Spencer, L. (2001) Improvement in service climate drives increase in revenue. In *a paper presented at the meeting of the Consortium for Research on Emotional Intelligence in Organizations*. Cambridge, MA, 19 April 2001. Online: Accessed: May 1, 2021.

Strominger, N. L., Demarest, R. J. and Laemle, L. B. (2012) Cerebral Cortex. *Noback's Human Nervous System*. 7th Ed edition. London: Springer.

Sun, M.-K. and Alkon, D. L. (editors) (2012) *Activation of Protein Kinase C Isozymes for the Treatment of Dementias*. Vol. 64. Academic Press.

The Electoral Commission (2021) *Results and turnout at the EU referendum*. Electoralcommission.org.uk website: The Electoral Commission. https://www.electoralcommission.org.uk/who-we-are-and-what-we-do/elections-and-referendums/past-elections-and-referendums/eu-referendum/results-and-turnout-eu-referendum Accessed July 13, 2021.

Trafton, A. (2018) *Distinctive brain pattern helps habits form: Study identifies neurons that fire at the beginning and end of a behavior as it becomes a habit*. MIT News Office: MIT. https://news.mit.edu/2018/distinctive-brain-pattern-helps-habits-form-0208 Accessed July 8, 2021.

Walsh, K. T. (2009) The First 100 Days: Franklin Roosevelt Pioneered the 100-Day Concept. *U.S. News & World Report*, February 12, 2009, https://www.usnews.com/news/history/articles/2009/02/12/the-first-100-days-franklin-roosevelt-pioneered-the-100-day-concept Accessed May 28, 2021

YCEI (2020) *Ruler: A systematic approach to SEL*. YCEI website: YCE. https://www.ycei.org/ruler Accessed May 1, 2021.

YCEI (?) *Ruler and Emotional Intelligence: Overview for Families*. [Online]: Schools.saisd.net. https://schools.saisd.net/page/open/81078/0/Introduction%20to%20RULER.pdf Accessed May 1, 2021.

About the Author

Pharm. Dr [Nze] Emmanuel Eni Amadi (B.Pharm, MSc, PGDip, MBA, PhD, MRPharmS) is an Author, Nanotoxicologist, Pharmacist & Leadership Consultant.

He is the Founder & CEO of AMADI GLOBAL™ Leadership Academy | Executive Education, Amadi Global Publishing (AGP), and Amadi Global.com – subsidiaries of AMADI GLOBAL LTD – registered in England and Wales.

The Amadi Global Leadership Academy | Executive Education is a UK-based premier Executive Education Institute aimed at transforming the Mindset of today's Managers into tomorrow's Leadership vessels through Professional Development Programmes.

He is a published author of two books on entrepreneurship and leadership: Starting a Successful £1Million Pound Business and Emotional Rulership - both are available on sale in Amazon.

Dr Amadi received his education from some of the world's best universities in the areas of Science, Pharmacy, Business, Management, and Leadership.

He studied in FOUR countries of the world (UK, USA, China, and Nigeria), and holds FIVE University Degrees (including TWO Master's degrees) plus over 40 Professional Certificates. He had travelled almost 50% of the European

Union countries. Dr Amadi is, indeed, a true Citizen of the world!

He obtained his Doctor of Philosophy (PhD) in Nanotoxicology, from the Department of Biomedical Sciences, University of Bradford, England, UK (2019) under the supervision of Professor Diana Anderson; Executive MBA (Executive Master's in Business Administration) (Lancaster University Management School, England, UK, 2011); MSc in Analytical & Pharmaceutical Sciences (Loughborough University, England, UK, 2003; Postgraduate Diploma in Pharmacy, University of Brighton, England, UK, 2006; and a Bachelor of Pharmacy with Distinction, University of Nigeria, Nsukka (UNN), Jan. 2000.

His professional development has seen him complete his Strategic Leadership training at Harvard University Extension School, Cambridge (USA, 2019), Aspiring Non-Executive Directors training, Bayes Business School (formerly Cass Business School) City, the University of London (2018), and the MBA Master Class of The Doing Business in China (DBiC)/International Business in Concept, Guanghua School of Management, Peking University, Beijing, China (2011).

Dr Amadi is a Founding Member of the Royal Pharmaceutical Society, London (29 June 2007) and a registrant with the General Pharmaceutical Council (GPhC), London, United Kingdom (2011).

He is a recipient of International Research Awards, including the Ebonyi State | HiPACT Overseas Full Scholarship Award, The European Cooperation in Science and Technology (COST) Research Grant, and The Leverhulme Trade Charities Trust, London, and a host of other awards.

He was a Guest Researcher at the Environmental Health Department, National Institute of Health (NIH), Porto, Portugal, in collaboration with the Director of the Institute, Dr João Paulo Fernandes Teixeira, where he worked on the DNA damage /genotoxicity of Graphene oxide nanoparticles on human blood samples.

As a Nanotoxicologist and Consultant in Pulmonary Nanotoxicology, Dr Amadi was an invited speaker at some of the world's conferences (UK, USA, China, and Poland) where he delivered his lectures on various topics which mattered in the worlds of Science and Business, including Nanotoxicology of Graphene Oxide on Human DNA, Gene expression of tumour suppressor and anti-apoptic genes in human lymphocytes from patients with Pulmonary diseases - lung cancer, asthma and COPD relative to healthy individuals; International Business Strategies, and Leadership.

He is married to his dear wife, Mrs Ewa Klosowska Amadi, a Polish-British Citizen. They are blessed with two boys - Michael Chidozie Amadi (aka Dodo) and Anthony Chibuike Amadi (aka Chibyke).

Books Published By the Author

Available worldwide on Amazon: http://getbook.at/SSB

Emotional Rulership: How Emotions, Principles, Laws, and Emotional Intelligence Affect You as a LEADER

How to Contact us

TO PARTNER WITH US, SPEAKING EVENTS, OR TO JOIN US IN ONE OF OUR LIFE EVENTS, PLEASE VISIT OUR WEBSITE:

https://www.amadiglobal.com/

To place your orders, please visit:

https://www.amadiglobal.com/merchandise/

FEEDBACK

Please don't forget to leave your reviews on Amazon about your thoughts regarding this book or any of my books.

www.AmadiGlobal.com

www.ingramcontent.com/pod-product-compliance
Lightning Source LLC
Chambersburg PA
CBHW030902080526
44589CB00010B/115